TRANSFORMING TRAUMA

A drugless and creative path
to healing PTS and ACE

The only people I would care to be with now are artists and people who have suffered. Those who know what beauty is and those who know what sorrow is: nobody else interests me.

Oscar Wilde

TRANSFORMING TRAUMA

A drugless and creative path to healing PTS and ACE

Heather L. Herington BSc, NMD, DHANP

With a foreword by David Schleich PhD

Hammersmith Health Books
London, UK

First published in 2022 by Hammersmith Health Books
– an imprint of Hammersmith Books Limited
4/4A Bloomsbury Square, London WC1A 2RP, UK
www.hammersmithbooks.co.uk

Disclaimer: This book is designed to provide helpful information on the subjects discussed. It is not meant to be used, nor should it be used, to diagnose or treat any medical condition. For diagnosis or treatment of any medical problem, consult your own physician or healthcare provider. The publisher and author are not responsible for any specific health or allergy needs that may require medical supervision and are not liable for any damages or negative consequences from any treatment, action, application or preparation, to any person reading or following the information in this book. References are provided for informational purposes only and do not constitute endorsement of any websites or other sources. Readers should be aware that the websites listed in this book may change. The information and references included are up to date at the time of writing but given that medical evidence progresses, it may not be up to date at the time of reading.

British Library Cataloguing in Publication Data: A CIP record of this book is available from the British Library.

Print ISBN 978-1-78161-225-5
Ebook ISBN 978-1-78161-226-2

Commissioning editor: Georgina Bentliff
Typeset by: Evolution Design & Digital Ltd
Cover design by: Madeline Meckiffe
Cover image by: ©naluwan
Index: Dr Laurence Errington
Production: Deborah Wehner of Moatvale Press Ltd
Printed and bound by: TJ Books Limited, Cornwall, UK

Contents

Foreword

Dr. Herington begins at the beginning in this book – that is, she does not assume that ours is the best of all possible worlds, given the perceived progress of biomedicine, so-called allopathic medicine, in the decades since Abraham Flexner's Report advocating this as the only effective approach to medicine was published in 1910; she does not accept holus-bolus the assumptions of the American Psychiatric Association's *Diagnostic and Statistical Manual of Mental Disorders (DSM)*, with its propensity for 'pathologizing any human experience'. Rather, grounding us in the history and early professional insights into PTS (post-traumatic stress or, as it is also known, C-PTS, 'complex post-trauma syndrome'), she considers the intricate old and new literature about medicine and health.

Tracing its roots and presentation to *The Epic of Gilgamesh* (the poet tale of King Uruk of Mesopotamia) and on to the prescient and powerful work of Harold Napoleon of the Alaskan Yuu'pik First Nation people, she takes care to clarify with considerable thoroughness how PTS is expressed. She gracefully shares a remarkable continuum of sources to do this, including significant contributions by psychiatrist Peter Breggin and researchers Stephen Porges and Rachel Yehuda, among many, many others.

In these pages, Dr. Herington elucidates the emerging conversations among healthcare professionals about the neurobiology of chronic stress, the role of inflammation in the trajectory of chronicity, the HPA axis (see page 84), the gut–brain axis and more. She stares down toxic psychiatry squarely with outstanding, well researched information, clinical pearls, and proven protocols.

Dr. Herington tells us a great deal about treatment paths other than conventional drug treatments, such as alternatives to the favored serotonin or chlorpromazine regimens so common in allopathic care for PTS or its comorbidities. She asserts: 'We in North America have generated one big mess in treating mental health and we have a lot of work to get it right.'

In Part Two, for example, Dr. Herington provides a succinct, immediately useful overview of the extraordinary utility of lifestyle, food, and detoxification options, 'drugless therapies', and a gold mine of naturopathic treatments: homeopathy, hydrotherapy, and botanical medicine, to name some of the material essential to this conversation about treating trauma, PTS and ACE (adverse childhood experience). With equal gusto, in the next sections, she delivers exceptional insight into the potential of still–point therapies, the mind–body connection, and the all-encompassing expressive arts.

This remarkable book is about what has been missing, about what, all this time, has been hiding in plain sight – natural medicine solutions in a world where, as the social critic Ivan Illich has contended, conventional medicine has severe limitations. In this rigorous discussion, Dr. Herington demonstrates successfully that PTS is hardly a new phenomenon and natural medicine comes equipped with a multitude of applicable solutions.

Valuable to consider and understand is the cumulative, full import of a work of this magnitude. This book is a touchstone for those healers and survivors wanting to employ (help patients using) drugless healing with PTS, ACE and many other conditions with psychological trauma at the core. She is among a small but growing number of naturopathic doctors with decades of clinical experience, research, teaching and learning among them, who are enthusiastically and meticulously writing about critical health topics. This community of scholarly naturopathic clinicians is well represented here by Dr. Herington.

Dr. Herington's work is as comprehensive as it is precise and functional. Her insights about contemporary sanctioned treatment of PTS are disciplined and noteworthy. Her book, written in elegant, clear, and often witty prose, is a strong statement of commitment to healing and teaching. Increasingly unmoored from inherently healthy roots in our culture, healthcare professionals and patients alike will experience Dr. Herington's work here as reassuring and prescient. She writes with such alacrity.

David J. Schleich, PhD
President, National University of Natural Medicine, USA

Dedicated to the memory of Denis Simpson,
Christopher Conti and Eky Zy

Introduction

Let us begin with a prayer to our ancestors whether Celtic, Viking, African, Persian, First Nation or Aboriginal, the lost tribes of Israel and so many others. Earth, a pulsing orb of chaos in the 21st century, needs this ancient wisdom, reaped from the experience of thousands of years, more than ever as its people are lost, struggling to make sense of it all, far from the natural laws it so keenly inhabits.

I grew up in what had once been the small Indigenous village of Hochelaga. Then, in Eastern Canada, the Maritimes I lived on land of the Mi'kmaq and now in Los Angeles, on that of the Chumash and Tongva who lived in a kind of Eden. I acknowledge the Iroquois Confederacy of Nations, its Great Law of Peace formed in 1722, a democratic creed to work together and respect each other, that influenced the United States Constitution. We need that kind of coming together now to right so many wrongs, concepts that can pull us together to benefit how we relate to each other and take care of each other. Hence this book.

There are so many ways to be harmed, to experience a trauma that leaves a legacy of pain difficult to counter, yet there are also many ways to heal from rape, childhood sexual abuse, bullying, drug overdoses, mass fear, intergenerational trauma, deadly shootings, war, natural disasters and the myriad of tragic personal and public responses to Covid-19 that have erupted from the fear and panic of an entity unseen by the human eye. There are so many ways to heal naturally without resorting to pharmaceuticals with their many potentially harmful effects.

And thank goodness for that because the number of people suffering what is generally labeled PTSD (post-traumatic stress disorder) continues an upward trend with no end in sight in 2021. The number of suicides, particularly by teenagers, already at an increase of 35% from 1999 to 2018 in the US, rose 67% in England and Wales between 2010 and 2017; Ireland has the highest incidence in Europe and suicide is the leading cause of death in younger people (first is Lithuania, then Estonia, Norway and Finland, with Ireland fifth), all seemingly only more so during COVID-19. These statistics are enough to break even the most hardened heart.

Yet do the general public or public health officials have this knowledge? Is it freely available and paid for by healthcare insurers? It would seem not as our mental health care crisis is off the charts and the need for new ideas (even if they are old) and new paradigms has never been greater. This time, over 120 years since the Flexner Report, which supported allopathic medicine to the exclusion of all other approaches (see page 50), must be a wakeup call to society, for all disciplines to come together to fix this tragedy and achieve the results we all want without what often gets in the way of a new possibility: the need for safety within our own controlled area of expertise.

Yes, these solutions may cause certain people trepidation, be outside a particular comfort zone and what we may have studied as professionals. To get it right, ergo, we must address the problem head-on, through the entire spectrum of medicine and healing, absent any skin or ego from the game and include both the importance of science in trauma and the essential contribution of our inherent creative expression, based on the body-mind connection.

It is my belief that psychological trauma is a natural response to an adverse event, whether experienced or witnessed. Accordingly, you will notice that I shortened the term PTSD (post-traumatic stress disorder) to PTS, dropping the D, siding with military vets who feel ostracized by calling a natural response a disorder. Second, by regarding PTS or ACE (adverse childhood experience) and any accompanying condition from this more humane, wider perspective, we may establish naturopathic medicine and the expressive arts as essential modalities in trauma recovery by strengthening the body-mind and allowing the pharmaceutical route to be circumvented. Both objectives are based on my three decades of experience in treating unresolved psychological trauma with a two-pronged approach: balance the biochemistry naturally with homeopathy, botanicals, nutrition and other drugless approaches, and tell (or revise) the underlying story through active expression from the realm of the arts.

Thirty years ago, a psychiatrist wrote that his profession was both toxic and out of control. Dr. Peter Breggin,[1] often called the 'conscience of American psychiatry', spoke about 'why therapy, empathy and love must replace the drugs, electroshock and biochemical theories of the "New Psychiatry"' via his groundbreaking book, *Toxic Psychiatry* in 1991; I hung onto it for life support because it acknowledged (extremely rare back then) that a profession as sacrosanct as psychiatry was flawed and creating major problems. Amazingly, to me, few people were questioning the possible dangers and potential brain damage from pharmaceuticals and other psychiatric treatments. I am also grateful for Breggin's almost decade-old book, *Psychiatric Drug Withdrawal: A Guide for Prescribers, Therapists, Patients.*[2]

I propose that my book, *Transforming Trauma*, underscores the missing links in treating the mental imbalances that continue to exist in the conventional medical approach, specifically around PTS and ACE and their comorbidities (other commonly associated problems) as the struggle to reduce overmedication amplifies, not just pertinent to the opioid crisis.

As a naturopathic medical doctor specializing in PTS/trauma (a term I use to signify the trauma at the core of many conditions and diseases) from sexual abuse, and a survivor myself, I have learned that for most patients a drugless approach works, even for difficult cases where the need for medications can be eliminated or, at the minimum, diminished. In fact, people do better in the short- and long-term care when, on first encounter, their physiological state – such as brain and gut chemistry, blood sugar, hormones, food allergies – is optimized and, second, a safe space is created to tell their story, listening without judgment, letting shame fall away, always encouraging the trust and risk-taking that inevitably lead to deeper expression. Between the arc of balancing blood chemistry naturally (naturopathic medicine) and encouraging self-discovery (psychotherapy and the expressive arts), we can implement tools to enhance a heightened sense of wellbeing that leads to an empowered mental state, letting go of fear and panic to manifest a strengthened self, one with clarity of vision and determined resolve. And we mustn't forget that experiences on the job, especially in healthcare professions (notorious for burnout), may lead to PTS. In fact, Canadian research shows that almost half of nurses can have symptoms of lingering persistent thoughts and feelings long after the event. And what about first responders?

Before naturopathic medical school, I spent summers with psychiatrists and psychologists who had trained with, or had been influenced by, Wilhelm Reich MD, and other visionary psychiatrists like Loren Mosher, who continued Quaker Moral Therapy,[3] a departure from the *de rigueur* of centuries of cruel, inhumane, and disempowering psychiatric treatment. In New York City I attended lectures by pioneering psychiatrists such as Rudolph Ballentine, MD, author of *Radical Healing: Integrating the world's great therapeutic traditions to create a new transformative medicine.* When the Vancouver Archdiocese contracted me to treat a person requesting drugless treatment as part of their settlement from sexual abuse, I had a background of many modalities to draw on.

Introduction

My personal story leveraged the possibilities for wellness: firsthand, I knew what optimal biochemistry through clinical nutrition could do, and how psychotherapeutic techniques and homeopathic and botanical medicine could address raw emotion. My own journey in meditation, visualization, and dance seemed the perfect complement to my blossoming practice. I eagerly created the retreat 'Moving the Pelvis to Healing' for my patients, who, referred by other NDs, MDs, psychologists as well as the Archdiocese, had been sexually, medically, or ritually abused. It was the 80s and stories of abuse were finally being expressed and were beginning to be taken seriously. But few professionals were excited or informed by this growing task.

All these years later, we, as a society, continue to find ourselves at a loss when treating mental imbalance, including PTS, addiction and other disorders that have anxiety and fear at their core. The hazards of the current allopathic approach are effectively presented in *Anatomy of an Epidemic* by Robert Whitaker,[4] a riveting account of the damage pharmaceuticals have created, and a book by researcher Peter C Gotzsche MD, *Deadly Medicines and Organized Crime: How Big Pharma has Corrupted Health-care*,[5] both underscoring the dangers and limitations of biomedicine.

Post-traumatic stress, a term that emerged after the Vietnam War, has been characterized as 'overwhelming despair, rage, and anxiety of living in a collapsing society'.[6] One consequence is that children are being prescribed pharmaceuticals at an alarming rate, without the prescriber acknowledging their underlying needs. Any possible experience of trauma is ignored, leading to further misunderstood negative emotions. In the case of adults, prescribers and patients can be too quick to turn to drugs at the first sign of distress. And now society continues to disintegrate to the point our brains and thinking are at risk. In the extreme, this may conclude in a similar mindset to brainwashing in torture, as the Dutch psychiatrist Joost Meerloo writes in his 1956 book, *The*

Rape of the Mind.[7] He invented the term 'menticide', a killing off of brain cells whereby we lose all reason and fall into a stupor, losing touch with reality and morality.

If 30 years ago, the amount of antibiotics prescribed to children for ear infections was alarming to me, that is nothing compared with the number of children routinely treated with psychiatric drugs for behavioral and/or emotional problems today. Now with the possibility of giving them an experimental gene therapy (that is, the mRNA vaccines), it makes my head spin and my heart revolt. Statistics show that over 14% of children (as young as 1 year old) and adolescents[8] are prescribed psychiatric drugs in the US, with 35% of foster children as opposed to 8% of non-foster children,[9] handing us the very definition of a world out of balance.

As far as the grown-up population is concerned, according to IQVia, a company associated with US physician prescribing data, as of 2020, almost 70 million adult Americans were on psychotropic drugs.[10] Clearly the American populace over-medicates, generally unconcerned with the possible consequences of future drug addiction or brain damage or a dangerous toxic load on the body and brain. The media may have opened our eyes to the problem of relying on pharmaceuticals, particularly opioid overuse in the form of heroin and prescription drugs such as Vicodin and Hydrocodone, but virtually nothing has been said about the limitations of our current mental health system, or alternatives that can sidestep the side effects of anxiolytic (anti-anxiety) drugs or antidepressants, chief among them those approved by the FDA in the US and NICE in the UK for PTS: the selective serotonin reuptake inhibitors (SSRIs).

Sadly, all the technology and material wealth we have as a society has not translated into being healthy individually or nationally. Truly the necessity to understand and address human needs is at an all-time high as the root of unresolved psychological trauma has been swept under the carpet in favor of pills for decades, creating one, gigantic, seemingly unsolvable, modern-day problem that can cloud our senses and dull our critical thinking, feeding into a deeper pathology, a nebulous mindset that has turned on authentic emotion to feed into destructive patterns.

The hard truth is, conventional pharmaceuticals are not doing what we need them to do. They merely suppress symptoms and do not treat the root cause of mental imbalance that may be a consequence of social, sexist and/or racial injustice, community and family disintegration, economic disparity, isolation, climate change, vaccine injury and now the ramifications of Covid-19.

What if we returned to Nature and its principles of wholeness, learned what it has to offer before leaping on the pill bandwagon? There are so many reasons to do so but none perhaps greater than to help our children. In psychiatrist Hyla Cass's article, 'Is it Drugs Not Guns that Cause Violence? A common thread amongst the most horrific school shootings of the past 25 years is that the majority of the shooters were taking psychiatric medication,'[11] she postulates that it is better to prescribe natural precursors such as vitamins, minerals, amino acids and botanicals to support the brain chemicals needed to restore balance.

To contextualize mental health care, to put the present in perspective and elucidate what is possible for the future, I turn to the past.

The history of medicine in the US

Splish, splash, what's that sound? People are waking up to the true history of medicine in North America, understanding that in the 18th and 19th centuries there was a diversity of healthcare providers: allopathic medical doctors (who called themselves 'regulars'); homeopathic medical doctors, many European-trained; Eclectic medical doctors, considered a forerunner of naturopathic physicians; as well as the first self-help movement in America created by farmer/botanist Samuel Thomson, who advocated 'every person his own physician',[12] often relying on plants and hydrotherapy learned from First Nations/Native Americans.

But this was not to be. According to the late E. Richard Brown – a nationally recognized public health leader, scholar, and UCLA professor – in *Rockefeller Medicine Men*: 'At the end of the nineteenth century laboratory scientists and elite (health) practitioners formed an alliance to promote scientific medicine, revamp the American Medical Association (AMA), win licensing legislation, and begin reforming medical education.'[13]

The Flexner Report of 1910 was published by The Carnegie Foundation for the Advancement of Teaching. Its full title was *Medical Education in The United States and Canada*,[14] and its findings were controlled by the Rockefeller Foundation. It was grounded in the threat to both the new pharmaceutical industry and their newly discovered products (e.g., coal tar), and to the conventional medical doctors, who saw the growth and successful application of homeopathy in treating epidemics in the late 1800s and the mounting public disgust with their practice of bloodletting, as a bona fide threat to their livelihoods.

Reforms were influenced not just by the AMA and its desire to shut down all competition from natural therapies but also by the pharmaceutical industry tied to the industrialist robber barons, Andrew Carnegie, and John D. Rockefeller. Their mission to dominate medicine succeeded absolutely and led to closures of homeopathic, naturopathic, chiropractic, midwifery, Black, and women's medical institutions. Linking corporate capitalism to medicine is a profound concern as these men unfairly placed their own interests at the heart of healthcare, without due process, commodifying medicine so intensely that the United States cost per capita for its health systems is the highest in the world today, notwithstanding a dreadful track record of chronicity, morbidity, and mortality. Bestowing huge grants on medical schools with the stipulation that only allopathic content be taught, they controlled the governance processes of medical schools, hospitals, and health agencies, and cemented conventional medicine and Big Pharma as bed partners to this day.

European roots

Klink, klunk – the sound of the prison cell-door slamming shut on dissident, psychiatrist, researcher and inventor, Wilhelm Reich, who died while incarcerated in 1957 after his books had been burned and his genius defiled. A cruel example of society's intolerance, this is emblematic of our inability to embrace novel ideas that can move us forward, to better understand the workings of the body and mind and their connection. In retrospect, the public's ignorance of this man who hailed from Vienna but made his home in America is catastrophic in terms of knowledge lost. He had much to offer the conversation on mental health and I offer him as an example of many brilliant people whose visions were cut short because of vested interests determined to sustain their position. To cut to the bone, the larger population has been prevented from seeing the whole picture.

These little-known episodes of repression in the history of North American medicine underscore the impediments to harnessing solutions for the present crisis by stopping the flow of ideas. There is little doubt that the decadent state of healthcare in America is largely a result of the monopolies granted by government leaders to health insurance companies, food corporations and so forth, as well as allopathic strongholds like the AMA, and the APA (American Psychiatric Association), through federal agencies like the CDC (Centers for Disease Control and Prevention), and the FDA (Food and Drug Administration). As a result, contemporary American culture is stuck in healthcare policies that don't consider both deeper causes and a more natural approach; treatment therefore becomes incomplete, spinning its wheels, and getting us nowhere in an increasingly desperate scenario.

Determined to promote what they supposedly believed to be the superiority of scientific medicine and modern medical education, the steel and oil barons (Carnegie and Rockefeller) were too quick on the draw, ultimately triggering a flawed and limited vision of science. The upshot of this system is that Americans have become used to the rush of diagnosis and treatment, to focusing on suppression of symptoms, and dependent on pills for everything, not just true emergencies, ignoring the ability of Nature—food, plants, water, miniscule or energetic doses (homeopathy), body work, and other natural therapies—to heal.

One hundred years later, we not only have Big Pharma but Big Agro with its toxic fertilizers, and adulterated, often genetically modified, food additives, none of which for all the sanctimonious entreaties to science-based medicine has ever been thoroughly studied for their effects on our bodies, and minds. These industries simply bought control of food sourcing, production, and distribution.

Like Rockefeller and the other robber barons at the turn of the 20th century, the contemporary food and health establishment, aided greatly by their skilled Washington lobby, ensures corporations will be able to spew ill-health through toxic products and thus continue to enjoy protected, growing profits, despite persistent reports about destructive markers such as the opioid epidemic or suicide rates, to name two of the most pernicious problems.

A plea for collaboration

Truthfully, the situation is that the dominant medicine today doesn't show any more signs of cooperating or collaborating with the purveyors of natural medicine than it did when its practitioners were anointed as society's saviors by the Flexner Report. In 1952, Adlai E. Stevenson, Jr. called for a widening of the boundaries for medical treatment.[15] Brian Klaas in his book, *Despot's Accomplice*, writes: 'Democracies, by definition, are inherently more collaborative and more willing to consider alternatives before launching new policies—a crucial advantage... Transparency is a key feature of a truly democratic state.'[16] (And now, at the time of writing in 2021, Covid-19 mandates abound in the US and Europe without any regard for medical choice and freedom as well as ignoring individual biochemical or genetic differences.)

In the US, the Community Mental Health Act, signed in 1963 by President John F. Kennedy, was meant to build a community-based system of mental health care that would integrate with social services. Sadly, this didn't happen; instead, hundreds of thousands of people needing help ended up on the streets or in jail or prison. This book addresses what can help them, as both balancing biochemistry and telling their story can help anyone able to get a decent meal and who has the ability to draw from their particular tragic circumstances.

There are many things to love and admire about conventional medicine, too many to mention, but it can't have it both ways. If your intention is to dominate as the exclusive public health option, then the orthodox medical establishment, its institutions, and public health officials, must be prepared to take the blame when things go wrong, because their approach isn't working. But that is not the case with our current mental health crisis. It is a simple observation of reality that their policies aren't succeeding and yet those in charge, the CDC and their like are in complete denial of the current situation and even worse, are doubling down on their refusal to let natural medicine do its thing.

To use a cliché, we don't need to throw the baby out with the bathwater. But we do need to understand and face the fact that political and social privilege has its limitations, that as a people, we need to reel in Big Pharma, its excessive and calamitous input into the lives of people suffering mental/emotional conditions that can range from anxiety to schizophrenia. While there are times when pharmaceutical drugs are needed, as a rule they are not.

Pre-Covid, Carolyn Dewa, MPH, PhD, of the Center for Addiction and Mental Health in Ontario, Canada, questioned the fact that there were so many treatments for depression (a common comorbidity of PTS or ACE) yet depression-related disability is on the rise.[17] As far back as the 1960s several European psychiatrists reported that drug-treated patients with depression over the long term were not getting better; indeed, although some medications helped significantly, there were many ruined lives and admissions of conflicted evaluations with pharmaceutical treatment.[4] Even healthcare insurers such as Blue Cross and Blue Shield in the US envisioned a more integrated public health system comprised of public health systems and insurance providers operating alongside the different levels of government for the communal benefit.[18]

A colleague of Dr. Breggin, psychiatrist Michael Gurevich, having noted a dramatic increase in chronic medical cases, also allowed for a more holistic viewpoint, emphasizing that the body and mind are inseparable.[19] Moreover, in *The Townsend Letter*, it is the hope of John Parks Trowbridge MD that allopathic doctors will soon be forced to acknowledge the vast array of options offered by non-conventional medicine to patients who have not been cured or healed by their drug-oriented approach.[20] Research of late tends to highlight two facts:

1. Psychiatric drugs are doing more harm than good.
2. Fraud in pharmaceutical research is rampant.

Danish researcher Peter C. Gøtzsche added: 'likely ... 15 times more suicides among people taking psychotropic drugs'.[5]

With research showing a higher suicide rate within the first days of starting antidepressant drugs,[21] the time has come for long discussions with all branches of medicine, beginning with the concern as far back as 1982 that psychiatric medications are often xenobiotics (chemicals foreign to the human body) that can induce abnormal brain states,[22] therefore unpredictable mental states. On the other hand, with the rise of both CAM research – so-called 'complementary and alternative' medicine (instead of its own true system) – and the healing qualities of creative expression, such as the positive effect of music on the brain confirmed by neuroplasticity and epigenetics, we have so much to take advantage of now in treating mental imbalance.

That the American Medical Association has attacked many elements of natural medicine for decades is indicative of its purpose: dominance in the health market. But over time, and more recently, this is happening: the migration of allopathic professionals to 'integrative, holistic and functional medicine' and the rise of board certifications for medical doctors, DOs and other biomedicine professionals, indicating that the 'regulars' of our day are not only using these descriptors to describe what they do, but are increasingly relying on drugless medicine to solve their patients' needs, both short-term and long-term. Hallelujah!

Let's face it: a pill cannot fix a pill epidemic. That ship has sailed. Knowing that drugless therapies have been muffled since the Flexner Report,[14] we can understand how natural medicine has been thwarted in what it can offer to stabilize mental health. At this point, we need to dig deeper, to understand the root(s) of the problem, to negotiate our way through often faulty and simplistic conclusions. Shot through our predicament is that we in North America have generated one big mess in treating mental health and we have a lot of work to do to get it right.

What this book offers

Within this book you will discover a detailed path to mental wellness, an unveiling of the vast continuum of the science of medicine and the art of healing. As an answer to the allopathic whitewash, this book weaves in the history of natural medicine while explaining how the body's immune system works to keep the brain functioning at a high level when energy-producing organelles in our cells – the mitochondria – the calming ventral vagus nerve system (see page 171) and the HPA (hypothalamic-pituitary) axis (see page 84) are threatened by the production of excessive stress hormones in the initial response to a traumatic event. In dealing with the biochemistry involved in my healing methodology, I prepare readers – be they general readers or clinicians – with the necessary brain science and biochemistry required to appreciate the effectiveness of clinical nutrition, homeopathy, botanicals, and hydrotherapy for good mental health. I also introduce the topic of unconventional psychothera-pies and the importance of nurturing the mind–body connection that will allow PTS victims to tell their stories in a supportive, less constricting manner.

Finally, in keeping with this book's drugless approach, *Transforming Trauma* introduces the expressive arts, once thought to be exclusive to the realm of the artist, for the most part usually privileged and extensively trained in their specific field, the process a well-kept secret, but now offered up as perhaps one of the best solutions for healing deep anxiety for those willing to take that first step into magic, armed with a muse, and guided by a qualified instructor, health practitioner or not.

Written to offer a path forward, this book was inspired by a conversation with Mary Minor, a naturopathic physician then in Alaska. Dr. Minor made me aware of Harold Napoleon's book, *Yuuyaraq: The Way of the Human Being*,[23] an extremely moving account of the Yu'pik, an Alaskan First Nation tribe that suffered a devastating loss in the 1918 influenza epidemic which ultimately decimated their former way of life because of unresolved psychological trauma on the entire community.

A once vibrant and extraordinary culture, the Yu'pik began

drowning in silence, alcoholism, and drugs. Over generations, anger and self-destructive behavior fed on *nallunguarluku* = 'pretending it didn't happen'. It was just too painful. Thanks to Napoleon, who instigated small community circles, the community started talking, beginning the healing process. Isn't it time we – all of society – followed suit?

Without a doubt, trauma recovery demands that healthcare professionals, lawyers, and government officials offer both compassion and insight. This means we take the time to reflect on our own traumatic experiences so we can empathize and not be triggered. With this we get ready to start talking, to gain the trust of the survivor, to open up dialogues, embracing new information and ideas. Owning our own situation as a professional we encourage curiosity about everything that can help mental imbalance.

Frankly, no type of medicine can stand alone. We must learn that conventional medicine is not the only game in town and realize that its ascendancy since Flexner has culminated in a healthcare crisis that is not only draining the gross domestic product of the US and many other countries of trillions of dollars every year but is leaving us in the dust in terms of a healthy population.

Whatever we believe culturally or politically, whatever threatens us as a community, a country, a planet, whatever medical system or modalities we have chosen to prevent sickness and maintain health, the reality is that we are all in this together. We need each other to cure our national ills, particularly in mental health. We must become aware of all that affects our state of wellness or illness. We need to understand that this holistic approach was not born in the Back-to-the-Land Movement or the Human Potential Movement or the Women's Movement but was alive and well long before the 20th century. We must honor the fact that Indigenous people have known this for thousands of years, as did pioneering naturopathic doctors, Benedict Lust and Louisa Stroeble Lust, and other medical reformers. Adding to this in 2022, I include those who understand frequencies and invisible energetics, realities rarely discussed.

It is time to reclaim our birthright to the full spectrum of healthcare, particularly mental health, understand the need to connect, to listen, to see the whole picture. We must realize we *can* recover from tragedy, whether from sexual abuse or another horrific event without resorting to pharmaceuticals.

Transforming Trauma attempts to shine a light on what is possible and relies on the fact that the body is always telling a story, that it never lies. Once our physiology is balanced, aided by the latest scientific research, we can investigate the event like a crime scene. We can let the evidence speak for itself when it doesn't further injure the survivor – when it's safe to do so. Or we can take the energy of the event and use the imagination to render it anew, generating an artistic venture that will promote resolution.

In the end, taking control and using an assortment of drugless modalities allows a sufferer of PTS or ACE to throw off helplessness, to become strong physiologically and psychologically with the best information out there, optimizing the ability to shed trauma that has threatened to override our resolve. Between balancing our biochemistry naturally and telling or revising our story, we make our way forward to re-empower ourselves. This is true holism. This is what we all deserve.

Part One

Roots and definitions

The little girl looked over at the man lying on the ground. She clutched the bear harder. Is this the way it was going to be? She was determined it was not the way her world would end.

Chapter 1

The history of the experience

War. Grief. Terror. Strangulation of thoughts.
Exhausted senses. Distortion of feelings.

Post-traumatic stress is not a new phenomenon. Not by a long shot. Severe anxiety and all the conditions that spin from its tangled web have been part of the human experience since the beginning of time. A presentation of schizophrenia – thought disturbances to the point of psychosis, a possible manifestation of PTS – can be traced to written documents in *The Book of Hearts*,[1] a part of the Ebers papyrus in ancient Egypt. The mind and heart were synonymous during that time with the disturbance remediated through various means, from listening to music to drilling a hole in the skull to release evil spirits. The Romans also had a specific deity, Angerona Dea,[2] who granted ease from anguish and secret grief. In Chinese medicine, *The Yellow Emperor's Classic of Internal Medicine*, circa 2600 BC, refers to 'any suspense which is similar to a disease'.[3]

Following his father's assassination in 336 BCE, Alexander the Great continued to engage in near-death combat while soldiers, including close friends, died around him.[4] His personality changed, his judgment affected, he became pathologically suspicious, all symptoms of PTS.

Sliding into the 20th century, it is a little-known fact that in England thousands of the two million soldiers in World War 1 were removed from combat duty when they exhibited psychological symptoms that included uncontrollable sobbing, stupor, and mutism. Army medics diagnosed the soldiers' state as

3

a neurological condition (it would become known as shell shock) but those in charge officially condemned them as cowards. Over 300 British veterans were executed;[5] it wasn't until 2006 that they were posthumously granted a pardon.

Women have, from the dawn of time, been claimed as collateral prizes, the victims of rape and other atrocities by victorious armies. Even the 'good guys' commit acts of atrocity: untold numbers of German women were raped by Allied soldiers after World War II on the emancipation of the concentration camps.

And what about events stemming from still current cultural norms that see women as vessels for men's pleasure? Nigerian women who are rescued from Boko Haram only to be raped and starved by the guards meant to take care of them?

And where are the reports on the lives that have endured generations of poverty, barely getting by, hardly able to articulate deep trauma. They struggle daily and pass it on. And on.

The fact is the impoverished and the wealthy have suffered trauma from all kinds of events. Grief, uncertainty, and social injustice continue to play a role in lingering psychological trauma.

Examples from literature

The oldest piece of Western literature that fits with a more specific diagnosis of PTS is from *The Epic of Gilgamesh*, a poetic tale of the King of Uruk of Mesopotamia, 4000 years ago. It describes the terrified king, Gilgamesh, after surviving a violent encounter that ended with his best friend dead. He rages, has trouble sleeping and experiences terrifying flashbacks of the event as well as feeling his future is doomed.[6]

The *Iliad*, circa 672 BC, reflects Homer's experiences during the Trojan War. He speaks of psychological trauma through Achilles' experience: 'Then said Achilles, "Son of Atreus, king of men Agamemnon, see to these matters at some other season, when there is breathing time and when I am calmer. Would you have men eat while the bodies of those whom Hector or Priam slew are still lying mangled upon the plain?".'[7]

Shakespeare's *Henry IV* deals with the psychological aftermath of a traumatic event. Hotspur's wife, Kate, complains about her husband's odd behavior after many mortal combats:

> *Thy spirit within thee hath been so at war,*
> *And thus hath bestirr'd thee in thy sleep*
> *That beads of sweat have stood upon thy brow*
> *Like bubbles in a late-disturbed stream;*
> *And in thy face strange motions have appear'd*
> *Such as we see when restrain their breath*
> *On some great sudden hest*
> *O, what portents are these?*[8]

This has all the criteria to meet a diagnosis of PTS in *DSM-IV (The Diagnostic and Statistical Manual of Mental Disorders)* produced by the American Psychiatric Association (APA)* and used as the ultimate authority on mental health diagnosis around the world.[9]

The descriptions of the Salem Witch Trials in colonial Massachusetts between February 1692 and May 1693, with 234 indictments and 36 executions,[10] underline the hysteria that led to intentional violence after a group of young girls claimed to be possessed by the devil and accused several local women of witchcraft. It was an intensely anxious period that led to delusions and ultimately the murder of innocent victims. Even the effects of their own neighbors' petty arguments led to poisonings through ergot, a fungus blight that can form hallucinogenic substances in moldy bread.[11] For those who survived we can only imagine the anxiety they experienced when women and men feared a death

---

* **Footnote:** Previously called Committee on Statistics of the American Medico-Psychological Association and the National Commission on Mental Hygiene.

sentence or minimally, had property confiscated. Clearly it was a time of mass psychosis.

Drawing on an instance from the US Civil War, Daniel Folsom, a tinsmith from northern New York, wrote about his experiences in battle. Having enlisted in the Union Army after the fall of Fort Sumter, he was a model soldier through long marches and difficult battles until the 1862 Battle of Fredericksburg when he became mentally disturbed. He stopped sleeping, became both manic and severely depressed, and eventually attempted suicide.

During this same 19th century time-frame, Harriet Ann Jacobs (1813-1897) detailed her profound experiences of trauma as a slave, including sexual abuse, in her autobiography *Incidents in the Life of a Slave Girl*,[12] one of the first books to recount the common abuse associated with the struggle for freedom. Yet, history tells us that this remarkable woman was able to shed her past sufficiently to become a leading abolitionist and reformer.

Some years later, the British writer and social critic, Charles Dickens, was involved in a terrible rail accident in London. Although he himself wasn't physically hurt, his daughter, Marnie, reported: '…my father's nerves never really were the same again… we have often seen him, when traveling home… suddenly fall into a paroxysm of fear, tremble all over, clutch the arms of the railway carriage, large beads of perspiration standing on his face, and suffers agonies of terror. We… would touch his hand gently now and then. He had, however… no idea of our presence.' Dickens died on the anniversary of the crash five years later.[13]

Stories of individual and collective horror fill our world. In Canada, First Nation children were torn from their families as late as 1966 to be placed in residential schools that have recently uncovered mass graves. In her book, *These are My Words: The Residential Diary of Violet Pesheens*, First Nation author, Ruby Slipperjack, a member of the Eabametoong, writes about how scared she was not just of being away from her family but of losing her traditions and of not having a name, just a number.[14]

And people trafficked, kidnapped over the centuries, where are their stories? And we can't neglect parents of sick children, particularly those vaccine injured, who bear the ignorance of the medical establishment and elected politicians.

Yes, so many stories of trauma, so many events with effects that last for years or a lifetime on the individual and the community: anxiety, depression, substance abuse, ensuing physical conditions, suicide. So many stories written only on the inside of someone's mind. So many tragedies that could be avoided. All what can be diagnosed as symptoms of PTS.

Early professional insights

Professionals witnessing trauma on the battlefield were the first to assess a presentation of ongoing distress. Beginning with the Napoleonic Wars (1803-1815), Dominique Jean Larrey, a French surgeon known as 'the father of modern military surgery', determined there were three distinct stages to what we now call PTS.[15] Known for his innovative care treating wounded men, Larrey noted that a traumatic experience was, first, a presentation of heightened excitement and imagination; second, a period of fever and gastrointestinal symptoms; and third, a feeling of frustration and depression. A very insightful and skilled observation, this may be the first holistic description of PTS by a health professional.

Soldiers during the American Civil War (1861–1865), as in Folsom's case, presented with an array of symptoms, including unexplained tremors, self-inflicted wounds, heart palpitations, paralysis, intense emotional distress, and even nostalgia, even when home.[16] The astounding number of war casualties resulted in the first public outcry for help, leading to the construction and opening of the first military hospital in Maine in 1863 for those diagnosed with psychiatric illness.[17]

A clinician by the name of Jacob Mendez DaCosta (1833–1900) joined in the call for improved care of the mentally-wounded Civil War veterans,[18] citing survivors experienced chest pains, palpitations, shortness of breath and extreme fatigue – with or without exertion – despite having no physical abnormalities to account for these symptoms. This constellation of symptoms became known as DaCosta's syndrome (also called 'soldier's heart', 'shell shock', 'battle fatigue' and 'combat neurosis') after he released his findings in his 1871 paper, *On Irritable Heart: A Clinical Study of a Form of Functional Cardiac Disorder and Its Consequences*.[19]

Although the writing of Sigmund Freud (1856-1939) was scant on PTS, one of his students, an American named Abram Kardiner, published *The Traumatic Neuroses of War* in 1941, a study considered by many to be the initial work on psychological trauma.[20]

Dutch psychiatrist Joost Meerloo in the middle of the 20th century wrote the book *The Rape of the Mind*, saying: 'stealthy mental coercion is the oldest crime of mankind' when 'human qualities of empathy and understanding' were exploited 'to exert power' over another.[21] His book goes into detail about 'menticide', unmatched psychic wounding, that affects us individually but also en masse when society experiences PTS, manipulated and brainwashed by lies and fraud, pulled away from bodily autonomy and our connection with nature and its offering of peace and balance, as we are now in 2022. Shorn roots leave us ungrounded in a sea of timidity where we become susceptible to pills or shaming or a myriad of other psychological forces that feed on our helplessness. We need to wake up and take back our rights. What our decisions today could manifest in years to come, particularly regarding our children, is particularly disturbing.

Intergenerational trauma

The new science of epigenetics proves that how our DNA is expressed can be transformed by the events of one's lifetime and this transformation can be passed on so that PTS can be transferred from one generation to the next, family to family, even community to community. Known also as transgenerational trauma, intergenerational trauma (IT) can go back many generations. In this way, we account for any of those whose genes have been exposed to trauma that remain unresolved – that is, until someone is brave enough or feels safe enough to breathe into it, to work through the held psychological pain, deeply and usually with considerable effort over time, and let it go (see Appendix 1).

A prime example of intergenerational trauma is childhood sexual abuse that can lead to an ongoing cycle of abuse, generation after generation. IT can also be transmitted through extreme poverty, the torture or sudden death of a loved one, or in a collective or historical trauma of an experience of cultural genocide, war, slavery, terrorism, or natural disasters that leave a psychic imprint on our DNA.

Descendants of a community trauma may also have altered stress hormones,[22, 23] undermining trauma recovery. An early study of 'PTSD' by Yehuda et al,[24] published in the 1980 edition of *The Diagnostic and Statistical Manual of Mental Disorders* (DSM-II) emphasized trauma exposure as a major cause in the appearance of severe stress symptoms that had been previously diagnosed as transient. Yehuda discovered that a mother could transmit PTS to her descendants, producing higher levels of an enzyme involved in the protection of the fetus, leaving them more at risk for age-related metabolic syndrome, including obesity, hypertension and insulin resistance. This syndrome influenced the diagnosis of PTS in the DSM-ll of that year. By 2009, as criteria for DSM-V were being considered, Yehuda encouraged the application of epigenetic methods to account for individual differences in response to trauma and would be included in DSM-V. [24]

Studies have determined that IT has affected those who survived the Holocaust in World War II and that it may occur anywhere genocide has been committed, resulting in the loss of daily love and comfort through family and traditions.[25, 26] Consider the terror innocent bystanders of current wars are experiencing through no fault of their own.

Harold Napoleon's book, *Yuuyaraaq: The Way of the Human Being*, exposed the legacy of an Alaskan community suffering from epidemics in the 1900s, writing, 'Not knowing of microbes, they (the ancestors) attributed these diseases to evil spirits and their own weaknesses. Blamed themselves and their way of life and abandoned themselves and their way of life as a result. But that did not end the suffering...'.[27] We now know the devastation was so complete they didn't speak of it for generations. 'So much suicide, domestic violence, imprisonments, alcoholism affected children, and deaths from disease attributed to alcohol... even though (they) never had it so good in terms of food, clothing, and shelter....'[27]

Further implications

There is more and more evidence to suggest that the parenting skills of those who suffer tragedy diminish following the event. Fear of intimacy, even subconsciously, puts distance between the parent and their children. Damaged parents can become hyper-vigilant thereby discouraging the child from taking normal childhood risks and participating in activities otherwise deemed normal. This can result in, often, a lifelong inability in these children to trust in themselves, damaging their sense of self-worth and curtailing their ability to manifest their own loving family, healthy friendships and positive careers. They exhibit anxiety and other negative behaviors that have manifested simply from being raised by parents or grandparents who had unresolved traumatic experiences.

Psychotherapist M. Gerald Fromm, who edited a collection of essays called *Lost in Transmission: Studies of Trauma Across Generations*, concluded: '...what human beings cannot contain of their experience—what has been traumatically overwhelming, unbearable, unthinkable—falls out of social discourse, but very often onto and into the next generation as an affective sensitivity or a chaotic urgency.'[28]

Ariann Thomas wrote, in *Healing Family Patterns: Ancestral Lineage Clearing for Personal Growth*: 'When we heal our physical, mental, emotional and spiritual traumas, illnesses and shortcomings we will affect all our family members because family patterns don't exist in a vacuum. They affect us all. We are related particles and matter in this world of quantum physics.'[29]

This inheritance of trauma can inform us every day, in our dreams or nightmares, our decisions, our manner of parenting or leading employees or students and the like. For those in leadership positions particularly, it's important this is investigated, to know what has come before us and influenced our own decision-making and behavior.

The following is a list of effects that can result from transgenerational or intergenerational trauma. As I scroll through these, I can track my own experience generated verbally by my mother and silently by my father. Can you relate to these in any way?

- Suppressed or delayed PTS due to communal shame
- Over-protective of children/hyper-vigilant
- Passing on the belief that something bad will happen again
- Avoidance of thoughts and feelings, a behavior that can lead to addictive behaviors or self-harm
- Generational violence: a cycle that may have been previously undefined as a source of trauma

- Living other people's memories (see Chapter 11: Writing and visual arts, for more).

A NOTE TO THE CLINICIAN

Be aware of signs and symptoms of trauma that may have been handed down through generations. There is usually one child within a family, often seen as the 'sensitive' or 'angry' one, who carries the grief of a traumatic lineage of ancestors or predecessors. Try to grasp the deeper issues that keep them from healing, and on different levels: physiologically, emotionally, and spiritually. I will show you the techniques to help them take action that will offer both strength and safety.

Learning to ask the right questions, to understand what has been left unexpressed, will offer a much deeper and more authentic picture of what is going on. Incorporate these same questions in your Subjective, Objective, Assessment Plan (SOAP intake form), expanding the moment when you ask about family medical history. There is so much to offer, particularly the troubled child of a once traumatized parent or ancestor. It begins with empathy and the acknowledgement of what came before. Digging into the lives of parents or ancestors may feel uncomfortable to many people, but can be a lifeline to vital information, giving us a more comprehensive understanding of the present situation, we have chosen to help transform.

It doesn't have to be a chore; it can be fun eliciting this information from various sources, whether from individuals or a community: stories, photographs, scrapbooks, journals, books, writings, artwork, jewelry, even old sports equipment, can offer the stories of the past that continue to live in the present. Who were these people

---

in our past, how did they think, how did they feel? What is their legacy? What strengths can be drawn on to build health individually and in community?

And if someone knows nothing of their past because of adoption or war, it is time to fill this void, create a history that gives them roots to be fed by. It doesn't have to be blood to feel a lineage. And this legacy doesn't even need to be human. It may be a grove of trees, a garden that relies on an aquifer, a boat that sails out to sea. Give this as homework and the roots of connection will grow a stronger, deeper and more complete healing on every level of being.

ASSIGNMENT #1

1. What can we learn from those who have gone before? Think in terms of values such as compassion, wisdom.
2. Explain transgenerational trauma and how that might affect someone with a challenging case of anger.
3. Is there any one person or group from your personal history that has affected you? Does this information change how you see the world, yourself? Describe.
4. Would the Amazon, the ancient female warriors, have experienced psychological trauma after a battle? How would the support of their community have fed the strong resolve and resilience they are known for?

Chapter 2

Present considerations

Helplessness. Unexpressed rage.
Suicide. Shame.
The core of a condition or disease.

For too long, those who have suffered what I refer to as PTS/ trauma, with its wide range of related disorders and comorbidities, have been alone in the darkness, limited to options dictated by the American Psychiatric Association (APA) and their *Diagnostic and Statistical Manual of Mental Disorders (DSM)*. First published in 1952, this has become, slowly over time, the standard classification for mental disorders around the world, acknowledged as such by conventional psychiatry which for decades now has upheld the prescription of psychotropic drugs as both the standard and the appropriate treatment.

With five major revisions by 2017, the *DSM*, its base firmly entrenched in conventional medicine, is on a collision course with the integrated path I shall set out.

From professional and personal experience, I firmly believe mental imbalance can be healed without pharmaceutical drugs, standard conventional (aka allopathic) care, when appropriate conditions are met. As you wind your way through this book, we will contemplate PTS as a normal response to a traumatic event that, due to its inflammatory nature and seismic effect on the brain's senses, transports the victim far from the borders of safety and strength into a chronic loop of mental anguish.

The path towards classification

The German physician and psychiatrist, Christian Friedrich Nasses, attempted to organize a classification system in his *Journal for the Healing and Diagnosis of Pathological Mental Disorders* back in 1818. Clearly frustrated, he had reported, 'Every worker dealing with mental disorders felt he had to offer a classification system of his own.'[1]

In 1840, the US Department of the Interior's census that was helped along through the US Marshall Service, had a question on 'idiocy', meaning insanity, at the time. The question posed was: 'Do you have any idiots in your family?' (Seriously.) Three years later, a letter of protest was sent to the US House of Representatives by the American Statistical Association complaining of the premise of the question in the classification of mental disorders. (Ah, a bit of sanity.) However, although there were other attempts to upgrade the classification (or 'nosology') of mental disorders continued to prove haphazard at best; nothing really changed... until *The DSM* was created in the 1950s.

Until the mid-fifties, the discipline of psychopathology, a term coined by the German-Swiss psychiatrist and philosopher Karl Jaspers in 1913, embraced the scientific study of mental health, including ways to define mental disorders, considered the expression of people's mental health collectively rather than individually. Its intention was to illustrate a 'static understanding'[2] of the mental state experienced and communicated by the client as well as what was observed by the clinician.

Later, in 1921, the American Medico-Psychological Association helped the Bureau of the Census create a standardized form to gather data designed to help mental health workers diagnose specific disorders. From this emerged the first edition of the American Medical Association's *Standard Classified Nomenclature of Disease (MASCND)*.[3] Of note, the US

Army voiced its objections, the first in a series of attempts by the military to intercede in the administration of mental illness, as many service members with some types of mental disorder weren't covered and didn't fit into MASCND's classifications.

The military's ongoing contribution

Following World War II, the military moved to the forefront of the mental-health discussion by virtue of the massive trauma suffered by many of its soldiers. By 1946, the army had developed its own classification system that led to an expansion in mental health services. The chair, William C. Menniger, supported the emerging field of psychology to aid the mental health of veterans and society in general, as seen in the *War Department Technical Bulletin: Medical 203*.[4]

The document focused on the idea or notion that life circumstances and stressful events could be the cause of mental illness in normal people, which concurs with my belief that psychological trauma is a 'normal' response that has looped through the affected psyche to become an ongoing reality perceived by the brain until we are able to break the cycle. Although the APA failed to support the army's classification, *DSM-I*, six years later, included the term 'disorder' as part of its proposed diagnosis for relatively normal people with symptoms from traumatic events (such as a disaster or combat), labeling it 'gross-stress disorder'.

Progression of the diagnosis

Despite growing evidence that trauma exposure was associated with psychiatric problems, the diagnosis of trauma as a 'gross-stress disorder' was eliminated in the *DSM-II* of 1968. The edition instead included 'adjustment reaction to adult life',[5] while severely limiting the diagnosis of trauma to three examples:

- Unwanted pregnancy with suicidal thoughts.
- Fear linked to military combat.
- Ganser syndrome—marked by incorrect answers to questions—in prisoners who face a death sentence. (Originally described by Sigbert Ganser in 1897, this is a rare and controversial disorder that could be malingering, or more likely psychosis due to the extreme stress of this experience.)

In 1980, the APA added 'post-traumatic stress disorder (PTSD)' in the publication of *DSM-III*[6] due to research involving returning Vietnam War veterans, WWII holocaust survivors, sexual trauma victims, and others. Links between the trauma of war and post-military civilian life were recognized and underscored a constellation of symptoms — nightmares, flashbacks, and intrusive memories of traumatic combat experiences. The *DSM-III* criteria for PTS (or 'PTSD' as they call it) were revised in *DSM-III-R* (1987)[7] to reflect continuing research and adding further classifications. One finding, which was unclear at first, was that PTS is relatively common, and is only becoming more so.

The following list represents the criteria highlighted in the 1994 *DSM-IV Manual*[8] to describe an ongoing PTS experience:

1. The primary source of trauma.
2. Recurring symptoms triggered by the initiating event:
   - Autonomic responses by the SNS (sympathetic nervous system) such as heightened sensory, sight, and sound perceptions.
   - A recurring, nightmarish memory loop including menacing images and overwhelming thoughts that recall the whole or parts of the traumatic scenario.
   - A general loss of focus and failure to remember anything associated with the life-shattering experience.

3. Prolonged bouts of hypersensitivity consisting of:
   - A continuous state of fear and nervous agitation.
   - Exaggerated emotional responses to socially accepted, experiential norms, and hyper alertness, sometimes verging on paranoia.
   - A heightened tendency toward irritable and angry reactions, and an internally normalized impatient attitude and distracted awareness.
   - Insomnia.
4. A growing tendency toward memory denial:
   - Passive and active resistance.
   - The persistent conscious or unconscious recognition of causes precipitating the traumatic event and to remember specific details, i.E., Important aspects of suffering.
   - Loss of interest in tasks and narrowing of formerly attractive projects or spheres of interest.
   - Reduction in search for previously proven sources of pleasure and gratification including an intimate relationship, and subdued range of feelings.
   - Preference for a 'doomsday' attitude with diminishing faith in the prospects of better things to come.
5. Extension of time frame for the period of illness beyond the previous limit of one month.

Unlike the DSM-IV criteria, the current DSM-V places post-traumatic stress disorder not in the anxiety disorder category but in a new category. However, this latest edition of DSM has been said to have arisen 'from a tradition filled with haphazard science and politically driven choices'.[9]

Critics

Even back in the late 1800s there was criticism of the nosology (categorization) of mental illness. Daniel Hack Tuke, a lecturer in psychological medicine at the Charing Cross Hospital Medical School in London, said: 'The wit of man has rarely been more exercised than in the attempt to classify the morbid mental phenomena covered by the term insanity. The result has been disappointing.'[10]

Today there is an ongoing chorus of disdain, many from the psychiatric profession itself, who are critical of the *DSM*. First, Karl Tomm MD, in his article *A Critique of the DSM*, maintains: 'As a psychiatrist, I have become increasingly concerned about the inadvertent pathologizing influence in our culture of a major psychiatric document (DSM) published by the APA.'[11] In addition, the complicit relationship between the governors of the DSM and the APA, Tomm questions the DSM's assumptions and its overreach in influencing our culture's interpretation (professional and lay) of mental imbalance with its many consequences.

Secondly, the description of PTS has been criticized as too vague regarding the compilation of symptoms relating to the disorder, as the late clinical and research psychologist, feminist and activist, Dr. Paula Caplan, explains in her book, *They Say You're Crazy: How the World's Most Powerful Psychiatrists Decide Who's Normal.*[12] In an expansive critique, she draws attention to the extent of disarray and ineptitude in the *DSM* culminating in a mental disorder not being anywhere near clearly defined.

To make my third point, the DSM's diagnosis of PTS as a group phenomenon is strictly confined to the military, thereby omitting a potential source of a vast array of PTS/trauma and comorbidities that could apply to a single person. Monnica T. Williams PhD writes: 'Currently, the DSM (DSM-V) recognizes racism as trauma only when an individual meets DSM criteria for

PTS in relation to a discrete racist event, such as an assault. This is problematic given that many minorities experience cumulative experiences of racism as traumatic, with perhaps a minor event acting as "the last straw" in triggering trauma reactions.[13]

Finally, what of the conflict of interest between those who instigate the Manual's use and the APA's association with the pharmaceutical industry? Consider the views of Danish medical researcher, Dr. Peter Gotzsche. In his book, *Deadly Medicines and Organised Crime: How Big Pharma has Corrupted Healthcare,* he writes: 'Psychiatry is the drug industry's paradise as definitions of psychiatric disorders are vague and easy to manipulate. Leading psychiatrists are therefore at high risk of corruption and, indeed, psychiatrists collect more money from drug making than doctors in any other specialty. Those who take the most money tend to prescribe antipsychotics to children... Most often psychiatrists are also "educated" with industry's hospitality more often than any other specialty.'[14] Agreeing with Tomm's earlier point, he goes on: 'This has dire consequences for the patients. The *Diagnostic and Statistical Manual of Mental Disorders (DSM)* from the American Psychiatric Association (APA) has become infamous.'

The corruption between the two parties had reached a level that, according to Allen Frances MD, chairman of the task force for DSM-IV (which lists 374 different ways to be mentally ill; up from 297 in DSM-III) believed the responsibility for defining psychiatric conditions needed to be taken away from the APA. Dr. Frances has warned that DSM-V could unleash multiple new false positive epidemics, not only because of industry money but also because researchers push for greater recognition of their pet conditions. He concludes that new diagnoses are as dangerous as new drugs because they can mean people will be treated by prescriptions they don't need.[15] As an epitaph, even an editor of the *British Medical Journal* asked the question, 'Who should define disease?'[16]

In sum, while the purveyors of *The DSM* fashioned a major contribution to the diagnosis of PTS, there is an ongoing debate regarding the dominance and validity of the DSM publications within scientific circles and the military. As noted, many patients, health professionals, and military leaders believe the stigma conveyed by the word 'disorder' contributes to many soldiers being reluctant to ask for help. They have urged a change to rename PTSD as post-traumatic stress injury (PTS or PTSI), a change I have implemented that is more in line with the language and thinking of our soldiers. As a further complaint to this rising power, the military environment needs to change so that mental health support is more accessible to soldiers and treatment more easily available. Furthermore, at the APA 2012 annual meeting, where the term 'injury' was proposed as a replacement, the majority adjudged it as too imprecise for a medical diagnosis in *DSM-V* instead deciding to stay with 'disorder' and the abbreviation 'PTSD'.

As the various publications and revisions emerged, *The DSM* cast itself as being more objective than subjective, based on scientific evidence gained from FDA approved research. But was it? Is it? I agree with psychotherapist Tracy Hutchinson: 'It may be irrelevant whether a person meets the full criteria [of a diagnosis of PTS] — what matters is if symptoms are causing problems in their life.'[17]

The data: what we know about the prevalence of violence, trauma and PTS worldwide

From multiple sources we can deduce that PTS is widespread and on the increase.

Major causes of lingering psychological trauma before COVID-19[18, 19, 20]

These are longstanding causes:

- childhood sex abuse in women
- neglect, physical and sexual abuse in children
- rape in adults (women and men)
- battered women
- personal assault
- car accidents
- military veterans, their experiences
- witnessing perceived or actual violence
- death of a relative or individual.

Countries with populations afflicted by PTS around the world

We can assume that wherever there is violence there will be PTS but the following lists international documented evidence.

- Canada (study of 24 countries) has the highest rate of PTS at 9.2%, followed by the Netherlands, Australia and the US with the lowest being Nigeria, China and Romania.[21]
- In the UK, one in three people who have experienced a traumatic event will have PTS.
- The UN estimates that more than 600 million women live in countries where domestic violence is not considered a crime.[22]
- In Mexico 25,000 women go missing every year. Mexico's Statistical Research Department reported on February 2, 2022 that there had been a 25% rise in domestic violence since Covid–19.[23]

General factors pertinent to affected populations

- Worldwide, 3.6% of the population suffers PTS.[24]
- PTS crosses all social classes and ethnicities.
- Women are twice as likely as men to have PTS or perhaps they are more willing to speak of it. And then there is the hormonal factor.[25, 26]

- Those living in wealthier countries are at a higher risk of developing PTS.
- However, those with social, economic or educational disadvantages and those subject to racism are more likely to experience PTS. [21]

Segments of the population most affected worldwide and in the US

- Altogether 35-70% of women worldwide have suffered either physical and/or sexual violence by an intimate partner or sexual violence by a non-partner at some point in their lives.
- Almost one-fifth of American women (16%) are sexually abused – from rape, attempted rape, or some other form of molestation – before their 18th birthday.
- Women and girls account for 70% of human trafficking.[27]
- One in 10 women experience cyber-harassment (European Union).[28]
- At least 200 million women and girls alive today have undergone female genital mutilation/cutting in 30 countries.[29]
- Every 68 seconds an American is sexually assaulted.
- The majority of sexual assault victims are under 30 years of age.[30].
- In the US, the ratio of PTS among females and males breaks down to:
  - Adults: women: 9.7%; men: 3.6%; overall: 6.8%
  - Children: Girls: 11% (1 in 9); boys: 1.9% (1 in 53). NB: High-risk children show higher prevalence of PTS than do adults.
- Each year, in the US, the majority of abuse reported, involving 5.5 million children, to Child Protection Services is due to neglect (65%), with 18% for physical abuse, 10% for

sexual abuse, and 7% for psychological/mental abuse (see causes, page 22).
- And now we have to include the effect of lockdowns, related suicides and vaccine injuries.

In the UK, Alexa Bradley, Centre for Crime and Justice, Office for National Statistics cites, stated: 'Child abuse is an appalling crime against some of the most vulnerable in society, but it is also something that is little discussed or understood... Measuring the extent and nature of child abuse is difficult because it is usually hidden from view and comes in many forms. Bringing data together from different sources helps us better understand both the nature of child abuse and the potential demand on support services.'[31]

Rape

The 10 countries with the highest recorded incidence of rape are:[32]
- Botswana (92.93% of total population)
- Australia (91.92%)
- Lesotho (82.68%)
- South Africa (72.10%)
- Bermuda (67.29%)
- Sweden (63.54%)
- Suriname (45.21%)
- Costa Rica (36.70%).

These are some of the facts on record about who is most at risk:
- 16-19 year-olds are four times more likely to be raped than the general population.
- 90% of adult rape victims are women.
- 18-24 year-old college students are three times more likely to be raped than the general population.[30]

- One in three females (one in four males) experienced attempted or completed rape: first time between ages 11 and 17.
- Females: 51% by intimate partners; 40.8% by acquaintance.
- Males: 52.4% by acquaintance; 15.1% by strangers.[33]
- Rape and PTS: One study found that, of women who had been raped, almost all – 94 out of 100 – experienced symptoms of PTS during the two weeks immediately following the rape. Nine months later, approximately 30 out of 100 of the women were still reporting this pattern of symptoms.
- Millions of men have been raped: one in 10.[30]
- Male (16-24 year-olds) college students in the US are five times more likely to be raped.

The violence factor

What we know about the experience of violence worldwide includes:
- Worldwide, an estimated 246 million girls and boys experience school-related violence every year, with girls being most susceptible.[28]
- One in four women in the World Health Organization (WHO) European region will experience gender-based violence at some point in their lives.[34]
- Approximately 100 to 140 million girls and women worldwide have suffered female genital mutilation (FGM).[35]
- Women and girls represent 55% of the estimated 20.9 million victims of forced labour worldwide, and 98% of the estimated 4.5 million forced into sexual exploitation.[36]

In addition to human trafficking, the never-ending shootings, the humanitarian crisis suffered by refugees (who are doubly traumatized by often being unwanted in their new country), we have the homeless on our streets and alleys, and now in 2022 those who have been forced into bankruptcy through no fault of their own, or who have been psychically damaged by lockdowns, hence traumatized by loneliness as well as forced vaccinations and mask mandates. We should not be surprised that the civilian PTS experience is ever increasing. The soaring rate of suicides, particularly by teenagers, during Covid-19 is another tragic reflection of poor decision-making by public health officials.

Indigenous women

In the US, the figures for Indigenous women are particularly troubling:

- In the US, the murder rate for Indigenous women is 10 times the national average, the third leading cause of death in American Indian and Alaskan Native Women according to Urban Indian Health Institute (UIHI) who wrote that the problem is that many cases are missing in law enforcement records.
- I quote UIHI: 'The challenges and barriers in accessing data on this issue from law enforcement severely impede the ability of communities, tribal nations, and policy makers to make informed decisions on how best to address this violence.'[37]
- Also, 'No agency has comprehensive data on the true number of missing and murdered Indigenous women and girls, and that further research is needed.' [37]
- And further: 'Tribal nations must have the ability to advocate for their citizens living in urban areas when they go missing or are killed. This is a courtesy extended to all other sovereign nations…'.
- The cultural genocide of Indigenous residential schools by government policies continues to cause tremendous suffering to this day, with Native Americans, First Nations,

Inuit, and Metis having the highest suicide rates in the world. In Canada, suicide rates for Inuit youth (extreme north) are 11 times the national average.

- For Native American youth the rates are 2.5 times the national average.
- Suicide in these groups was very rare historically.[38]

The suicide factor

Rates of suicide, as reflected in the data above, tell us much:

- The CDC (Centers for Disease Control and Prevention, US) has reported that in 2017 38,000 people between 16 and 64 died by suicide in the US.[39]
- This is a 40% increase from 2000.
- Overdoses have been calculated at over 100,000 for the last year as of November 2021. This gives us a horrifying glimpse into the mental and emotional pain that is only increasing.
- In the US, 132 suicides occur every day from PTS.
- Eight suicides occur every day in the UK and Ireland.

We are clearly at a crossroads in history, experiencing a whole new reality that includes extreme divisiveness in families and long-term friendships because of the loss of liberty and medical freedom and the differences in how to protect or heal, that can boil down to what medical system is adhered to. Teenagers have been especially hit hard with this reality, with many trying or in fact being successful in ending their lives. And the increase in addictions and domestic violence are also impacting families.

The experience of military Vets[40]

- **Operations Iraqi Freedom (OIF) and Enduring Freedom (OEF):** Between 11 and 20% have PTS in a given year.

- **Gulf War (Desert Storm):** 10-12% have PTS in a given year.
- **Vietnam War:** It is estimated that about 30% of Vietnam Veterans have had PTS in their lifetime; 4-5% reported recent symptoms 20-25 years later.
- Among Veterans who use VA healthcare, about 23 out of 100 women (or 23%) reported sexual assault when in the military.
- 55 out of 100 women (or 55%) and 38 out of 100 men (or 38%) have experienced sexual harassment when in the military.

People most susceptible to PTS

- Transgender women
- Prostitutes
- Veterans
- Police officers
- Firefighters
- Journalists
- First responders (rainn.org and www.delraybeachpsychiatrist.com/7-professions-risk-post-traumatic-stress-disorder.

In addition, we know that transgender individuals are four times more likely than cisgender to experience violence (rape to murder).[41]

Common signs and symptoms of PTS

There are so many symptoms and signs that may have their basis in PTS and in ACE and can be expressed or appear in the many other conditions and diseases shown in the list below, based on my clinical experience and other sources. Once we trace back to the event, we can often confirm the cause of unacknowledged symptoms. This is the intent of this book. For instance, I have seen many women who had various symptoms following sexual abuse. Headaches and vaginitis were very common and can come from both a bad diet but also the repression of the event. Therefore, a mind–body approach to healing PTS and ACE is essential. Common symptoms of other sources include:

- adrenal fatigue and exhaustion
- agitation, anger issues
- any unresolving symptoms such as laryngitis or vaginitis
- autoimmune disorders, cancers, and fibromyalgia
- eating disorders
- emotional distress such as anxiety (often unexplained), depression, aggression, rage, behavioral disorders
- fragmented thoughts, feelings of being dissociated
- frequent urination
- gastrointestinal disturbances
- headaches
- increased heart rate such as in Graves' disease. insomnia, nightmares
- insomnia, nightmares
- memory and concentration problems
- psychotic episodes
- psychological numbing
- severe anxiety to the point of suicide
- sexual dysfunction: intimacy reluctance or sex addiction
- skin disorders.

Lingering psychological trauma often goes unnoticed or is not spoken about with a clinician. For this reason, unexplained psychological and physiological symptoms become key to digging further to the root cause. As I have said, a main thrust of this book is to expand the arena of PTS victims available for treatment by natural medicine.

Adverse childhood experience (ACE)

It's hardly a surprise that research has found childhood adversity, whether through government policy, emotional neglect, sexual or physical abuse, poverty, chronic feelings of shame, parents who are depressed or addicts, and the like, affects health later in life. The term 'adverse childhood experience' or 'ACE' was coined by physicians Vincent Felitti and Robert Anda in 1995 and written about extensively by Donna Jackson Nakazawa. ACE represent cumulative prolonged trauma with a similar pattern of changes to the sudden shock of PTS: similar brain locale, such as the amygdala and hippocampus, and release of toxic levels of hormones such as cortisol, all of which will be discussed in Chapter 4: The brain on fire.

Although ACE may not have the exact same effect on the brain, studies, albeit controversial, show that the amygdala and hippocampus can either be enlarged or reduced and that the vulnerability to the brain and subsequent risk of ACE-related disorders are associated with sensitive phases of development that relate to the type and timing of abuse. It seems alterations in synaptic organization are at play, affecting neural networks, and that the hormone, estrogen, may be protective. So although not a classic PTS experience, the experience of ACE can result in unresolved psychological trauma with symptoms and behavior that present for our purposes with little difference.[42, 43, 44, 45]

Key knowledge of ACE includes:

- Studies show that almost two-thirds of participants had experienced four or more traumatic childhood events that included emotional abuse and neglect, with most occurring within the family and can include having a parent in prison or with mental illness.[46]
- Several studies of ACE show almost all participants who had suffered even one adverse childhood experience could have

a comorbidity of schizophrenia diagnosed as an adult.[47] And that this can increase suicidal behavior.

- Another egregious factor is the devastation of maternal stress on fetal brain development that can generate mental and emotional dysfunction over a lifetime and even generations.[48]
- And then there is the horror of domestic abuse[49] that has risen dramatically from an already intolerable prevalence because of restrictions during Covid-19.

Complex-PTS (C-PTS)

A severe form of PTS, complex-PTS (C-PTS) or 'disorder of extreme stress' includes survivors of kidnappings or torture, people who have experienced protracted trauma, or a situation of 'life or death' over a long period of time. Violent or not — the mere act of being held against your will implies violence — terror has provoked intense emotional lability (aggression, rage, severe panic attacks) and possibly mental derangement, such as dissociation, fragmented thoughts, and amnesia. The terror can turn inward and result in self-destructive behavior such as addiction, cutting, or self-mutilation.[54]

Dr. Marylene Cloitre, author of three books on trauma, has analyzed data from a wide number of projects. She noted that, although trauma history, childhood trauma, and sustained and repeated trauma are risk factors for C-PTSD, 'they are not, in themselves, determinants'. She explained that 'context, ecological factors and individual factors could all make a difference to an outcome diagnosis'.[50] And for that we can rejoice… no matter how bad a situation there are always factors that can shape and lead to healing.

Comorbidities

Comorbidities are any conditions associated with an illness. I reiterate, in terms of PTS, a traumatic experience can be at the core of many conditions or diseases, including many that are simply not considered. Obvious examples include severe anxiety coupled with depression, an eating disorder or addiction, but its manifestations are many, from an unexplained itch to the paranoia of schizophrenia.

According to the Irish Dr. Robert Graves (mid 1800s) and the British Dr. Caleb Parry (early 1800s), Graves' disease is a constellation of symptoms that has its roots in a great fright (or great grief) resulting in a serious disturbance of the normal functioning of the thyroid gland.[51, 52] Digging into what these two observant doctors learned 200 years ago, I was able to save my own thyroid from being removed or irradiated. I don't know of any research on this yet, but it will come. And, in my belief, there is so much more to discover. In fact, an originating emotional distress is far more common than we can imagine in both physical and mental health.

The following list highlights common comorbidities of PTS:
- Depression
- General anxiety
- Panic
- Social anxiety
- Agoraphobia
- Drug abuse.

I firmly believe that, as we become more aware of probing the root cause – investigating people with particularly difficult and unresolved cases – more symptoms and diseases will be traced back to a traumatic event. For example, genitourinary or lower abdomen/pelvic area problems are easily considered in sexual assault, but we can also extend the link of a traumatic event to cancers. Here we can look to the work of the German oncologist Dr. Ryke Geerd Hamer, who discovered a set of healing principles that included reducing conflict anxiety as a primary step in healing. In his work that he called New German Medicine, he explained that he believed (as I do) that if the shock of a grief or ongoing destructive behavior or relationship has not been dealt with on an emotional level, it manifests on the physical. (His epiphany came when he was diagnosed with prostate cancer a few months after his son was killed in a car accident.)[53]

An endless list of cases, not yet considered or counted by the medical establishment, has resulted in an invisible epidemic. This lack of perception of the root cause is leaving people with daily struggles that may lead to a lifelong disability. Yet when this is probed it may lead them, often very quickly, out of their pain. For example, comorbid conditions of physical illness — whether viral, bacterial or fungal — and of the many central sensitivity disorders — fibromyalgia, ME/chronic fatigue, multiple chemical sensitivity disorders, physical pain—may arise from trauma. These may have their source in a dysregulation of the limbic system, autonomic dysregulation, and immune inflammation, perhaps through an infectious or physiological pathway but may have a psychological or emotional precipitant. (These pathways will be detailed in Part Two, beginning on page 59.)

As noted, because of the huge role it plays in American life, the military has had extensive input into the diagnosis of trauma. Most recently, O'Donovan et al at the San Francisco VA Medical Center underlined the thesis of comorbidity with the following statement: 'Our findings... contribute to the growing literature highlighting the increased risk of other chronic physical diseases with PTS and other psychiatric disorders.'[54]

Research: Disorders that can have trauma at their core

The following links have been supported by published research:
- **Autoimmune disorders:** O'Donovan et al found a two-fold increased risk of an autoimmune disorder in individuals with PTS compared with those with no psychiatric diagnosis.[54]

- **Eating disorders:**
  - Emotional eating attempts to suppress an emotion or soothe our distress. (Really the same thing)
  - Anorexia, bulimia, or simply overeating, creates a burden on our brain and body either without enough or too many nutrients.
- **Heart disease:**
  - DaCosta's syndrome[55, 56] was confirmed in a 1990 study: a form of cardiomyopathy known as takotsubo cardiomyopathy, occurred in those who had significant psychological trauma.[57]
  - Cardiac arrhythmias are linked to excess circulating levels of catecholamines/neurotransmitters, an indication of psychological stressors that can lead to adverse physical effects, including cardiovascular events.
  - Further clinical and epidemiological studies[58, 59] indicate people with PTS may have an increased risk of cardiovascular disease. Increased activity of the physiological connection between the sympathetic nervous system and the adrenals plays an important role. (Aha! Adrenal involvement!)
- **Metabolic syndrome:** The link between PTS symptoms and metabolic syndrome was first observed in police work.
- **Sexual dysfunction:** PTS can cause sexual dysfunction even when the trauma is not related to sexual assault. Clinical psychologist, Amy Lehrner, writes: 'It is clear that PTS is associated with sexual problems, even among relatively young people regardless of the type of trauma they experienced… PTS and sexual desire compete for the same hormonal and neurological networks. Sexual arousal mimics the physiological experience of fear, and once these associations have been forged in the intense experience of trauma, it can be difficult to uncouple them.'[60, 61]

- **Vaccine injury:** Any illness or death of a loved one, of course, creates trauma. An illness of our own creates trauma. But what if a society continually chooses to ignore its mistakes by refusing to recognize the harm being done? Simple answer: It, meaning the catastrophe, hits everyone involved even harder because of the lack of compassion that has been generated by fraud in medical research. For example, William Thompson of the CDC admitted only after nine years to Dr. Brian Hooker whose son was harmed by the MMR vaccine that studies on autism and MMR had been manipulated. See my podcast, episode #5, for Brian's story.[62, 63]
- **Gender dysphoria (GD):** Trauma can accompany every stage of the distress of the possibility of gender dysphoria (GD). This is heightened by the lack of support and understanding in society and the level of violence that transgender people may experience. Watching and waiting has been the norm but now, with 30 years of experience and debate, this has become controversial.[64, 65, 66] (See my podcast with Walt Heyer a man who transitioned to a woman and then back to a man on my podcast in Season 2.) Whatever your opinion in this debate, GD can cause moderate to severe PTS/trauma at any step and all considerations and possibilities must stay on the table. With children especially we must address underlying trauma – it might not be GD at all.
- **Addiction:** Trauma is almost always at the deepest root of an addiction and leads quickly to unbalanced biochemistry (see Chapter 15).
- **Schizophrenia:** Recent findings show that psychotic symptoms, typical of schizophrenia, occur with a higher-than-expected frequency in people suffering PTS (see Chapter 15).

- **Neurological conditions** such as autism and PANDAS (pediatric autoimmune neuropsychiatric disorders) are beyond the scope of this book, but I need to mention them briefly here because they are associated with such severe anxiety, among many other symptoms. 'PANDAS associated with streptococcal infection' comes under the umbrella of PANS – pediatric acute onset neuropsychiatric syndrome. These conditions include a rapid onset of severe anxiety (with many other symptoms that involve the brain), often after a strep infection, and are an example of how a toxic substance like a bacterium or a vaccine can affect the brain. This is in fact a perfect example of the body–mind (brain) connection because if we address the gut (accessing the gut–brain connection), boost the immune system, and detoxify the toxin we can see a change in tics as well as anxiety and the myriad of other symptoms generated. Therefore, a holistic approach is imperative, one that covers nutrition and allergies and balances energy (homeopathy).

More subtle occurrences

Intergenerational trauma aside, the standard definition of PTS is that it occurs after an individual experiences a terrifying, life-changing event where physical or psychological harm occurred or was threatened. (Or, as in Graves' disease and other conditions where one feels a misfit, with the ensuing negative societal perceptions.) This is true, but it is important to under-stand that PTS can occur after more subtle events or situations where boundaries have been crossed. While the experience may not be terrifying, it may result in a profound and chronic nega-tive response that overwhelms the survivor's physiology. This may be difficult to ascertain.

Insufficient reporting

Until recently, studies on PTS have been either poorly written or contained insufficient reporting, often because of one, very powerful emotion. That emotion is *shame*. And that is not just shame on the part of the survivor but of a medical professional or public official who, perhaps triggered themselves, has swept the seriousness of what has happened under the rug, ignoring the devastation of the person sitting across from them.

Thankfully, in the last few years, mainly due to the heightened awareness of the suffering of veterans and the #MeToo and #TimesUp movements, as well as a rise in Indigenous and non-indigenous healing circles, less *shame* and more *compassion* has been framing public perception. In this, society is educated to the reality that PTS is not a mental illness, that the shame of being vulnerable to anxiety or depression or any other symptoms of PTS is a normal reaction to a terrifying situation. This has allowed survivors to come out of the shadows and shine without ridicule or another victim-blaming experience, perceived or real. It has been a very exciting time for those of us who have suffered emotional pain not only in silence but in the hurt of misunderstanding, rejection, and prejudice for years.

And now, in 2020-2022, the world has been exposed not just to a virus that may be little worse than a bad flu (for those without underlying conditions) but to damage by often uninformed political decisions. Fear is generated daily by the media no matter what the presentation or solution. People are stepping up to fill vacuums of disinformation but, depending on their knowledge base, we can't be sure anyone really knows the facts or has the power to put the truth into action. People have lost so much, not only jobs and the comfort of community but the safety of a world, however previously illusory, that has gone, to be honest, berserk, and will need a lot of help to right itself.

Chapter 2

The more we reflect on and tease out the truth of our predicament, the better off we will be individually and collectively. This situation is a global condition and layers the already precarious situation of climate change that is triggering flooding and fires (and recently snow in Texas); heightened violence whether domestic, human trafficking, police shootings, racism; LGBTQ; hunger; loss of work through no fault of the individual; and so much more.

It is indeed a tangled web, and because of that, it has been a particularly difficult time for people who already had PTS or generalized anxiety before Covid-19. Layer upon layer of community or national/international pathos manifests personally in panic attacks, uncontrollable anxiety, nightmares, even psychosis including schizophrenia, and suicide. Physiologically, the presentation is endless: obesity, diabetes and other underlying conditions are not being addressed and healed (something naturopathic and integrated physicians excel at).

NOTE TO THE CLINICIAN

Emotion casts a wide net and psychological pain is the source of many illnesses, far more widespread than is generally realized. To dismiss it out of hand could have far-reaching consequences and is not the direction in which to go. When we take the time to track back to the original event and allow for any possible unveiling of a condition or disease that we may not initially have suspected as PTS, we may be closer to getting the results we and the survivor are looking for.

If asking questions directly is a problem, my advice is to go slowly, and to start by getting to know the person generally and focus on trust. No one is going to answer you honestly unless they feel safe with their story. It may be that as a professional you need to do your own emotional work to stay centered and strong.

I have always appreciated Jung's thoughts that a wounded doctor is best. When you realize that your deepest understanding of another's situation motivates the best of both of you in the direction of health, we all win. Remember that everyone has a distinct personality, and that it is impossible to predict either the reactive path of a terrifying event or the resilience in response. Stay open to discovering the thread or key that unlocks a person's pain.

ASSIGNMENT #2

1. If we accept that someone has trauma, what needs to be transformed?
2. What can we do to reach in and touch a wounded heart? What parameters might we need to consider?
3. Consider a personal experience with physical symptoms. Can you track them back to a psychological event? Who was there for you and how did that make you feel?
4. Take time to reflect on your thoughts regarding the present *DSM*. Does this classification of PTS cover your personal experience of this condition or of treating survivors?

Chapter 3

A divided perspective

Differing paths. Reductionism. Vitalism. The laws of Nature. The chemical explosion.

The historical divisions and differences in medicine continue to inform our preferences for treatment in the present time. We'll get to the Flexner Report (page 50), the event that changed the trajectory of medicine, but first let's look further back in time to realize the philosophies that have underlined the roots of medicine for centuries, and why a full spectrum of healthcare, particularly in lingering psychological stress, is essential to attain true wellbeing.

Quite simply, the separation of mind and body represents the reductionist, allopathic approach of conventional medicine that separates each body part from the whole. This means treatment of the digestive, nervous, cardiovascular systems, and so on, and omits any connection between them as well as ignoring underlying causes, whether physiological or psychological. Vitalism, on the other hand, sees a unified whole and believes the mind–body is dynamic and ever changing. This perspective – what naturopathic medicine and other drugless systems are based on – assumes an innate intelligence within that is designed to heal the body, each system coordinating with the others, and the inherent holistic ability for restoration through natural medicine, that in our case includes creative means. Both schools of thought and practice were influenced by Greek medicine, which viewed the mind–body both as a dynamic whole and as consistent with distinct mechanistic parts.[1]

These differences – reductionist versus vitalist (as well as sexism, racism, and other injustices) – have informed medical theory and treatments for centuries and have created a haphazard approach to addressing mental health. Contrary to Indigenous and Eastern cultures, historically allopathic medicine's perspective on mental distress has dictated Western culture's perception: the mentally ill were bad and must be physically abused in one manner or another, burned at the stake, or locked up in an asylum, and now, overly medicated. By understanding the missing pieces, we can generate a more holistic system for treating PTS and all its comorbidities that also includes justice and kindness, and connections to each other and the community at large that will undoubtedly lead to higher recovery rates.

The historic view

As early as 400 BCE, Greek physicians proposed a unified or holistic vision of health (except for 'female hysteria', their idea that the womb wandered around the body causing havoc mentally and emotionally.) Hippocrates introduced the idea of encouraging those he deemed having 'disturbed physiology' to participate in quiet activities like reading and walking.[2] The one accompanying prescription was the botanical purgative, *hellebore*, to clear the body of 'noxious build-up'. Another approach came from Aristotle, who felt watching a dramatic play at the Theater of Epidaurus could, by releasing emotion, create a catharsis.[3] Interestingly, 2500 years later, the ideas of quieting the mind, expressing repressed emotion, and clearing the body of toxins are making a comeback to help stabilize a person's mood.

Before long, another Greek, the physician Claudius Galen (129–210 AD), came up with his theory of 'heroic' medicine that would form the foundation of Western conventional medicine. This philosophy advocated balancing the four humors – blood, yellow phlegm, and yellow and black bile – through various treatments: starvation, bloodletting, purging and vomiting.[4, 5, 6] The term 'heroic' denoted extreme treatment and aggressive dosages of toxic substances in medical practice; I assume also one was seen as a hero to undergo these types of medical treatment!

During the 17th century in America, physicians such as Thomas Willis encouraged bloodletting to treat mental illness, believing a biochemical variance was the cause of altered states. Used extensively[7] by Benjamin Rush (1745-1813), one of signers of the Declaration of Independence, bloodletting came to be symbolized in the barbershop pole – red for advertising the procedure, and white for the tourniquet.

During these years, insane asylums started popping up where those considered mentally disturbed would be housed with criminals, as opposed to centuries of being cared for at home. (Rush, considered by some to be the Father of American psychiatry, was not an advocate of shackles and chains.) The injustices beyond being tethered in these asylums were numerous; patients including victims of senility, syphilis or other neurological disorders, were subjected to obscene practices that included high-pressure showers, injection of metallic salts, horse serum, even arsenic, teeth removal, with the cruelest being barbaric surgeries such as removal of diseased female genitalia.

In the face of the ongoing challenge to human decency and good medical practice, there were several reformers who have withstood the whitewashing of what has been presented to the public as definitive medical history. During such abysmal times for the mentally ill there were those who came forward with kindness and insight, as Hippocrates had.

First, there was Samuel Hahnemann MD, founder of the medical system of homeopathy in the 1700s, who made the first step towards compassion when he accepted an offer from the reigning Duke of Saxe-Gotha to take charge of an insane asylum. At the time, the mentally ill were put in dungeons, chained, and whipped. 'I never allow an insane person to be punished,' he said, 'either by blows or any kind of corporeal chastisement... these sufferers only deserve pity and are always worse after such rough and cruel treatment.'[8] He also opposed the large and repeated doses of nauseating medicines that inmates were forced to swallow.

Within a year of being in charge, Hahnemann had 'established a dramatic cure of a patient, Herr Klockenbring,' the Secretary of the Chancellery of Hanover, who had been treated previously for insanity, presenting with 'eccentricities, delusions, and a tendency to destroy his clothing, the furniture, piano',[8] without success by the Hanoverian court physician, Herr Dr. Wichmann. Hahnemann, perhaps, was the real pioneer of psychiatry, the first physician to advocate a 'treatment of the insane by mildness rather than coercion'.

Hahnemann wasn't the only one to suggest a more humane approach, however. Fifteen months after Hahnemann's Gotha asylum success, the French physician Phillippe Pinel, who had also taken over an insane asylum, 'exchanged shackles for sunshine and exercise'.[9]

In the 1800s, when psychiatry became a medical specialty,[10] psychiatrists focused on disturbed individuals continuing to be confined to asylums or hospitals. Many had physiological conditions ranging from hypothyroidism to seizures. Treatment was again barbaric, continuing to reflect the ignorance and consequences of 'heroic medicine'.

In opposing this status quo, Pinel in France,[11] and William Tuke[12] in England founded the 'moral therapy' movement, a mental health approach based on humane care and perpetuated in the United States by the Quakers and, later, the psychiatrist Loren Mosher. History tells us that in 1844, 50% of the mental health patients in a Philadelphia asylum administered 'moral therapy' were discharged within a year of entry, with many never returning.

Three women

Like the poor, or those of another skin tone, women have historically been viewed as 'closer to nature', not a term viewed with respect or implying elevation of status. Yet it was women who traditionally cared for the mentally imbalanced at home before prescriptions of torture and asylums dictated another standard of care.

It is a well-known fact that women have been discriminated against in the medical profession, but they continue to surface and remind society to wise up. Three women figured prominently in attempting to right these wrongs. First, Dorothea Dix[13] in 1840, a lay woman living in Massachusetts, who, after witnessing the mentally ill imprisoned like criminals, where they were left naked, often chained in the dark without heat or bathrooms, and often beaten, became a political advocate for prison and mental healthcare reform. Dix lobbied for improved conditions, working tirelessly for 40 years to establish state hospitals that would treat patients with dignity and respect. She even had an audience with Pope Pius IX to encourage him to investigate the observed cruelties that included hollow wheels, needle cabinets, Utica crib and a wide assortment of water tortures and terror that were inflicted on people considered wild animals. Often chained to walls in dungeons, such treatments ensured those inmates who weren't already certifiable surely would become so.

Elizabeth Jane Cochrane, a pioneer of investigative journalism, went undercover in the late 1880s, targeting Blackwell Island (now Roosevelt Island), to write the book, *Ten Days in a Madhouse*, under the pseudonym Nellie Bly. She 'fooled various doctors and authorities into deeming her insane and admitting her to the asylum'.[14] Upon her escape — she lasted 10 days as her book title suggests — she raged: 'That such an institution could be mismanaged, and that cruelties could exist 'neath its roof, I did not deem possible.' Having shed her disguise, she published her findings, proudly announcing: 'The City of New York has appropriated $1,000,000 more per annum than ever before for the care of the insane. So, I have, at least, the satisfaction of knowing that the poor unfortunates will be better cared for because of my work.'

A third example of a pioneering woman during the 1800s regarding medical practices is Clara Barrus MD (1864-1931), one of the first female medical doctors in the US. A homeopath, after graduating from Boston University in 1888, she practiced at Middletown State Hospital of Homeopathy for several years. Her book, *Nursing the Insane*, published in 1915, is an extremely valuable resource in that she acknowledges the demand on nurses of 'mental and nervous invalids', and goes on to say in the patients' defense: 'to be always under lock and key, deprived of liberty, subjected to the necessary rules of a large institution, to the authority of the superintendent and the other attending physicians, to the directions of the supervisor, and sometimes also to the tyranny of attendants, who too often exercise an unwarrantable dictation over patients whom they are expected to care for, to guide, to console, and to encourage, but never to dictate nor command.'[15] This gives us a window into the need at that time for kindness (see page 113).

Allopathic asylums

Despite attempts by reformists to separate the mentally ill and convicted criminals, the latter were admitted in great numbers to allopathically run asylums. While all this was going on within prison-like walls, in the realm of general medicine the public began to voice its disdain for and fear of the use of 'heroic' medicine, the practices of which included bloodletting and the toxic usage of substances like calomel (mercury) – the reductionist method in the extreme – and became increasingly resistant to a model of medicine that tended to kill rather than to cure. Hence allopathic physicians needed to find another way to practice medicine; they began to rely on the growing scientific emphasis on, and application of, reductionist methods. Unfortunately, they were not influenced by the moral nature or the example of a gentler medicine or treatment, as in the homeopathic hospitals. (Although baseball games did seem to be a commonality between certain allopathic and homeopathic asylums.)

The rise of natural medicine

Interlaced with this reductionist takeover in the US and Canada were the early naturopathic doctors and homeopathic medical doctors like Barrus who inherently understood the term 'mind-body medicine'. Although at the time called 'mental culture', this generated the holistic model we rely on today: 'shared beliefs in valuing the mind and spirit for healing intentions.'[16]

To understand the difference between the 1800s and now, consider what life was like in the 19th and early 20th century: a much harder, more physical life for many, with few rights for people in general and none for women or people of color, yet it was a time when people were connected, whether they liked it or not, to the land. The 'earth beneath our feet' was literally the earth beneath their feet and not as now, at our fingertips. People felt close to nature in a way we can hardly imagine anymore unless organic farming is your honorable profession. Far more than in this past century people relied on Nature Cure, trusted it because they understood the workings of their body – that it could heal without pills. This remains so in countries in Europe like Armenia or Hungary, or in Asia with centuries old tradition of acupuncture and herbal medicine, but in America it is suspect. I had one patient say to me: 'Natural medicine is not normal'. We have lost so much of what we can do ourselves with the help of nature, as we have seen in two years of Covid-19 where there was no mention of sunshine or vegetables or exercise to boost our immune system. (Hence my book *Surviving a Viral Pandemic Through the Lens of a Naturopathic Medical Doctor*.) COVID-time is all about external solutions: standing six feet apart, masks, and vaccines, or rather experimental gene therapies that were not tested properly.

Gentler treatment

As noted, Dr. Hahnemann advocated kinder treatment in 1700s Germany and, towards the end of the 19th century, homeopathic asylums in America followed this tradition. One such hospital was Middletown Homeopathic State Hospital[17] in New York State, which included therapeutic sports and expressive art activities along with individualized treatment with homeopathic medicines. They did well for years but, as these institutions became overcrowded, it was difficult to maintain the patient-centered care that is so necessary in homeopathy. This sadly, in the end, led to the need for mechanical restraints that they had tried so hard to minimize.

Around this same time, the New Thought movement flourished in America, including in the newly formed naturopathic profession, maintaining the opinion that thought was the first step in healing. It also advocated justice in all aspects of society, believing in equality for all, universal suffrage, medical freedom, humane working hours, the rejection of stifling dress codes, healthy food options and, ultimately, a desire to return to nature. Early naturopathic doctors believed that negative thought affects the body and is a major factor in producing ill health. (Their beliefs were strong, including that vaccination and vivisection were both immoral and detrimental, and went to prison for them. Louisa Stroeble Lust was wealthy and bailed many out while her husband Benedict was imprisoned 18 times. Prolific writers and healers, they were also visionaries.[18, 19, 20, 21])

Chapter 3

'Thought,' wrote Benedict, 'first, last, and all the time, causes, perpetuates, and consummates Pain, Disease, and Death, Worry, Poverty, and Fear, Failure, Error, and Hell.'[22] They believed, 'Close communion with Nature is necessary to our being and keeps us on the right path.'[22] They relied on the term *Vis Medicatrix Naturae* – Latin for the healing power of nature, a principle that grew out of vitalism, which harnesses the idea that the body–mind can heal itself given the opportunity. They practiced the popular Kneipp Water Cure that Benedict had brought from Germany and were able to create schools, spas, and publications to promote natural healing that also included homeopathy, plant medicine, and 'mental culture' – the inherent mind-body-spirit connection. Louisa believed Nature Cure could stand on its own but Benedict, ever practical, chose to obtain his MD degree so that he would stop being arrested for practicing medicine and performing surgery without a license.

While attending medical school, Benedict was continually taunted by his fellow students and even a professor. Not only did they prank him and call him a 'quack' and 'Hydrotherapy Ignoramus', hoping to be rid of him, but when he shared copies of his *Kneipp Water Cure Monthly* they treated him like a criminal, saying this was 'radical propaganda'. His determination didn't waver; he went on to get his MD degree to 'fight to bring the freedom of choice of treatment I believed the American Constitution guaranteed'. (What would he and our founding fathers think of this time during our loss of medical sovereignty?)

Benedict called 'allopaths professors of the irrational theories of life, health, and disease who treated their victims with dangerous drugs and animal vaccines and serums. Their magic pills, potions, and poisons,' he wrote, 'attacked the ailment and suppressed the symptoms instead of addressing the ailment's real causes.'

Both Louisa and Benedict were friends with writer and naturopathic ally, Louis Kuhne, who published several books on his experiences, including the 1884 *The New Science of Healing*, so popular it was published in 25 languages. Kuhne believed that 'foreign matter' in the body was the cause of disease. Henry Lindlahr (1862–1924), known for his prolific works and definition of Nature Cure, borrowed much from Kuhne's philosophy and theory. All these early naturopathic thinkers rejected allopathic/orthodox medicine for its inability to get to the root causes of disease, relying instead on nature and its power to heal.

Contrast this with the standard procedures forced on patients by allopathic doctors in the not-too-distant past for what were considered deviant emotions and behaviors: electroconvulsive therapy, lobotomies, hysterectomies, ice baths, insulin shock, not to mention bloodletting. Even so, conventional medicine has characterized natural medicine as folklorist nonsense (while they continue to rely on psychotropic medication that, for one, has led to the opioid epidemic). This widespread, wholesale misrepresentation, begun in the 1800s and carried forward to the present day, was amplified and subsequently immortalized by the publication of the infamous Flexner Report in the US in 1910 (see next) and its effect in other countries.

The Flexner Report

The Flexner Report,[23] with its 384 pages, posited among many things that mental disorders are brain diseases and emphasized pharmaceutical treatment to target presumed biological abnormalities. In the process, the Report transformed America's medical educational system from a proprietary (ownership based) model to a biomedical model as the gold standard of medical training and precipitated the prolonged obscurity of all previously recognized drugless medical systems, beginning with

Chapter 3

homeopathy and extending to the practice of naturopathy, chiropractic, traditional osteopathy, herbalism, and midwifery.

Among other lasting impacts of the Report, which advocated
reducing the number of medical schools and of doctors being
trained, all but two 'negro' medical schools were closed and
American universities reverted to male-only admissions to
reduce their student intake.

When Abraham Flexner, an educator, not a physician,
was commissioned by the Carnegie Foundation to inspect
medical schools of all types in the United States and Canada,
his recommended 'medical reform' ripped away systems of
medicine that had rich and enduring traditions as well as success
in non-drug modalities that now, in the 21st century, have
science to back them up as evidence-based medicine.

Commissioned by Andrew Carnegie, a 19tth century
industrialist who had made his fortune in steel, and
perpetuated by John D Rockefeller who made his in oil and
railroads, healthcare via the implementation of the Flexner
Report (with no vote, only money and power dictating)
took a distinct turn against the adage *Vis Medicatrix Naturae*
by limiting the practice of medicine to the 'regulars' who
graduated from medical schools that guaranteed a 'scientific'
education with its inclusion of a laboratory and an adjoining
hospital with ironically the same 'active principles' from what is
usually either a plant or mineral.

This more materially based interpretation of medicine
became *de rigeur* in medical schools in Europe; Flexner was
particularly impressed by the well-organized system of German
laboratories, less so by the British and French medical schools
as he saw them as less orderly, more chaotic. When the Flexner
Report was widely distributed in Europe by an influential trustee
of the Carnegie Foundation for the Advancement of Teaching, it
got the attention of both the British and French medical schools,
and they sprang into action to clean up their laboratories.

The Flexner Report and the actions it subsequently led to effectively sabotaged the full scope of natural modalities, and dovetails with why even licensed natural medicine doctors continue to be shamed and disparaged to this day.

To bolster their domination of the medical market, the Carnegie and Rockefeller Foundations would only provide major funding for medical schools that complied with the scientific and allopathic frameworks detailed in Flexner's approach. (To further ensure his dominance, Rockefeller, personally a proponent of homeopathy, monopolized his 'philanthropic' medical work by insisting that one of his own had a seat on the Board of Directors of each hospital sanctioned by his crony, Carnegie.) Clearly, the drive for increased 'scientific' reforms and research was primarily profit driven as healthcare moved to become a monetized industry in the early 1900s. Rockefeller's empire of Standard Oil, highlighting its coal tar–petrol derivatives, made sure psychotropic/ psychiatric drugs remained on the top of the list as the answer to mental wellness. Reforms were influenced not just by the American Medical Association (AMA) with its desire to shut down all competition from natural therapies, but also by the pharmaceutical industry that was tied to Carnegie and Rockefeller.

Medical schools had historically been in the private realm so government hadn't got involved until that time. We might wonder why Carnegie and Rockefeller got away with having this influence, but the obvious answer is these powerful industrialists, the 'robber barons', were able to monopolize political policymaking in many spheres. We see such interference in healthcare from those successful in business today.

Don't get me wrong, technological advancements – the foundation of allopathic medicine over the last almost century – can be perfect in a physiological crisis, with drugs being 'miraculous' when truly needed, but natural medicine best engages the patient preventively and in the long term, getting to the source of the condition or disease through a holistic model, particularly in mental health.

The rise and fall of natural medicine

A single-minded diabolical force emerged with the Flexner Report, having dismissed the possibility a level playing field for other approaches to medicine. Yet, despite being disparaged as 'quackery' by the leaders of the medical establishment during this period, specifically the head of the AMA, naturopathic medicine was very popular spanning the years 1918 to 1937, as witnessed by the 1920s naturopathic medical conventions which attracted over 10,000 practitioners. Thriving naturopathic journals promoted the achievement of a healthy lifestyle through disease prevention and a good diet, botanical supplements, and homeopathic alternatives, while advocating a truly holistic approach through Nature Cure, the effects of optimism, thought, rest, play, a sense of humor, music and civil rights.

While we all truly benefit from advances gained from valid research, Flexner's medical reform came at the cost of incapacitating society's knowledge and power of natural medicine. The Flexner Report initially disabled the numerous homeopathic medical schools that never recovered to a licensable degree and the naturopathic medical colleges closed their doors in the 1940s, only to reopen in 1956, starting with the National College of Naturopathic Medicine (now National University of Natural Medicine) in Portland, Oregon. In 1979 three of its graduates founded John Bastyr College of Naturopathic Medicine (now Bastyr University) in Seattle, Washington. As to how the schools are faring today, the situation is complicated and they are hampered by not being government funded. As well, it is disappointing to me that Bastyr, my alma mater, has turned more allopathic, including newer graduates eager to inoculate patients with the Covid-19 jab, a situation that couldn't be further from our roots as per Benedict Lust going to prison for being against vaccines.

The continuing dilemma

The practice of psychiatrist Charles Burlingame offers us a glimpse of the divisive nature of mental medicine. In 1931, Burlingame took over the Hartford Retreat in Connecticut, one of the oldest mental hospitals in the US (later renamed the Institute of Living) and sought, with little success, to 'resocialize' patients, a term commonly applied to prison reform. He wrote: 'I can envisage a time arriving when we in the field of Psychiatry will entirely forsake our ancestry, forget that we had our beginnings in the poorhouse, the workhouse, and the jail... when we will be doctors, think as doctors, and run our psychiatric institutions in much the same way and with much the same relationships as obtained in the best medical and surgical institutions.'[24]

Burlingame may have wanted the best possible care for his patients but by the late 1930s he was participating in the so-called 'miracle cures' that involved insulin coma therapy, electroconvulsive therapy and frontal lobotomies that were being used to treat schizophrenia, severe anxiety, depression and obsessive disorders, a long way from the gentle compassion many past reformers had advocated.

The chemical explosion of the '40s

Strategically, allopathic medicine quickly hitched its philosophy and methods to the burgeoning scientific discoveries of the 1940s, incorporating biomedical sciences and experimental science into the curriculum and clinical training of its students and interns. They grabbed on to the growing medical technology and pharmaceutical drugs to offer what most people came to believe was a superior or 'easier' method of treatment, a final nail in natural medicine's coffin. In the case of mental health care, as these 'miracle' psychoactive drugs, advocated by the rising psychiatric profession, caught the public's attention and steered it even further toward allopathic medicine, drugless therapies were increasingly ridiculed and disdained.

World War II

The War Department, by virtue of caring for its wounded, has played a prominent role in determining the state of mental healthcare in the US as noted in an earlier chapter. In 1945, following the end of World War II, as soldiers were returning home, it became obvious that many were suffering from what we now call PTS. General Lewis Hershey concluded: 'Mental illness was the greatest cause of non-effectiveness and loss of manpower'[5] during the years of fighting. The General's report to Congress made politicians aware of the need to change the way it had cared for victims of psychological trauma. Almost half a million people were locked up in psychiatric wards.

There seemed to be no turning back with the publication of photojournalist Albert Deutch's book, *The Shame of the States*, in a 1948 *Life* magazine, photograph after photograph highlighted decrepit facilities exposing unbelievable neglect. Deutch was '...reminded of the Nazi concentration camps at Belsen and Buchanwald...'.[25]

Going forward I can only hope that what we are going through now will cause reflection and we will allow truth, backed by the transparency of real science, to point us to compassionate and gentle medicine, as Hahnemann so beautifully and bravely exemplified almost 400 years ago.

A NOTE TO THE CLINICIAN

As we dig ourselves out of a soaring mental health crisis, we can turn back to basic truths in healing, knowing that medicine in North America and the rest of the world has not always been governed by the pharmaceutical industry or dominated by allopathic doctors. We can use the extraordinary treatments and techniques that have a positive effect on the mind that are based in nature and 'do no harm'.

Although research now confirms the scientific basis of naturopathic treatments, these remain unlicensed in many states and provinces; yet naturopathic physicians are the pioneers of functional and integrative medicine and every day another group or individual takes credit for what we have been practicing for a very long time!

Today, many psychiatrists and psychologists from the conventional approach may sense that mindfulness and other still-point therapies (see Chapter 8) will somehow be beneficial to relieve mental and emotional suffering. Perhaps these natural techniques will encourage them to understand what plants, and other natural medicines, including the expressive arts, can do. As we balance the biochemistry naturally, we can then turn to telling or revising the story of what created deep mental disruption. This two-pronged approach is a truly holistic path and is, in fact, a no-brainer for gentle, non-addictive and empowered healing.

It is time for those who practice vitalism, including naturopathic medicine and the expressive arts, to take our rightful place in helping those with mental health needs that have PTS/trauma at their core.

ASSIGNMENT #3

1. Discuss one woman who helped change the terror of the asylum.
2. What does the term *Vis Medicatrix Naturae* signify?
3. What is Mental Culture and how does it affect health and healing?
4. Discuss the Flexner Report and how it denied a holistic approach to treatment.

Part Two

Setting the stage

She prepared her work like a picnic. She had books, many that were hard to reach. She would build a ladder all the way to the stars if she had to.

Chapter 4

Brain on fire

Underactive prefrontal cortex.
Overactive amygdala. Internal chaos.

The physiological root of trauma

Mental-emotional wellbeing starts with taking the time to be informed on how to nourish cells and tissues while maximizing elimination processes to generate calm. Sounds easy? Not when thoughts and feelings are crying out for attention and we return the favor by eating too much and feasting on 'comfort' food: sugar, bad fats, too few micronutrients and enzymes, and so on. Our inflamed bodies continue to hold onto traumatic experiences, affecting us unconsciously until we can bring them to at least some level of balance before tapping into them consciously.

It all starts with the brain[1, 2, 3, 4, 5, 6, 7] for a person with PTS and any of its comorbidities. By highlighting organs and pathways, neurological and systemic, while nourishing the adrenal glands and the mitochondria, balancing neurotransmitters, the HPA (hypothalamic–pituitary–adrenal) axis and the vagus nerve, we optimize trauma recovery through biochemistry naturally. This is the first part of my two-pronged approach.

The concept of fostering wellbeing through natural means has been the basis of naturopathic medicine and other systems of natural medicine for centuries. It is how naturopathic physicians practice — maximizing physical and mental health by adhering to the laws of nature. Just as the naturopathic doctors of the late 1800s did, we promote a healthy lifestyle with a clean environment as well as positive thoughts, beneficial foods (often fermented for optimal gut health), detox protocols, botanical medicine, hydrotherapy, and the like. These are now more and more scientifically verified – methods and substances that have in fact been utilized for centuries. The relatively new science of epigenetics (the study of changes caused by the modification of the expression of our genes in response to our behavior and environment) together with neuroplasticity (the ability of the brain to form and reorganize synaptic connections) confirms that the brain can heal itself, underscoring the use of drugless therapies.

How liberating and affirming it is that DNA is not destiny. Life is completely alive in the moment – acknowledging, discovering, negotiating, concluding, and conducting!

We can modify behavior and the thoughts that drive it, by what we ingest. We understand that even intergenerational trauma – changes passed on from generations before – can be coaxed to a healthier expression. The brain can change itself, allowing us to implement a treatment plan with confidence.[7]

This becomes another 'Aha' moment in trauma recovery – that genes and their expression are not static, not stuck in place. Whatever type of medicine we practice, to view the cellular level that may stem from adverse events, and add or subtract what's necessary, is the gift of epigenetics. It may show us the science that lies beneath what we already knew worked but didn't know exactly why. It offers us – clinicians and survivors – another way to confirm what needs to be done.

This is the most important part of this book to understand: by giving adults, adolescents and children affected by trauma access to drugless treatment and creative expression, we can help their brain heal and their behavior to transform without medicating them.

Now let's look at what we have to work with to set things straight for the results we are looking for.

Initiating action

The action in the originating event of PTS is a quick, sudden response to danger. This forceful impact affects key areas of the brain – they atrophy (shrink) or hypertrophy (expand), altering pathways and nerve cell levels and functions. The brain's architecture also changes through adverse childhood experiences (ACEs) with the repeated release of toxic hormones from feelings of terror or intense fear and helplessness that have occurred over a long period of time. One neuroimaging study has found that in pediatric PTS[8] there is again abnormal structure and function in neural circuitry in the frontolimbic area that leads to increased feelings of threat and weaker emotional regulation as children age. Many studies confirm that the brain is altered in ACE.[9, 10] How this is differentiated in PTS or causes crossover between PTS and ACE is not entirely clear yet, but various emotional responses to trauma are in reality the same and result in unbalanced biochemistry. Therefore, in both scenarios curbing inflammation and balancing gut function and hormones through nutrition, implementing emotional safety and protection, or guiding creative expression to release negative emotions will transform behavior.

Female hormones and PTS

One study[11] has discovered that women are twice as likely as men to be susceptible to PTS: '…earlier studies highlighted estrogen during fear extinction learning. It is possible that progesterone directly and indirectly exerts memory-enhancing effects at the time of trauma, which is an effect

---

that may not be necessarily captured during non-stressful paradigms. We propose a model whereby progesterone's steroidogenic relationship to cortisol and brain-derived neurotrophic factor in combination with elevated oestradiol may enhance emotional memory consolidation during trauma and therefore present a specific vulnerability to PTSD formation in women, particularly during the mid-luteal phase of the menstrual cycle.'

Chronic looping

In lingering trauma (PTS), the brain doesn't get the message that the threat is over; physiological changes persist while the calming parasympathetic nervous system via the ventral vagus nerve is inhibited and all the main stress activators, including cortisol, stay high.

The transfer of power from the executive function of the prefrontal cortex (PFC) to the survival instinct of the amygdala is quick. As the PFC shrinks and loses control over cognition and memory in the face of trauma, more primitive brain circuits take over. Basically, the PFC has weighed the external traumatic event and has internalized it, succumbing to the amygdala (part of the limbic system) which becomes the star of the show, overreacting and signaling fear to the hypothalamus (part of the limbic system as well) that responds with an autonomic response. We then experience emotions like fear and/or anger. Another part of the limbic system, the hippocampus, responsible for the ability to store and retrieve memories, shrinks. These organs and the systems in which they function serve as ground zero for the inflammatory basis of emotional disruption that generates our behavioral and psychological responses. Consequently, these areas comprise the highest level of control over the physiological activities we are attempting to manipulate through drugless therapies in PTS. [12,13]

Chapter 4

It is in children with trauma that we uncover the most grievous findings as it is the frontal and limbic areas that show abnormality, with declining hippocampal volume, increasing amygdala reactivity, and declining amygdala-prefrontal coupling with age.

The effect on memory

Both short- and long-term memory are affected by chronic looping. When the emotional stress response is activated, the amygdala inhibits short-term memory and concentration and stimulates long-term memory. To go into more detail, any sensory input we experience – visual images, sounds, smells, tastes and textures, inner awareness and/or external stimuli – are translated into electrical signals and directed to different areas of the cerebral cortex, such as the prefrontal cortex. In PTS the signal reaches the pair of amygdala, one in each cerebral hemisphere, that then send the signal to other parts of the cerebral cortex that manage sight, sound, and other senses. At this point, the neurons form new connections to place the memories in long-term storage in the hippocampus.

The process described can be protective – you want to remember in case it happens again – but if this activation goes on too long, as in PTS/trauma, it can cause further injury and distress. When we witness the homeless on sidewalks, as they shuffle in place, move in unnatural ways, we can bet that the PFC, the brain's analytical part, and amygdala, which control the processing and expression of emotions, especially fear and anger, are hanging by a thread, pathways to their muscles and speech affected in ways we can't imagine. Yet I would also bet that, although barely functioning, their brain harbors a story to be told, and that once their body is nourished, at least to a certain extent, may set them free.

The role of oxidative stress and inflammation

Going to the cellular level we appreciate that 'PTSD is a traumatic stress-related emotional disorder linked to chronic low-grade inflammatory reactions in the body and brain'.[14, 15, 16] That means that any lingering negative psychological event begins with the physiological, inflammatory-derived symptoms that won't shut off.

Inflammation through free radicals or ROS (reactive oxygen species) affects not only the amygdala in our brain but the totality of our organs and interconnected systems that are at play. This results in continual re-experiencing of the trauma through sensory triggers and memory and their stress-related neurobiological pathway. Elevated levels of this oxidative stress ultimately target cell membranes and cause a continual loop of destruction. If allowed to continue, this excess activity results in ongoing cellular damage and is one of the major reasons people with PTS/trauma fail to heal. The totality of this experience has been called the cell defense response (CDR). To sum up, chronic inflammation and oxidative stress constitute a prolonged CDR. (See mitochondria, page 79, for more on the CDR.)

Cytokines

Cytokines are signaling molecules secreted mainly by white blood cells to regulate immune responses throughout the ANS (autonomic nervous system). In PTS or ACE, behavioral and emotional conditions influence the activation and numbers of cytokines in the brain and body.[16]

These high levels of cytokines, coupled with insufficient cortisol regulation, soon to be discussed, perpetuate a process that won't turn off.

The autonomic nervous system

Let's back up for a minute by identifying the major systems in the body that are involved in psychological trauma. The central nervous system (CNS) refers to the brain and spinal cord. The peripheral nervous system includes the cranial nerves and nerves outside the CNS and is divided into two main parts:

- The autonomic nervous system (ANS): This oversees involuntary bodily functions and regulates glands such as the adrenals.
- The somatic nervous system: This controls muscle movement and relays information from the ears, eyes and skin to the CNS.

The ANS is made up of the SNS (sympathetic nervous system), the PNS (parasympathetic nervous system) and the enteric nervous system that controls digestion, also called the gut–brain axis. The SNS is where the action starts in a lingering traumatic event and in any state of arousal. The PNS, through its ventral vagus nerve, attempts to lasso the SNS, in order to pacify it – that is, to bring the mind and body to calm. It is its calming partner when safety conditions are met

As noted earlier, the hypothalamus activates the ANS in PTS and triggers it in ACE and this pathway can be manipulated.

In more detail, the SNS responds to danger or stress with its fight-or-flight response. Acting through the hormone/neurotransmitter epinephrine, aka adrenaline, the SNS functions to increase cardiac output and to raise blood glucose levels to get you away from danger quickly. (It can result in the release of too much blood sugar and increased risk of heart disease, stroke and other damaging conditions.) In contrast, the PNS can, among other things, slow the heart rate, relax muscles, and regulate digestion, allowing the SNS to fade in a healthy response. The essence of lingering PTS means the PNS has failed to return to a relaxed state after the threat or danger has passed.

The PNS runs along the vagus nerve, labelled cranial nerve X, the longest nerve in the whole ANS. It carries both sensory signals to the brain (about 20% of its capacity) and motor signals from the brain to almost all organs: heart, lungs, abdomen, digestive system, pancreas, liver, spleen, and pelvis. It engages the neurotransmitter GABA (gamma-aminobutyric acid) that passes chemical messages from one cell to the next throughout the entire nervous system, making this thoroughfare (and corresponding side streets) a true friend to someone with trauma (except when it goes into FREEZE mode as will be discussed).

Other players are the pituitary and adrenal glands, along with the hypothalamus, which make up the hypothalamic–pituitary–adrenal connection or 'HPA axis'. This axis plays a vital part in the release and balance of the major stress hormone, cortisol (see below), into the bloodstream. Because the HPA axis has a link to the thyroid gland, this is another hormone we must consider in trauma recovery.

We then have the hormones and neurotransmitters, both of which act as chemical messengers within the body. Hormones help manage our metabolism and are affected by stress and changes through the balance of fluid and minerals. Too much or too little of any hormone harms the body. It's all about balance.

Neurons

Neurons are nerve cells which transmit signals within the brain and the nervous system. They are responsible for receiving sensory input from the external world and sending motor commands out to our muscles, and for transforming and relaying electrical signals at each step of the process.

A typical neuron consists of a cell body or soma, dendrites, and a single axon like a long tail. The soma is a compressed organelle, and the axon and dendrites are filaments extruding from the soma. Dendrites are usually branched and extend a few hundred micrometers from the soma.

A single neuron contains about 50 billion proteins. These proteins are needed for the essential functions of the neuron but are also used to alter how the neuron responds to inputs, a process called synaptic plasticity. These alterations in the proteins at synapses underlie learning and memory.

Neurotransmitters

Neurotransmitters are chemical messengers that help neurons transmit messages, whether between neurons or from neurons to muscles. These chemicals and their interactions are involved in a wide range of functions in the nervous systems and the body.

Neurons rely on neurotransmitters via activation or inhibition of an 'action potential' – that is, a nerve impulse through a junction or synapse between two neurons, one 'pre-synaptic' where the neurotransmitters are stored, and the other 'post-synaptic' (on the other, receiving side of the synapse). This process, known as 'exocytosis', can release neurotransmitters in less than a millisecond.

Most neurotransmitters are either small amine molecules, amino acids, or neuropeptides. There are about a dozen known amines and more than 100 different neuropeptides.

Action potentials

For an action potential to communicate information to another neuron, it must travel along the axon and reach the axon terminals where it can initiate neurotransmitter release. These nerve impulses happen when there is a sudden increase in membrane permeability. This results in an influx of ions along a concentration gradient hoping to cross the neuron's membrane. Finally, because there are more sodium ions than potassium on the outside of the nerve cell, sodium ions rush into the neuron.

For a healthy cell membrane

Keeping cell membranes healthy is super-important in healing of any kind. They are made up of omega-6 and omega-3 fats which is why supplements and foods high in these substances can help support healthy function. More on this later, but remember, DHA and GLA (omega-3s), fat-soluble vitamins A, D, E, and K, and vitamin C help to nutrify and detoxify, keeping cell membranes strong and efficient.

Neuromodulators

We should also be aware of neuromodulators, substances that do not directly activate ion-channel receptors in cell membranes and so are not restricted to the synaptic cleft between two neurons. These can affect large numbers of neurons at once and, acting together with neurotransmitters, can enhance the excitatory or inhibitory response, albeit over a slower time frame.

Important neurotransmitters

The important neurotransmitters to know in PTS and ACE are:
- norepinephrine (NE) or noradrenaline
- epinephrine (E) or adrenaline, synthesized from NE
- dopamine (DA)
- serotonin (S).

The first three, commonly referred to as 'catecholamines', are synthesized from the amino acid, L-tyrosine, produced by the adrenal gland at the sympathetic–adrenomedullary axis (SAM).

The SAM axis interacts with the HPA axis, according to the following sequence:

L-tyrosine → dopa (dihydroxyphenylalanine) → dopamine → norepinephrine (noradrenaline) → epinephrine (adrenaline)

The exact relationship between catecholamines and PTS has elicited many hypotheses but there have been inconsistencies in studies as to their exact nature. What we do know is that catecholamines are released at high levels, quickly weakening the cognitive function of the prefrontal cortex – remember, normally the boss – while augmenting the emotional and instinctive responses of the amygdala (as well as the corpus striatum).

The properties of these key neurotransmitters are:

Norepinephrine:
- most likely to be the hallmark of chronic stress, in terms of a neurotransmitter on overdrive.
- involved in the physiological and pathological responses to stress, panic, the sleep-wake cycle, mood alterations and local blood flow.
- has a specific action on receptors in the amygdala, hippocampus, and PFC, all of which may play a role in debilitating symptoms indicative of PTS/trauma-like nightmares and flashbacks.
- is released from the locus coeruleus (LC), located in the upper part of the brainstem, to finally morph into long-standing symptoms of PTS.

Epinephrine:
- is a marker for acute stress, and a crucial part of the body's fight or flight response. (See Appendix for Acute stress, page 333.)

Dopamine:
- has the ability to regulate the fear response.

- plays a role in hyperresponsiveness and hypervigilance – fear, memory, nightmares, impulsivity and more.
- may account for a lack of a normal feeling of pleasure (anhedonia) seen in people with anxiety and depression.
- in chronic stress, poor nutrition and other factors may inhibit the conversion of dopamine to norepinephrine.

Serotonin:

- is a crucial player in the brain's effort to check chronic stress and inflammation.
- stabilizes our mood, enhances feelings of wellbeing and happiness, and can modulate the amygdala. Involved in sleep; it also regulates sexuality.
- formed from the amino acid tryptophan, serotonin was initially thought to influence blood pressure via vascular tone (blood serum + tone = serotonin). Only later was it found also to act as a neurotransmitter.
- An imbalance of serotonin can lead to depression and/ or obsessive behavior and/or anger/aggression and/or suicidal thoughts and suicide.
- Too much serotonin (called serotonin syndrome) can lead to seizures and death. (Allopathic practitioners should avoid prescribing L-tryptophan and 5 hydroxytryptophan (5 HTP) in conjunction with the antidepressants SSRIs (serotonin reuptake inhibitors) as they may increase their efficacy and toxicity.)

Other neurotransmitters to know

Glutamate or glutamic acid, a powerful excitatory neurotransmitter:

- occupies almost 90% of all brain synapses, sending signals between nerve cells.
- under normal conditions, plays an important part in learning and memory.

- is produced by the body and abundant in foods: mushrooms, soy and other beans, veggies, meat, fish, dairy.
- can convert to glutamine, an amino acid that helps cells of the gut.

GABA – the major inhibitory neurotransmitter in the brain:

- is amplified by the PNS and the ventral vagus nerve and is the body's best friend due to its calming effect.
- can paradoxically be increased by glutamate.

Glycine – the smallest amino acid but the **major inhibitory neurotransmitter** in the brainstem/spinal cord and so acts on both motor and sensory pathways:

- promotes relaxation.
- enhances detoxification by amplifying glutathione production.
- regulates the action of glutamate.
- along with glutamate, GABA, and taurine, it helps make serotonin.
- is found in turkey, chicken, beef, fish, dairy, eggs, and legumes. (Vegans may need to supplement.)

Unconventional neurotransmitters

These neurotransmitters designated 'unconventional' are not stored in the synaptic vesicles, but carry messages backwards from post to presynaptic neurons, and break down into two classes:

Endocannabinoids: See Cannabis in Botanicals section (page 121).

Gasotransmitters, the soluble gases, such as nitric acid/oxide (NO). These can cross the cell membrane, acting directly on molecules inside the cell instead of the norm of interacting with the receptor on the membrane of the targeted cell. This is important because NO has many positive abilities, including as a vasodilator that can lower blood pressure and allow smooth muscle relaxation that is so necessary in trauma recovery. (See Chapter 5, page 93, for foods that supply NO.)

Other worker bees

Glutathione – the brain's most abundant antioxidant and detoxifier:
- Dysregulated in people with PTS. Decreases with age.
- Made up of three amino acids: cysteine, glutamic acid and glycine. (Can take its precursor n-acetyl cysteine, NAC, as a supplement.)
- Said to be the **most reliable blood-based biomarker for PTS** (through measuring the enzyme glutathione transferase).
- This confirms the fact that what we need are high levels of antioxidants to quench free radicals as well as to detox daily.
- Made in cells but also available in sulfur-containing foods and cruciferous vegetables and is augmented by vitamin C (which takes the load off glutathione's work as a free radical scavenger).

Oxytocin – the major bonding hormone, influences physiology and behavior:
- The hypothalamus releases oxytocin into the bloodstream via the posterior pituitary gland and other parts of the CNS, and in response to cortisol.
- It is released via the posterior pituitary gland between mother and child at birth.
- Activated in human bonding and affects both social functioning and learning in conjunction with serotonin by modulating the amygdala and other brain regions.[17, 18]

- The dysregulation of oxytocin early in life can lead to social attachment 'disorders' as well as a predilection to addiction.
- Helps produce calm; levels increase in response to stressors including conditioned fear stimuli.
- Decreases anxiety and blood pressure.
- Stimulates positive social interactions.
- Also increases the pain threshold.
- Nicknamed the love hormone, oxytocin will increase through joy or feeling happy while connecting with another, although also shows increased levels when lonely or unhappy. (Is the hormone trying to help?)

The hormone, cortisol

Cortisol is the star stress catalyst:
- Produced in response to signals from the hypothalamus and the pituitary gland, cortisol attaches to glucocorticoid receptors (GR or GCR) in almost every cell of the body.
- The most important glucocorticoid (hormones that affect the metabolism of carbs, also fats and proteins), cortisol is produced in the adrenal glands after being stimulated by stress. Excessive amounts can result in chronic inflammation and play the key role in determining our long-term response to stress that in time may result in disease.[19]
- Cortisol levels naturally fluctuate throughout a 24-hour period, normally peaking at 8:00 am and reaching their lowest point around 4:00 am.
- Cortisol levels at night need to be low when we sleep and high in the morning when we wake, giving us energy throughout the day. In people with PTS or ACE, the circadian rhythm is distorted because of variable cortisol levels due to the stress response being activated without coming back to rest. [20, 21]

- Cortisol's job is to influence metabolic processes and its capacity to act as an anti-inflammatory is both key and confusing. (Hence, the cortisol paradox theorem, coming up.)
- If circulating cortisol is not balanced, negative effects include:
  - blood sugar imbalances
  - decreased muscle mass
  - high blood pressure
  - increased abdominal fat leading to metabolic syndrome – heart attacks, strokes, high levels of LDL, low levels of HDL
  - lowered immune function
  - sleep disruption
  - slow wound healing
  - thyroid dysfunction (hypo or hyper)
- Individuals with PTS can have chronically low levels of circulating cortisol which may manifest in:
  - adrenal fatigue
  - blood sugar imbalances
  - brain fog, mild depression
  - inflammation
  - low blood pressure
  - lowered immune system
  - sleep disruption
  - thyroid dysfunction (hypo or hyper).
- They can also have high levels which may stimulate and lead to a burden on the epinephrine or adrenaline output being continuously hyper.

The cortisol paradox
The first published observation on cortisol in PTS was in 1986 by John Mason and colleagues at Yale.[22] They found that:

- Cortisol can bring down the high levels of epinephrine (aka adrenaline) released during fight or flight. In other words, having enough cortisol to completely bring down the sympathetic nervous system is very important to calming a person.
- People with PTS showed significantly lower cortisol levels both on admission and discharge than other mentally ill patients. Low cortisol may partially explain the formation of traumatic memory or generalized triggers as epinephrine and norepinephrine have been shown to be responsible for memory formation and arousal.

Rachel Yehuda, a neuroscientist and director of the traumatic stress studies division at Mount Sinai School of Medicine in New York, explains that people with lower peritraumatic cortisol levels have an increased likelihood of developing PTS.[23]

Slovakian neuroscientist and researcher Richard Kvetnansky, and colleagues,[24] have observed that the paradoxical effect may be due to the loss of the feedback system of the HPA axis:

- Lower cortisol levels at the time of the traumatic event may prevent terminations of the sympathetic stress response and consequently prolonged noradrenergic activity.

In a study of mothers with PTS, both the mothers and their babies displayed lower cortisol levels, leading to the following possible conclusions:[17]

- Cortisol levels showed more significance if the stress occurred in the middle of the second or third trimester.
- Mid second trimester, an enzyme (11B-hydroxysteroid dehydrogenase type 2) in the placenta blocks conversion of cortisol to its inactive metabolite, cortisone.
- This process protects the fetus from the detrimental effects of maternal glucocorticoids (i.e., cortisol and others) that

could overwhelm the body's capacity to metabolize cortisol to cortisone.

- It also enables mothers to 'transmit' different vulnerabilities or resilience to offspring.

Points of entry

Now that you have a sense of the players in PTS and ACE let's look at the many points of entry to neuro and systemic inflammation, the starting gate and perpetrator of physiological disruption. This happens not only in the physical manifestation of injury and disease but also in lingering emotional and mental imbalance. Happily, we can manipulate this pathway through natural medicine. For example, unbalanced microbiota (bad bacteria predominating in the gut) will generate inflammation, challenging our immunity to disease and, in this case, mental disruption by leading to an increased sensitivity to food and poor intestinal motility and digestion; this can include malabsorption of nutrients, as well as the decreased production of the bacteria that produce the calming neurotransmitter GABA, essential to our feeling of wellbeing.[25] We now have scientific research findings to indicate what long-lived communities have known for centuries: fermented foods spawn beneficial bacteria and are a primary factor in maintaining a normal gut–brain axis.

Another example is the lymphatic system, the garbage disposal system of the body; in the brain it is called the glymphatic system. Inflammation in the brain can result from bad food as well as environmental pollutants – car emissions, pesticide exposure, water and food contamination. The glymphatic system, discovered in 2012, provides glial-dependent lymphatic transport, and has been termed a 'pseudo-lymphatic' perivascular network. It detoxifies harmful metabolic waste from the brain nightly during slow wave sleep through a process called 'autophagy'.[26] Hence the importance for the health of the brain of getting a good night's sleep, and the need to start with that consideration in any treatment plan.

Both our gut and our garbage disposal system are pivotal parts of our immune system that help detoxify contaminants that can disrupt a healthy brain's metabolism. The next chapter on prevention and treatment will suggest a variety of natural anti-inflammatory compounds to reduce the synthesis of these inflammatory mediators and/or modulate the inflammatory pathways.

Thus, while the catecholamines, cortisol and various other factors can activate and feed the stress response, other participants – cellular organelles (see next) along with specific pathways – play an important role in the initiating setup of the cell defense response (CDR), a natural and universal cellular reaction to injury or stress, a theory proposed by neuroscientist Robert Naviaux to explain the continuing manifestation of PTS. These include:

1. Mitochondria
2. The ventral vagus nerve
3. The hypothalamic–pituitary–adrenal connection (HPA axis): Adrenals are the home of cortisol and, as the bellringers of many diseases, must be considered; adrenal depletion easily causes fatigue affecting the entire body.
4. The gut–brain axis and associated supplements.

1. Mitochondria

Healing our mitochondria is an essential first step in trauma recovery as these organelles (microstructures within nearly all our cells) play a role in almost every metabolic function by generating most of the energy needed to power a cell's biochemical reactions. This energy, stored in a small molecule called adenosine triphosphate (ATP), affects every cell and organ, thus our every movement, every breath, every thought, every second.

The brain represents about 2% of our weight but accounts for about 20% of calories consumed by the body. It relies for energy on the mitochondria, the first group of organelles to be overwhelmed in PTS/trauma. Therefore, these need to be in top shape to slow or halt an agitated state. We honor this tiny but mighty powerhouse, giving it a starring role in treating PTS/trauma, one that will need nourishment for it to regain its numbers and strength. (It has also been theorized that myelin has a role here, that it is able to consume oxygen and produce ATP, adding to the energy stores through mitochondrial fusion with the myelin but this is beyond the scope of this book.)[27]

What happens when mitochondria are targeted by the chronicity and exhaustion of PTS and become dysregulated and unable to function optimally?

- First, without the help of the mitochondria, the alternative pathway for producing ATP (the glycolytic pathway) produces only two ATP molecules from one glucose molecule. Contrast this with the 36 ATP molecules that can be produced with the mitochondria's help, via the Krebs cycle. Scientific evidence[28, 29] has recently revealed that the mitochondria play a role through synaptic neuroplasticity (change that occurs at synapses (see earlier) that allows neurons to communicate). The idea that synapses could change, and that this change depended on how active or inactive they were, was first proposed in 1949 by Canadian psychologist Donald Hebb. Because of synaptic plasticity's probable contribution to memory storage, it has since become one of the most intensively researched topics in all of neuroscience.[30]

- The mitochondria are engaged in every step, with neurotransmitters counting on them for fuel/energy.

- Hence, mitochondria are the first element in the cells to be overwhelmed by the rush of the CDR, theoretically a metabolic response meant to protect cells from harm.

According to research scientist, R. K. Naviaux PhD,[31] the CDR is the body's initial attempt to maintain homeostasis (metabolic balance) as it tries to deal with any attack on the mitochondria. If this healthy response does not occur and the defining traumatic event lingers, the CDR appears to loop indefinitely in the nerve cells in the brain. That's the theory. This leads to chronic stress with its host of symptoms and behavioral disorders until we can find a way for the amygdala to cease and desist... and balance with the prefrontal cortex, the decision-maker that has shrunk in response to trauma.

Yet, any threat, whether psychological or physiological, causes the release of excessive amounts of the currency of our bodies, ATP (adenosine triphosphate) and ADP (adenosine diphosphate), depleting them. (When ATP converts to ADP, stored energy is released for biological processes to use.) In almost all systems and pathways, this leads to chronic inflammation and oxidative stress, in theory a prolonged CDR that affects the HPA axis, gut–brain axis, and our innate immunity.

All of these processes can therefore perpetuate the continuous loop of chronic stress seen in PTS/trauma. We must always address the state of the mitochondria to lessen the overactivity of the amygdala and heal trauma, whether the symptom is anxiety, depression, suicidal thoughts or another prevailing symptom or underlying cause of a comorbidity.

Vulnerability:
- The phospholipid membrane of the mitochondria (and of the cell itself in which the mitochondria are positioned) is vulnerable to damage from toxins – that is, toxins can generate lipid peroxidation.
- Toxins come from prescription and over-the-counter drugs as well as alcohol, meth, cocaine and the like.

- Also from environmentally-based heavy metals, such as lead, mercury, arsenic etc, many man-made chemicals, and mycotoxins from molds.

Repair:
- To help our precious mitochondria, we implement a daily detox (Chapter 5, page 90). We also need to supplement coenzyme Q10, an essential participant in cellular respiration and the 'electron transport chain'.
- You can also add glutathione and PQQ (pyrroloquinoline quinone) or NAC (N-acetyl cysteine), its precursor. Selenium stands out as one of the most important minerals (best from Brazil nuts) while methylated B vitamins are essential if you have a certain form of the MTHFR gene that inhibits your body from processing folate (vitamin B9) and can also affect vitamins B6 and B12. Some health conditions result from a mutated MTHFR gene because it can inhibit detoxification; methyl-folate is critical to methylation, a process that informs the production of DNA and metabolism of hormones, as well as proper detoxification. For example, in pregnancy women with a mutated MTHFR gene may have a higher risk of miscarriage, pre-eclampsia, or having a baby born with birth defects related to the 'neural tube' (skull and spine), such as spina bifida.
- Exercise supports mitochondrial growth and repair. Walking or gentle exercise is best so as not to tax the adrenals further.

2. The polyvagus nerve

The polyvagus/polyvagal nerve, the main component of the parasympathetic nervous system (see page 67), controls a huge array of bodily functions, including mood, heart rate, digestion and immune response. It supplies a connection between the brain and the gastrointestinal tract and sends vital information about the state of the inner organs to the brain via afferent fibers. For now, consider that the vagus nerve has two sides, the dorsal and ventral.

As I will explain, the dance between the sympathetic nervous system (SNS) and parasympathetic nervous system (PNS) involves the ventral vagus to calm the mind. The primary route to recovery, this situation will be investigated further down the line. For now, to give you an idea, the essence of lingering PTS is that the PNS has failed to return to a relaxed state after the triggering threat or danger has passed. However, according to research psychologist, Dr. Stephen Porges, it will need to coordinate with the SNS to heal and it is the ventral vagus nerve we need to activate for resolution of PTS/trauma.[32] (More on the dorsal vagus nerve later – see page 148.)

Through the PNS, the ventral vagus nerve harnesses GABA, the calming neurotransmitter which travels from brain to face and thorax and down to the abdomen, innervating the digestive system. From the word, 'vagrant', the vagus nerve is a true wanderer, the longest nerve in the body with the widest distribution with these essential roles:

- Activates the PNS.
- Calls on the brain to release calming neurotransmitters (i.e. GABA) when cytokines (inflammatory proteins) threaten to increase inflammation.
- Calms the amygdala.
- Reduces stress by reducing the heart rate, blood pressure and blood glucose.
- Stimulates digestion and all the other metabolic processes that are activated when we are relaxed.
- Can literally make or break the process of trauma recovery.

To me this is the *piece de resistance* in trauma recovery because we can use something as simple as breathing to acti-vate the ventral vagus nerve and therefore increase the calming neurotransmitter, GABA. By controlling (slowing) our breathing, we can engage the PNS (remember, the calming side of the ANS), via the ventral vagus, while observing the outbreath and lengthening it. We will discuss this further in a later section (see page 285).

Influenced by breath work, the ventral vagus nerve also responds to:

- gargling
- cold water immersion
- meditation
- yoga and other still-point therapies
- certain exercises like Qi Gong.

3. The HPA axis

Since the HPA axis controls hormones such as cortisol, the primary stress hormone, it is at the forefront of the brain's chronic stress response. With our mitochondria (the source of energy in cells as we have seen), the HPA axis is our first responder in a traumatic event, cooperating to the fullest of its abilities to quell the metabolic disturbance initiated in the brain.

The process of cortisol release from the HPA axis follows these three steps:

- The hypothalamus releases corticotropin releasing hormone (CRH).
- CRH stimulates the anterior pituitary to produce and secrete adrenocorticotropic hormone (ACTH).
- ACTH stimulates the adrenals to produce cortisol.

My favourite botanicals in PTS/trauma are *Glycyrrhiza glabra* (licorice) and ashwagandha as they support the adrenal glands and balance cortisol.

If the stress begins in childhood, whether from neglect or negative emotion, physical or sexual abuse, grief from the loss of a parent or caregiver, these sources of biochemical change can lead to long-lasting distress due to alterations in the prefrontal cortex (which has the overseer function in the brain), levels of oxytocin (from the hypothalamus) and cortisol (from the HPA axis) and emotional regulation (by the amygdala) that often translates into adverse behaviors such as aggression and attachment disorders as well as lingering states of anxiety, depression, addiction and, most tragically, suicide. Thankfully, natural medicine has many treatments to change this depressing picture.

Summary so far

The sound of alarm by the CDR, the cell defense response, sets the stage for chronic inflammation by damaging cells throughout the body. This damage is the result of oxidative stress, with insufficient antioxidants to douse the free radicals generated, affecting oxygen conservation, cell membrane fluidity, and electron flow to name a few metabolic processes. This is the impact of PTS all the way down to our cells and their mitochondria that will register the damage of the event.

A NOTE TO THE CLINICIAN

To summarize: Retriggering the loop, survivors often have higher levels than normal of arousal hormones such as epinephrine and dopamine but lower levels of cortisol, which, in effect, is needed to calm the response even though the threat of trauma seems to be no longer present. This may calm down after one to three months (depending on who one reads). Therefore, a diagnosis of PTS should only begin at least three months after an acute stress attack occurs.

Once we understand the metabolic processes – in both brain and body – we can target so much. We may want to do neurotransmitter testing or add GABA to the treatment protocol. Taking a four-point cortisol test can pinpoint adrenal fatigue. Genetics may play a part through the MTFHR gene, disrupting normal methylation, so a test for this SNP (single nucleotide polymorphism – a DNA sequence variation) can tell us to add methylated B vitamins. And we can understand why it is so important to exercise, meditate etc to increase the parasympathetic tone. We can also give our patients advice to gargle and/or throw cold water on our faces knowing calm can be elicited.

Also, knowing the inflammatory pathway is no different in PTS and perhaps ACE as in a physical injury. (Remember that from biochemistry class?) Above all, to know the role mitochondria have and how they can be helped by certain nutraceuticals and activities will give a survivor the energy to make the changes they would like to make but have been too exhausted to take forward.

Understanding the body and its pathways, its miraculous organs, cells, organelles and molecules gives us so much power – peaceful ammunition to spread hope, trust and empowerment.

ASSIGNMENT #4

1. Discuss the over- and under-reactivity of the areas of the brain affected by lingering psychological trauma.
2. Discuss the ANS. What do the letters stand for and what role does it play in generating stress and calm.
3. Name five ways to stimulate the ventral vagus nerve.
4. Why are the mitochondria such an important organelle in trauma recovery?

Chapter 5

Optimizing our metabolism

Toxins. Nutritional deficiencies. Stagnant lymph.
Leaky gut. Free radicals.

The key to optimizing our metabolism is balancing our biochemistry.[1, 2, 3, 4, 5, 6] This first-prong approach to treating PTS is twofold: harness both the gut–brain axis and the lymph/glymph system to diminish inflammation in the brain and thereby the body.

Louis Kuhne, author of *The New Science of Healing* in the late 1800s, was correct.[7] Toxins, internally created or externally sourced, are the cause of most diseases and a layer we must address in PTS/trauma. This reality is even more apparent today in our artificial, polluted world coupled with our diminished capacity to detoxify, with the result that our bodily systems can adversely affect our mental health. Tremendously.

Heavy metals, pesticides, molds that generate mycotoxins, harmful chemicals in food because of 'Big Ag' and toxic consumer products, cosmetics, cleaning products, vaccinations, polluted air, deficient soil, water in need of filtration and energizing, all burden our bodies and can do lasting damage through excess free radicals that lead to inflammation. (This is why glutathione, the major antioxidant in the brain, is so important – see page 74.)

Minerals on receptor sites on cell membranes may be replaced by toxic molecules; this has the potential to change the brain's messaging and pathway signaling. Vitamin depletion lowers organ function, especially that of the adrenal glands. Studies link poor diets to many comorbidities of PTS/trauma, including diabetes, metabolic syndrome, and cardiovascular disease; these conditions affect brain chemistry and regulation, including the functioning of the hippocampus,[8] which can result in cognitive impairment. And PTS affects our emotions profoundly through under-and over-reactivity in areas of the brain, as we saw in chapter 4.

With a traumatic event or a lifetime of trauma that has disrupted homeostasis and rides shotgun with anxiety and so many other symptoms that weigh us down, we need to do all we can daily to turn the situation around to nourish our bodies, to encourage our gut to break down food freely and happily to communicate all is well with our brain.

Whether our goal, when dealing with a variety of underlying conditions or diseases of PTS/trauma, is to encourage energy production, regulate blood sugar, sleep more soundly, or ferret out food allergies, we begin with a diet that is calming and supports digestion. We do this, as is explained in greater detail in this chapter, by eating organic food, added minerals (consider fulvic or humic acids to increase mineral absorption and increase detoxification), prebiotics, probiotics, fermented foods to heal a leaky gut, neuroprotective antioxidants, fatty acids such as omega-3s (DHA, EPA and ALA), and medium-chain triglycerides (MCTs). Becoming more aware of optimal vitamins and minerals, and brain supplements such as CoQ10, PQQ, glutathione, methylated B complex, vitamin D, quercetin, magnesium, and zinc, we can curb neuro-inflammation and oxidative stress so our brain has a chance to manifest the mental outlook that will serve us best.

Eat organic only. Glyphosate (see MIT scientist, Dr. Stephanie Seneff's book, *Toxic Legacy*,[9] or my podcast interviews with her) and other toxic chemicals are wreaking havoc in our brains (even in utero), contributing to neurological impairment and cognitive decline and problems with mood and behavior.

Parasites are infecting one out of three Americans, often called 'neglected' parasitic infections because they usually occur within extreme poverty and can be the cause of schizophrenia.[10]

Best practices

A traumatic event (or a lifetime of distress) can negatively affect our microbiome, the ecosystem within, leading ultimately to an increase in hormones like cortisol, amplifying the experience of psychological trauma. Whether you choose to eat a vegan or keto diet, for example, just know food affects mood, and this can be intense. It also affects sleep, which is one of the most challenging issues for someone with PTS/trauma because we are prone to have nightmares and to be hypervigilant, keeping us up or waking us up.

The discoveries of Weston A. Price

It is a person's choice to eat vegan, keto, Mediterranean or any other diet but there is no denying that someone in recovery needs to feed their brain with healthy fats. One person who has my deepest respect is Canadian dentist, Weston A Price. He travelled the globe in the 1920s and '30s with his wife, visiting traditional peoples, including Polynesian islanders, Aborigines of Australia, the Maori of New Zealand, African tribes, Indigenous peoples in North and South America and Gaelic communities in the Outer Hebrides, and discovered that ancestral foods, diets rich in good fats and the 'activator' fat-soluble vitamins, A, D and K2, were the key to robust health. These foods included organ meats and full-fat dairy (raw with enzymes) that offered far more nourishment than the typical modern SAD (Standard American Diet), a processed diet filled with sugar, the root cause of our ill-health that is 'worse with each generation'. The SAD seems to be the main culprit of our brains leaning away from good decision-making and healthy relationships and is, in my view, why this planet is in such a mess. So, whatever you eat, feed your brain. Don't believe modern-day advertisers. You need saturated fats, and cholesterol-rich foods, the right ones. Our ancestors have work-shopped a traditional diet for the best health, beginning with our babies for centuries. It's time we paid attention to the dentist who went the extra mile to find out why certain people have such healthy teeth and bone structure that they often don't have to brush their teeth!

Maintaining the gut-brain connection

A balanced microbiome, made up of microorganisms – bacteria, viruses and fungi – is so important that the gut has been called the first brain. It seems gut neurons evolved independently to control gut function and communicate with its surroundings as well as the brain.

The ongoing biochemical signaling between the gastrointestinal tract and the central nervous system, via the GBA axis, is bidirectional. Therefore, the interchange between our brain and belly depends on what we eat and drink, as well as digestive enzymes properly breaking down food to optimize gut function.

- Stress can make our bellies ache and our minds foggy because of systemic dysregulation that leads to inflammation.
- Good food can help us deal with stress by reducing inflammation.

Brain function is tied to the health of our gut microbes, the health of which is tied to the quality of the foods, more particularly the fiber, we eat, the ones we eliminate, the way we sleep, how we manage our stress, and our daily detox. Our gut, intimately connected to our brain through its many nerve fibers, has tight barriers in its lining, allowing only the smallest molecules to pass through. Stress can allow these junctions to weaken and so allow bad bacteria or immune complexes to infiltrate the circulation and body, causing havoc. Thus, if we want to think or feel balanced in a state of PTS, it behooves us to eat well to make our inside community happy.

Healthy gut bacteria may enhance vagus nerve function by:
- stimulating its fibers
- positively affecting the microbiome.

It is essential to focus on organic nutrient-dense foods you *like* and will eat, not feeling deprived. It can take time to hone this, learn new recipes to substitute for old, cherished comfort foods. But it can be done. Add to your goals the reduction of any underlying health conditions that need to be addressed. Again, you can find substitutes for old favorites that are healthier for you. For example, if you have or have had an autoimmune disorder, you are going to need more protein, vegan, or carnivore; just make sure it is organic and, in the case of meat, grass-fed. If you live in a toxic location, you will need to tailor your meals to be in accordance with a detox diet. So many foods can help detox the liver and cells. The bottom line is to adopt an anti-inflammatory organic diet. (See dietary plans in my book *Surviving a Viral Pandemic*, written with Dr. Alec Peklar. Or read books by Weston A. Price or those he influenced.) I know this is difficult for people who want to eat only vegan, but you can eat mostly vegan and eat the healthy saturated fats. You can also supplement with ALA (alpha-linolenic acid) that converts to DHA, the primary structural component of your brain and retina, an essential (can't be made by the body) omega-3 fatty acid. Brain (neurological) development and cognitive support are impeded with a deficiency of this fatty acid, which is in fish and animals that are grass fed. It is much easier to figure this out with a naturopathic or integrative physician who will also include lab tests to pinpoint any immune issues and/or elemental deficiencies.

Reactive hypoglycemia

Low blood sugar within four hours of eating a meal is a major contributing factor to anxiety and depression. Most people become irritable if they don't eat, getting 'hangry', a symptom of their blood sugar (glucose) levels falling. This is reactive hypoglycemia. And while the craving for and resulting ingestion of sweets relieves symptoms initially, a few hours later blood sugar levels become exacerbated and hard to manage. Symptoms include anxiety, trembling, heart palpitations, sweating, hunger, and irritability.

It works in the following way. The sympathetic nervous system is triggered by a lack of sugar in the blood and releases epinephrine and norepinephrine which restore the glucose level toward normal but also induces the 'fight or flight' reaction.

Recommendations for addressing this include:
- Avoid refined sugar.
- Avoid caffeine, found in coffee or energy drinks and sodas; (in one study, patients saw improvement in hostility, suspiciousness, anxiety, and irritability by eliminating caffeine[11]).
- Avoid dark chocolate – if eaten in quantity, it can manifest in a similar scenario to reactive hypoglycemia.
- Eat enough protein to maintain even blood glucose levels.
- Carry seeds, such as sunflower, or pumpkin, or nuts, such as almonds.

Chapter 5

Brain foods

These foods help mitochondria, create new brain cells, help fight free radicals (remember, these unstable molecules cause inflammation and affect blood flow); incorporate them into your daily diet. Here are some examples:

- Beets: increase nitric oxide (NO) that increases blood flow to the brain.
- Berries (all): one of the foods richest in antioxidants.
- Foods with color and antioxidant and anti-inflammatory properties: for polyphenols and minerals eat dark green leafy, dark green, orange or purple vegetables; broccoli and other cruciferous vegetables for sulforaphane; quercetin is present in onions, garlic, and apples; avocado provides carotenoids and tocopherols; mushrooms, especially Chaga and Shitake, but all kinds are good.
- Non-vegans: fatty fish for omega-3s – salmon, sardines, mackerel, halibut.

Super-foods

Also add these detoxifying super-foods to your diet:
- Phytoplankton (Nannochloropsis gaditana), seaweed, a star of the show contains:
  - antioxidants: zeaxanthin and beta carotene
  - amino acids
  - DHA, EPA, nucleic acids
  - omega-3 fatty acids
  - vitamin A, vitamins B1, B2, B6, B8, B9 and, most importantly for vegans, B12
  - minerals such as copper, iodine, magnesium, potassium, and zinc.

OR

- Spirulina: similar to phytoplankton but from freshwater. Contains iodine but the amount varies widely.

Protective brain supplements

Glutathione

This is most important! Its precursor is NAC (N-acetyl cysteine), a major antioxidant in the brain, needed in high amounts.

Features of glutathione include:
- called mitochondria's best friend
- repairs damage to cells caused by inflammation
- helpful in sleep
- regulates production of pro-inflammatory cytokines
- recycles antioxidants vitamins C and E
- high in avocados, asparagus, carrots, garlic, onions, cabbage family, spinach, squash
- intravenous glutathione therapy is also available in some countries.

Glutathione's enzyme, glutathione transferase, is a biomarker for PTS.

Nrf-2

Production of antioxidants like glutathione is triggered by transcription factor Nrf-2, a protein that binds to DNA to activate genes and acts as a switch to turn on protection when a cell is damaged. This will decrease inflammation. Phytonutrient-rich plants such as broccoli sprouts (see list below) that contain glucosinolates activate detoxification enzymes via Nrf-2.

Nrf-2 tells the cell that oxidative damage is occurring, thereby turning on your body's defense mechanisms that help the cell to produce protective antioxidant molecules. Interestingly, the highest levels of Nrf-2 are in the liver and kidneys, the main organs of detoxification, so Nrf-2 supports these detox pathways (mainly Phase ll in liver metabolism) and curtails damaging cytokines, like NF-κB, further reducing systemic and neural inflammation.

Foods containing Nrf-2 include:

- broccoli and broccoli sprouts
- cabbage, kale, collard greens, cauliflower, bok choy, Brussels sprouts (sulforaphane)
- garlic and onion (sulfur)
- grapes, cranberries, blueberries, mulberries, lingonberries, bilberries, jackfruit
- peanuts, chocolate (resveratrol)
- olives including olive oil (oleuropein)
- pomegranate (delphinidin, cyanidin, pelargonidin)
- green tea (epigallocatechin-3-gallate, EGCG).

You can see why a Mediterranean diet can be a good choice, especially if needing to detox.

Alpha-lipoic acid (ALA)

This short-chain omega-3 fatty acid breaks down adrenal hormones so they no longer cause 'fight or flight' feelings. It chelates certain metals (binds to them and removes them from the body) and potentiates antioxidants like glutathione, vitamin C and vitamin E.

ALA is rich in red meat and organ meats plus nuts, especially walnuts, flax and flaxseed/linseed oil.

Alternatively, you can supplement: 200-1000 mg/day, or intravenously with the help of a health professional.

Pyrroloquinoline quinone (PQQ)

This is a calming antioxidant and redox cofactor, able to carry out 20,000 catalytic conversions compared with only four for vitamin C. It is neuroprotective and promotes the development of new nerve cells and new mitochondria. It is rich in parsley, green peppers, kiwi fruit, papaya, tofu, and green tea.

Common food allergens

Food allergies or food intolerances are particularly troubling in someone with PTS/trauma of any kind as they burden the immune system through over-reactivity, a contributing factor to anxiety as well as playing a role in dissociative disorders. Rare before the 20th century, food allergies now affect most Americans. They can lead to leaky gut syndrome that in turn leads to incomplete protein nourishment, and can form immune complexes in the blood while wreaking havoc in joints and other tissues.

Since a large percentage of the population doesn't experience an acute physical reaction to these substances, many aren't even aware they have a food intolerance or allergy. These reactions are often challenging to connect back to a specific food as they can occur days, rather than minutes, after the food has been ingested. Hidden or masked food allergies trigger a wide range of emotional disorders. An IgE and an IgG food allergy test are essential, or if one is not available or affordable try an elimination diet with the support of your naturopathic physician.

Common food allergens include:
- dairy, milk (casein)
- eggs
- fish
- peanuts
- soy
- shellfish
- wheat (gluten/gliadin).

More subtle and wide-ranging reactions include:
- anxiety
- lethargy
- joint pain
- indigestion
- headaches

- migraines
- fatigue
- itchy skin
- fast pulse.

What to do

It's best to eliminate gluten[12] from all sources along with wheat, rye, and possibly oats. In a study of women with schizophrenia (often trauma-induced) and celiac, the elimination of gluten in the diet led to the disappearance of psychiatric symptoms (and the reversal of hypoperfusion of the left frontal area of brain).[13]

Stay away from grains or add cautiously. Schizophrenia, often trauma-induced, is reported to be rare in regions where grain consumption is rare.

Prior to the widespread enrichment of refined grains, 100 to 200 mg of niacin a day eased anxiety and other symptoms in patients with functional digestive disturbances.

Soak grains, nuts, and seeds or buy them already sprouted. This way phytic acid won't grab onto minerals and make them unavailable by decreasing absorption.

Add B complex vitamins if going grain-free.

Help the lymphatics

Addressing the lymphatic system (throughout the body) and glymphatic system (in the brain) is essential as these drain cells and tissues through a filter system of lymph nodes and vessels, removing dead bacteria and other poisons. Without this system in tip top shape, inflammation throughout our body will rise dramatically. You know that sick feeling when you eat the wrong foods and feel achy? Or you are toxic with pesticides and heavy metals? You have generated free radicals that are missing their mate, causing chaos in your bloodstream and brain. This system is not given enough attention in healing but it is super-important, just as is taking out our own garbage from our home.

What to do

- Massage or exercise is the best way to get lymph moving: start exercising gently like jumping on a trampoline to get your lymphatic system activated.
- Drink alkaline water or a cup of water with a pinch of baking soda.
- Eat sauerkraut or kimchi.
- Make sure to have regular bowel movements.
- Eat raw food for the enzymes to support the immune system, gut and liver functioning properly. You can add digestive enzyme products. Exercise through sweating promotes enzymes needed for detoxification.
- Consume at least 40 grams of fiber daily through fruit and vegetables.
- Go to sleep early and wake up early. The body detoxifies and repairs the damage at night when we rest.
- Spend as much time outdoors in green spaces, as indoor air is generally considerably more polluted.
- Learn breathing and stress-reducing techniques as these reduce the oxidative stress on the body.

If the focus is on detox[14, 15]

- Add liver botanicals such as dandelion or *Silybum marianas*. Ayurvedic medicine has a product called Shilajit, a tar-like substance from the Himalayas.
- Foods high in Nrf-2 (see page 95).
- Add fulvic acid: this transports and attaches minerals that will maximize mineral uptake and increase the elimination of pesticides and heavy metals.

- If available, take a sauna, preferably far infrared, at least two times per week and, if you live in a city, almost every day.
- Try colon hydrotherapy. If this is new to you or you are older definitely be under proper supervision of an experienced professional.
- If fasting, do so very carefully since the adrenals are already taxed.
- Reduce exposure to electro-magnetic pollution (EMFs) – there are protective devices available.
- Include herbs and spices for high antioxidant activity. Grow pots of basil, oregano etc. on your window sill or balcony; pick them off to add to a salad.
- *Nigella sativa* (black cumin seed or oil) is good, especially if you have been eating junk; it helps reduce neuroinflammation.
- Ginger: increases NO (nitric oxide). (Green, black or white tea contain caffeine and may be too stimulating; better ginger tea; add turmeric).

Help your gut

Prebiotics

Prebiotics are indigestible fibrous plants that allow the healthy microorganisms in our gut to flourish by feeding the good bacteria like bifidobacteria. These also help with detoxification, reduce constipation, and improve mineral status.

Good food sources include:
- apples
- almonds
- asparagus
- beans and legumes
- burdock root

- chicory
- dandelion root and greens
- garlic
- jerusalem artichoke
- kiwis
- konjac root
- onions.

Three prebiotics that are found in foods are:
- **Inulin** found in roots (the rhizome) and many of the foods above (too much at first may upset some people's gut so go slowly).
- **FOS** (fructooligosaccharides, often used in natural alternative sweeteners).
- **Pectin:** We probably all think of apples but pectin is also in berries, green beans and peas, sweet potatoes, carrots, bananas, and peaches.

Butyrate

Butyrate is a short-chain fatty acid produced by healthy gut bacteria when they break down fiber in fermentation. (It is also in butter.) Its beneficial properties include:
- Protects brain and spinal cord
- Anti-inflammatory
- Main source of cells in the colon
- Helps stabilize blood sugar levels.

Probiotics

As opposed to *prebiotics*,[16, 17] *probiotics* are live microorganisms, commonly found in fermented foods that support our microbiome. Naturally high in Nrf-2, fermented foods that naturally contain high levels of probiotics include:

- brine pickles (almost any vegetable can be fermented)
- kefir
- kimchi
- miso
- olives
- sauerkraut
- tempeh
- yogurt.

Two probiotics, *Lactobacillus helveticus R0052* and *Bifidobacterium longum R0175,* are bacteria commonly found in our GI tract. Together, they have been shown to contribute significantly to reducing anxiety and depression by calming pro-inflammatory cytokines and balancing hormones in the brain, including the HPA axis – that is, cortisol and ACTH (adrenocorticotropic hormone).

Lactobacillus rhamnosus is another common probiotic.

All of these are present in fermented foods in varying amounts; you can also buy capsules or powder of them.

With new studies coming daily, there are many probiotics that are known now to reduce anxiety and depression and, in general, to have these remarkable benefits:

- A dramatic reduction in symptoms of mental illness.
- A 49% decrease in distress.
- A 50% decrease in depression scores.
- A 60% decrease in anger-hostility scores.
- A 13% decrease in urinary free cortisol.
- An increase in BDNF (brain-derived neurotrophic factor); this protein promotes the survival of nerve cells.
- Intestinal permeability dropped by 57%.

My experience is that fermented foods and prebiotic fiber are better than taking capsules of probiotics to encourage a healthy microbiome and studies are now confirming this.

Increasingly, studies are also confirming evidence of a leaky gut in depression and anxiety.

It is worth noting that children born by Caesarian section or fed with formula may be at increased risk of conditions later in life and that this is thought to be related to not acquiring the mother's microbiome through descending the birth canal and breastfeeding.

Other considerations – fats and fatty acids

Sixty per cent of the brain's dry weight is fat. High levels of fats, with fat-soluble vitamins A, D, E and K2, are essential for brain health. For dietary fats, always eat organic and if, beef or poultry, also grass fed. Never eat farmed fish due to parasites and the chemicals used to counteract them.

Medium-chain triglycerides (MCTs)

- Found in coconut (all forms), human breast milk, cow's milk, goat's milk.
- Healthiest source of fats for the brain: neuroprotective and calming; also help in digestion and boost the immune system.
- Unlike long-chain fats, they are easily absorbed.
- The liver converts MCTs to ketones and releases them directly into the bloodstream. (Ketones can be used for damaged brain cells since these cells can't utilize glucose.)
- The best fat for cooking is coconut oil; it is stable at high temperatures.

Fatty acids

Essential unsaturated fatty acids are important components of all cell membranes. These comprise omega-3 fatty acids and omega-6 fatty acids. They are called 'essential' because we cannot make them – they have to be consumed, and that should be in a ratio of about 1:4.

Omega-3s are anti-inflammatory and play an important part in healthy brain function through the mitochondria. Specifically, they include:
- ALA (alpha-linolenic acid, not alpha-lipoic acid) (see earlier – page 95). If we have the right enzymes we can break ALA down to:
  ○ DHA (docosahexaenoic acid): the most abundant fat in the brain.
  ○ EPA (eicosapentaenoic acid): like DHA, a long-chain fatty acid; we can make DHA from EPA.

Both EPA and DHA are found in phytoplankton (ocean) and spirulina (lake). They are also found in cold water fish like:
- salmon
- mackerel
- sardines
- halibut
- shellfish
- cod.

Omega-6s play a crucial part in brain function too and have many important metabolic functions including in the immune response's initial inflammatory phase. Unfortunately, the Western diet just has too many foods containing them; unless someone is starving, a deficiency in omega-6s is hard to come by.

Vitamins and minerals

Vitamin C is essential, preferably liposomal, as is vitamin D. Minerals can be had from various sources, as noted, as well as from bone broth or, for vegans, a broth made from vegetables and miso.

A note on B vitamins and the mitochondria

B vitamins work together, and so, being deficient in one of them will affect the whole process of ATP production (page 79) in our mitochondria, so necessary for optimal brain function and mood as we have seen. They all can manifest a deficiency through visible signs such as rashes, and tongue changes, and through what you can't see – malabsorption – or what you feel – nerve tingling – as well as increased homocysteine as a biomarker.

Particularly think of **riboflavin (vitamin B2)**, the source of FMN (flavin mononucleotide) and FAD (flavin adenine dinucleotide), both coenzymes in the Krebs cycle (remember biology class), absolutely necessary for conversion in so many enzymatic reactions.[18, 19] If riboflavin is depleted OR you aren't absorbing nutrients due to a leaky gut or a disease like Crohn's, or high stress, inflammation, infection or pancreatitis (look at toxins), then you will feel fatigued. Signs of a deficiency include painful cracks at the corners of the mouth, and a dark purple tongue.

NB: B vitamins should be taken as a complex, not singly, because they work together as I have said, unless your integrated health practitioner advises an intravenous drip. Even in this case I recommend trying a methylated B complex first and eating fermented foods.

A NOTE TO THE CLINICIAN

Emotional eating creates eating disorders leading not only to depletion of the adrenal glands, but also to poor mitochondrial function and poor gut terrain, as has been discussed. Understanding basic healthy intake (the good stuff in: what you eat and what you do) and outtake (metabolic waste; detoxification) will affect the body's level of inflammation and this will make a huge difference in mood and behavior, particularly anxiety.[20] Hence, to

---

reduce and with any luck resolve PTS/trauma, we must first implement an anti-inflammatory nutrient-dense diet to change our biochemistry. Whether a survivor chooses a keto, vegan or Mediterranean diet or follows Weston Price, a more traditional diet globally, this decision must be left to an individual's choice, optimally working with an integrated health professional. (An anti-inflammatory diet and a daily detox together are also the key to decreasing physical pain and therefore a reliance on pills.[21])

Creating an individualized plan is essential because, although some foods have the same negative action for all of us, others are specific to our DNA or metabolic needs. By consuming more alkaline foods and water, and super-dense nutrients, introducing live cultures to our gut, sleeping more soundly and managing stress, we can take control, decrease inflammation and regulate cortisol to optimize brain function.

And remember, when you are working with survivors, be sure to find ways to encourage changes without seeming to feed any feeling of deprivation. This is the reason to listen, not label, their story, their feelings, and their intent.

Refer to a weekly farmer's market, help to adapt favorite recipes to include healthier ingredients and discover tasty new recipes; incorporate fun into the transition.

ASSIGNMENT #5

1. Design a basic health protocol for an adult family member with anxiety. What is the reasoning at the forefront of your plan?
2. Discuss the role of the gut in optimal health of someone with PTS/trauma.
3. Design a daily detox for yourself. Include reasons why.
4. What can you do if changing the diet is met with resistance?

Chapter 6

The healing power of nature

*Natural inclination drew me to science; severe
sickness and sad experiences with orthodox
(allopathic) physicians led me to Nature Cure.*

Louis Kulne, late 1800s

The pioneer of integrated and functional medicine, Naturopathic
Medicine honors an ancient lineage of philosophy and treatments. These gifts of modalities include clinical nutrition (see
Chapter 5), homeopathy, hydrotherapy, botanical medicine,
and body mind therapies. The belief that everyone possesses
the innate ability to heal naturally was the basis of Nature Cure
in the 1800s that led to forming the independent profession of
Naturopathic Medicine. In the early days many in the profession, as is true today, were against vaccination, vivisection, and
any invasive allopathic treatments.

Today we can be grateful for modern science's recognition
of Naturopathic Medicine through evidence-based research,
defined as the 'integration of best research evidence with
clinical expertise and patient values'.[1] This means that
when health professionals, including primary-care trained
naturopathic physicians (aka 'naturopathic medical doctors'
(some US states) or 'naturopathic doctors' (UK)) make a
treatment decision with their patient, they base it on their
clinical expertise, the preferences of the patient, and the best
available evidence, using proven therapies to help heal on a
physical and/or mental level.

Little known history

Traditional Chinese Medicine (TCM), Ayurvedic medicine (with its roots in India) as well as the health practices of Indigenous cultures, enjoy a legacy of thousands of years of healing with plant knowledge and natural techniques such as hydrotherapy or the manipulation of Qi/energy meridians (i.e., acupuncture). These were distinct systems of medicine long before 20th century miracle drugs and technological advances took precedence around the world.

As early as circa 400 BC, Hippocrates rejected the rituals of the priests and used hellebore, a plant that induces vomiting, to alleviate madness – fears and terrors. Although there is a question whether this hellebore was white hellebore, *Veratrum album*, or black hellebore, *Helleborus niger*, this is of interest for two reasons. First, because of the importance of detoxing, of ridding the body of poison, essential for a healthy brain promoting positive thoughts and feelings, mood and behavior, and second, because both plants can be made into homeopathic medicines to treat mental imbalance.

Hydrotherapy was a system of medicine (see page 125) unto itself in the 1800s and, according to Cayleff's book *Wash and Be Healed*, was 'one of the most celebrated alternative forms of medical care in an age generally characterized by more dramatic therapeutics' (in other words, bloodletting).[2] The Water Cure offered psychological relief for nervous disorders and emotional malaise, as well as physiological relief. So how, in the Western world, did we get to a place in history that shuns Natural Medicine?

First, there was the fact that there were three main kinds of physician who practiced medicine in America during the 1800s. Allopathic medical doctors, as we saw in Chapter 1, called themselves 'regulars' and misused the word 'heroic' to describe their use of bloodletting and mercury-based formulas, based on the four humors; they fell out of favor with the public due to injuries and fatalities. The other two types were the homeopathic medical doctors and the 'eclectic' physicians who relied on a mix of Nature Cure (hydrotherapy, diet, fasting), medicinal plants and homeopathic remedies. Crossovers occurred between the three, including conversions of allopathic doctors to homeopathy, while allopaths could add eclectic medicine to their practice.

Chiropractic and osteopathy emerged towards the end of the century, as did the naturopathic doctors. The birth and growth of Naturopathic Medicine and its opposition to the toxic so-called 'heroic' medicine underscored the principle, *Vis Medicatrix Naturae*, the healing power of nature, attracting the homeopaths, hydropaths and eclectics.

One aspect that many don't realize is that the early naturopathic doctors understood the concept of energy medicine, a truth that is only today becoming more commonly understood. Early naturopathic doctor, Ludwig Staden, wrote in *Naturarzt* (German for Naturopath) in 1901: 'Taking into consideration that physical life and health are based on the vibrative process in the cell, which we call change of matter, there is no doubt that all disease is simply a disturbance of harmonious vibration within the cell.'[3] As Dr. Sussanna Czeranko wrote in *NDNR*: 'As part of the early naturopathic worldview, the nature cure physician incorporated "vibration" as a bridge to unify science and the principles of naturopathy into an understandable paradigm.'[4] This was an early acknowledgment of energy medicine and shows that those who profess to be energy field healing pioneers of late don't know this history.

Staden received letters from around the world in response to his column, 'Naturopathic Advisor' in a Benedict Lust publication. In 1902, he wrote: 'A true Naturopath before all must be a teacher of health.'

1. Homeopathy

Homeopathy is my first and favorite modality in treating PTS/ trauma. It can wipe years of angst and depression away, renewing the vital force of the survivor.

Homeopathy is a medicine based on the Law of Similars – 'like cures like' – a medical system founded by Samuel Hahnemann MD (1755-1843), although the concept can be traced back to Hippocrates. I never stop being amazed by what homeopathy can do for people with a challenging case, often individuals who have been undergoing therapy for years and have tried all available allopathic treatments to no avail, when, *voila!*, a shift in energy leads to changes in thoughts, feelings and behavior.

The beauty of homeopathy, for those suffering PTS, is that it gently heals the emotional wound, redressing the physiological and psychological imbalance of the initiating event without suppressing symptoms, through the science of resonance and nanoparticles, recognized now by physicists.[5] The objective is to correct the underlying disturbance of the body's 'vital force' and its subsequent symptoms with an energetic medicine, in stark contrast to the allopathic goal that advocates suppressing symptoms with a material substance.

Treatment requires excellent observation skills as one needs to be open to what the patient is experiencing, and then be able to translate it to the individualized treatment.

There is also prevention in homeopathy that considers 'obstacles to cure', another term coined by Hahnemann. Dovetailing with the naturopathic adage, *Vis Medicatrix Naturae*, these could be:
• poor choices in food
• environmental contamination
• other harmful lifestyles.

If called upon, non-suppressive modalities like clinical nutrition, botanical medicine, psychological framing and the expressive arts, can be employed to clear these obstacles before prescribing homeopathically.

Homeopathy was the first medicine to employ what we now know as frequencies and nanoparticles; its subtlety of action, its inherent energetics, can act so extraordinarily that sometimes it's just too hard to believe... until you've experienced its effect personally.

Hahnemann and other forerunners

Hahnemann, a genius pharmacist and linguist (he spoke seven languages), came to understand homeopathic principles and medicines by studying plant tinctures systematically. He noted their effects on healthy subjects before experimenting with dilution of these tinctures to the point they contained no mole-cules, only the 'energetic layer' that strengthened the substance – 'spirit-like energy and life force'. Over time, he noticed that his herbal preparations proved more effective after a day of bounc-ing along beside him in his horse-drawn buggy as he attended house calls. Hahnemann also noted that the least amount of medicine had the better effect.[6]

Wm. Henry Holcombe MD (1855–1892), another extraordinary homeopath, had tremendous success in the yellow fever epidemics of the 1800s in Louisiana. A convert from allopathy to homeopathy, he also realized the importance of the mind–body connection.

> *The part which the mind has always played in the cure has been ignored, or not recognized, because of the prevalent and dominant spirit of materialism. The mind (thought) has been all the time counted out, while it may have been the chief and perhaps the only factor in the case. When one has grasped the idea that, by creative laws, mind (thought) is dormant*

(nevertheless at work) in all things of the body, the minutest changes of which are organic manifestations or showing forth of mental conditions, many things before incomprehensible become clear. Emotions (which are produced by thought) can determine the most rapid changes in the secretions of our body. Fight turns the hair gray. Terror poisons the mother's milk. Great mental excitements or the slow torture of mental anxiety write their baneful effects upon the tissues of the brain....[7]

When we are confronted with cures of the most remarkable character, cures entirely beyond the reach of our best medication, we attribute them to imagination, faith, hope, expectations. And we do rightly; for imagination, faith, hope, expectation are states of mind, are the mind itself in substantial activity and creativity energy, and when these vital forces can be evoked and directed there is no limit to the possibilities that lie in store for us.[8]

An additional quotation to illustrate homeopathy comes from Ethelbert Petrie Hoyle MD (1861–1955), a British physician who lived in San Francisco periodically between 1895 and 1910 and converted to homeopathy:

One great difference between the two schools of medicine is that orthodoxy (allopathy) is always flirting with the "maximum" dose. We homeopaths always aim at giving the most minute medical stimulus, never harmful, which will arouse the vital reaction towards natural repair. We have a guiding rule (similia) on which to base every prescription.[9]

Albert Einstein PhD (1879–1955) famously remarked, 'There is a particle and a wave to everything'.[10] Homeopathy is the wave. A study[11] of quantum physics appears to clarify this idea and is also in line with Nobel Prize winner Luc Montagnier's statement: 'Homeopathy is the future of science and medicine,' an idea he came to after witnessing his physicist friends work in nanoparticles.

Homeopathic asylums

It might surprise you to know there were homeopathic asylums. Middletown State Homeopathic Hospital in Middletown, New York, opened in 1874 and Homeopathic State Hospital, Gowanda, in 1898, in Collins, New York. The beauty of these asylums was that they chose not to use violent methods for treatment, adhering to kindness as an alternate means of approaching their patients.

Regulations

Today it is more than a shame that misinformation about homeopathy still abounds, with unfair regulation by government and health insurers. Dana Ullmann puts it best in his article, 'Critique of Proposed Regulations of Homeopathic Medicines and Alternative Proposals'.[12]

> ...the common potato has more belladonna alkaloids in it than any homeopathic medicine on the market today. At a time when many regulations are being questioned and reduced, it is a bit odd that the FDA is choosing to significantly increase the regulation of homeopathic medicines, despite their 200-plus years' history of safety. When we consider the serious problems related to drug use, it would seem that there are many other much more serious problems facing the American public:
>
> • The opioid crisis.
> • The overuse of antibiotics.
> • The epidemic of polypharmacy (the use of many drugs concurrently).

- *The ineffectiveness and real dangers of many prescription drugs.*
- *The high costs of select drugs.*

Homeopathy takes time to learn but one remedy is important in terms of a public psychological traumatizing event, and that is **Aconitum**. See Appendix 2 for a list of my favorite homeopathic medicines for PTS/trauma.

A NOTE TO THE CLINICIAN: Homeopathy

Learning homeopathy isn't easy; it can take years to understand (see Resources (page 349) for recommended classes and books). That said, to be able to refer a survivor for this modality to give their vital force an energetic nudge to come to terms with their negative experience(s), can be life-altering. Not only can the right homeopathic medicine help them grow stronger, but it can also help them articulate the trauma and ultimately heal from the experience more quickly.

Constitutional (aka classical) homeopathy, rather than acute prescribing, is best with trauma survivors. Although you may prescribe acutely, if the overwhelming symptom is nightmares; then you could prescribe solely on this one strong symptom (perhaps *Stramonium*). Or, if they can't stand noise – it seems to penetrate their body – you might try *Theridion*.

Knowing that homeopathy can not only help a person with PTS/trauma, but it is in fact the best modality for transformation gives you a path to healing you might not have considered. You don't have to practice it, but you can be confident to refer someone with PTS to receive it. Do the appropriate research for different practitioners' training and years of experience and then reach out to see if they feel comfortable treating PTS/trauma.

I have heard many stories of how psychotherapy became far more effective after treating someone with a constitutional homeopathic medicine.

There are so many good teachers of homeopathy. I have included schools in the US and elsewhere in Resources (page 349).

One thing you might want to know is that many homeopathic teachers say strong smells, like eucalyptus and coffee, to name two, can counteract homeopathic remedies. This lies in the fact we all have varying degrees of sensitivity. However, I have never found them to be a problem. I have seen strong emotion block a homeopathic medicine. Just be aware.

Assignment #6A

1. What is the Law of Similars in homeopathy?
2. What scientific description did Nobel Prize winner, Dr. Luc Montagnier, refer to regarding the healing power of a homeopathic medicine?
3. In your own words, what are you looking for in determining a homeopathic medicine?

2. Botanical medicine

The scent of lavender lingering in a bath, the smell of a forest after a rainfall, the shredding of a root of ginger to soothe a distended belly, picking an herb to increase antioxidants in our salads, are all ways to harness this powerful modality and are a testimony to the resurgence of plant medicine and our connection to the earth.

A little history

There were literally thousands of Eclectic doctors in the 1800s. They utilized botanical medicine, hydrotherapy (water therapy), homeopathy, and good nutrition while advocating less stress and positive thinking. They wrote about it extensively in books and publications that are available today.

The Eclectics were the first officially recognized school of medicine to admit and graduate both women and African Americans. Although the last school standing, Eclectic Medical College of Cincinnati, was forced to close by 1940, it did so long after the naturopathic medical schools. Moreover, the Eclectics' Lloyd Library in Ohio held on to its legacy in what is regarded as the greatest botanical library in the Western world. These doctors were ultimately funneled into the medical herbalists and naturopathic physicians we know today, as naturopathic medicine evolved into a distinct profession.

My favorite botanicals for PTS

Withania somnifera (ashwagandha)[13, 14]

History: 4000 years of traditional use in its native India, Pakistan and Sri Lanka.

Description: A member of the Solanaceae family, it is a Medharasayan, the Ayurvedic category of foods and nutrients that promote learning and memory retrieval; an adaptogenic and tonic herb, its botanical name is *Withania somnifera*. Popularly known as Indian ginseng or winter cherry; Ashwagandha translates roughly to 'the smell and strength of a horse'.

Habitat: A small shrub that grows to 1.5 meters tall; it is found in dry areas of India and Africa.

Active ingredients: The root and leaf contain the highest number of steroidal compounds; these include the lactones withaferin A, and carbon-27-glycowithanolides, known collectively as withanolides. It also contains a fair amount of alkaloids including tropine, pseudotropine isopelletrine, anaferine, and saponins.

Function: Traditionally used in conditions of debility, emaciation, impotence, and premature aging, it helps the body resist both physical and psychological stress. It acts on the inflammatory system; nourishes the neurological/ nervous system; and can reduce agitation and insomnia, symptoms of trauma, especially in an overactive state of fatigue. Calming and rejuvenating, it helps calm thoughts, encourages healthy sleep and supports the thyroid, adrenals and immune system.

Research: The NIH cites five studies assessing trials for the treatment of anxiety in the *Journal of Alternative Complementary Medicine*; the journal concluded that ashwagandha resulted in significant improvements versus placebo in outcomes on anxiety or stress scales.

Dosage: Traditionally, ashwagandha is taken with equal amounts of ghee and honey (1:1).

- As capsules (most common today): 1-2 x 300-mg capsule once or twice a day.
- As a powder: before bed, one can take ¼-½ teaspoon of powder or once or twice a day; can put as much as 2 teaspoons in two cups of milk (preferably coconut, almond or flax) on a low heat for 15-20 minutes; add stevia or raw honey and cardamom or cinnamon if desired.
- As a liquid extract: add 30 ml or 1 dropperful to hot water one to three times daily.

Side effects: Ashwagandha, in my experience, is very safe and seems to have no interactions with any medications.

Cautions: Large doses of ashwagandha might cause stomach upset, diarrhea and vomiting; up to 1200 mg/day is safe.

Glycyrrhiza glabra (licorice)[15, 16]

History: From the Latin term 'liquirtia' that was based on the Greek term 'glukos riza' or sweet root; used for centuries in China and Rome for respiratory troubles and intestinal complaints.

Description: Small, pointy leaves and flower clusters.

Habitat: Europe, Asia, North America, South America and Australia.

Active ingredients: Glycyrrhizin is the active ingredient; 50 times sweeter than sugar although it has an aftertaste some don't like; licorice candy is a misnomer as the taste comes from anise; licorice contains at least eight compounds that are monoamine oxidase inhibitors.

Function: *Glycyrrhiza* can act as a potent antidepressant; it nudges the immune system to secrete more interferon, an antiviral chemical; licorice is *the* botanical that nourishes the adrenal glands in PTS or any autoimmune disorder and is recommended in the third stage of adrenal exhaustion; it also soothes the stomach, can heal ulcers and yields extensive health benefits due to its flavonoids, lignans and other phytochemicals, even when the active ingredient is removed to avoid hypertension because of 'potassium sparing'. (This is because of the potential for K+ (potassium ions) to decrease, leading to heart arrhythmias due to glycyrrhizin in licorice; it is therefore best if licorice has been deglycyrrhizinated.)

Dosage: ¼ tsp extract three times a day or ½ to 1 tsp tincture a day.

Cautions: Just be careful with people with hypertension. I have never had a problem when administering it in small doses. Use small doses and sparingly to avoid headaches, lethargy, water retention and excessive loss of potassium and high blood pressure. Beware – it interacts with many pharmaceuticals so don't use if someone is on pharmaceutical medications.

More favorites

All the following soothe the nervous system, calming feelings of anxiety. They can also be used for insomnia.

- *Passiflora incarnata* / passionflower – shown to be as effective as benzodiazepines.
- *Eschscholzia* / California poppy – indigenous to California and used by Indigenous people.
- *Lavendula officinalis* / lavender – nervine, calming, anti-depressant.
- *Matricaria recutita* / chamomile – also good for the digestive system, anti-inflammatory.
- *Melissa officinalis* / lemon balm – not to be used with people with hypothyroidism.
- *Piper methysticum* / kava kava – similar in effects to a benzodiazepine.
- Rose – uplifting, great to use in a spray.
- *Scutellaria lateriflora* / skullcap – nervine, very calming, in extreme stress and rage.
- *Valeriana officinalis* / valerian – same as Passiflora.
- *Avena sativa* / oats – nervine, nourishes the nervous system.

- Wild lettuce (*Lactic virosa* and *L. altissimo*) Also called bitter lettuce or lettuce-opium (no opiates and no constipation or excitement of the brain) – contains milky juice inside (lactucarium).
- *Morus alba*/white mulberry - reduces anxiety.[17]
- Skookum root or hellebore (*Veratrum viride*)[18] The Haida and other First Nations use it in Northwest British Columbia; said to help reduce scary dreams.

Entheogens

Entheogens are plants with mind-altering capabilities that should be used with extreme caution and are not available in many countries. These are not advocated as a self-help approach but only with the guidance of an experienced practitioner and availability of these plants very much depends on where you are geographically. Do not buy anything from dubious online sources under any circumstances. I include these here for completeness given the help many PTS sufferers have found from them.

Many veterans have found profound relief with cannabis, while other survivors report over-thinking and paranoia. Ayahuasca is a spiritual tea that can allow insights at the expense of feeling horrible. Mescaline (peyote) is another naturally occurring entheogen, found in certain cacti in the American southwest, Mexico and South America with similar properties to LSD.

Ayahuasca/Banisteriopsis caapi[19, 20, 21, 22, 23]

> **Description:** Also known as yagé, this is a woody vine of the family Malpighiaceae. It is an ancient Amazonian psychoactive botanical extract originally composed of several different plants. It is used as a tea for religious/ spiritual and/or medical purposes.

Habitat: Amazon rainforest in Brazil; also grows in Peru.

Active ingredients: The leaves contain the hallucinogenic compound, DMT, short for 'N, N-Dimethyltryptamine', a common plant alkaloid, as well as psychoactive beta-carbolines found in the leaves, stem and roots.

Research: Many studies show positive benefits in PTS/trauma, including for anxiety and depression,[19] highlighting the mechanism of action along epigenetic lines and healing traumatic memories.[21]

Positive anecdote: A woman repeatedly raped as a child, had had an abortion, compounding her grief. She recounted she was able to speak to the aborted girl, 'the process was excruciating' but in the end she 'felt totally wholesome and complete in mind'.[22]

Caution: Little is understood about the potential dangers of ayahuasca or its potential therapeutic activity in psychiatric and neurological disorders as a neuromodulatory botanical drug. I know people who ultimately had a very positive experience guided by shamans in the Amazon but for many it can be a ticket to a mental/emotional hell.

Cannabis

There is sufficient research to confirm that cannabis, in its various forms, reduces anxiety by decreasing amygdala activity.[24, 25, 26, 27, 28, 29, 30, 31]

History: Both *C. indica* and *C. sativa* (see below) were used to make hemp fiber and **for the seeds** for food in Europe and Asia. Both grew wild in India where its drug effect was discovered and processed for hashish. American farmers grew hemp to produce rope during World War II, then considered it a pesky weed after it was made illegal.

Description: There are two main variants or strains plus two hybrids:

- *C. indica* is short and bushy with wide leaves. Generally regarded as a sedative: treats anxiety, insomnia, chronic pain and loss of appetite.
- *C. sativa* is tall with thin leaves. Thought to have a positive effect on creative blocks, fatigue, lack of focus and depression; however, there is more evidence that the cannabinoids and terpenes, two of the many compounds found in cannabis, are the deciding factors.

Active ingredients: Although both strains are considered psychoactive there is no high from pure hemp extract.

- People with PTS seem to have reduced levels of cannabinoids, chemicals produced naturally in the brain through the endocannabinoid system or eCB.[32]
- Thus the plant can fill this deficit.

CBD (cannabidiol):
- discovered in 1940, derived mostly from hemp but also present in small amounts in cannabis.
- one of 113 cannabinoids identified.
- accounts for up to 40% of the hemp plant's extract and provides medicinal value.

THC (tetrahydrocannabinol) (as opposed to CBD):
- produces the 'buzz' as this is the principal psychoactive constituent.

Function: Depending on its chemical constituents, it helps to relax and/or energize; war veterans, in particular, cite its benefits.

Dosage: CBD oil is not regulated as a medical treatment for anxiety, so dosage is unclear. Some suggest 12 drops twice a day. Everyone is different. Best to start with a low dose and work up to see what works.

Research: Shows CBD can reduce anxiety while helping to decrease fear memories.[26, 27] While research is difficult to perform, since CBD triggers many pathways in both the body and the brain, studies – albeit with small sample sizes – are showing it to be a strong anti-inflammatory and antioxidant, and that it increases both serotonin levels (through 5-HT1A serotonin receptors) and GABA.[28] Martin A. Lee, author of *Smoke Signals: A Social History of Marijuana – Medical, Recreational and Scientific* and director of Project CBD, reports: 'Scientists have determined that normal CB-1 receptor signaling deactivates traumatic memories and endows it with the gift of forgetting. But skewed CB-1 signaling, due to endocannabinoid deficits (low serum levels of anandamide), results in impaired fear extinction, aversive memory consolidation and chronic anxiety, the hallmarks of PTSD.'[29]

Cautions: 'Cannabis use is generally considered safe; still beware, since different strains of marijuana have different amounts of THC, dosing a suitable or safe amount of marijuana may prove difficult.'[30]

Again, be cautious and be prepared

It is imperative that the ingestion of any plant (or substance) with psychoactive properties is carried out in a safe environment to minimize risks and abuse potential; in addition, the quality of the substance must be verified. I would never want anyone to experience an entheogen in the atmosphere of a rave or anywhere that has the potential to be unsafe and unsupported. But in a controlled setting it can be very useful to deepen and subsequently heal a difficult mental and emotional state.[31, 32]

More from the earth

Forest bathing: Walking in a forest gives benefits, decreasing cortisol and other biomarkers.[33]

Earthing: Grounding ourselves into the earth's energy is something Indigenous people have tapped into for centuries.

- Adolf Just, an early pioneer of Nature Cure, wrote about this in his book, *Return to Nature* in the 1800s when the natural health movement was strong.[34]
- The earth's natural electric charge influences the regulation of physiological processes and is best and most potent if connected to water like the ocean, a lake or even a swimming pool.
- This decreases inflammation, optimizes the immune system and helps in autoimmune disorders.[35]
- Ocean water is an added benefit from the salt with other electrolytes (minerals) dissolved in it.
- Or swim in a lake, or a swimming pool.
- Walk barefoot or nap on the grass.
- You can purchase bed sheets, shoes and other articles that promote earthing. See Resources, page 349.

A NOTE TO THE CLINICIAN: Botanical medicine

If you are not trained in botanicals, I suggest trying one (non-entheogen) plant at a time before prescribing to someone else. Try a capsule or tincture that has been standardized (meaning the pharmacy has assured the active ingredient to a certain potency) to make sure it has the effect on you that is desired. Start dosing low, follow the product's suggested dose. Be careful if you want more; medicinal plants can cause havoc if taken at too high a dose.

Learn all about the plant before it was a capsule or tincture. Taste it. Feel it. Pick it. Draw it. Grow a medicinal garden or pots of herbs on your balcony. As you start seeing the action they are intended for, put them in a category such as adrenal support, thyroid calming, liver cleanser, mitochondrial or vagal support, and so on. You will begin to trust them as you feel their effect.

In the early years of my practice, except for licorice, I only used plant medicine for detoxification. Homeopathy, food, hydrotherapy in terms of naturopathic modalities were enough. However, living in Los Angeles for the past 20 years has given me the opportunity to use many plants not just in detox but in terms of manipulating the HPA axis. The adrenals also need vitamin C and the thyroid, iodine, but a plant medicinal like ashwagandha can be a godsend. Adding rhodiola, maca, magnolia and kava kava on a regular basis doesn't have to interfere with an energetic modality like homeopathy.

There are so many ways to use plants to comfort and heal no matter what your part in trauma recovery. Be curious, make it an adventure, an experiment to learn more!

Assignment #6B

1. Describe the benefits of ashwagandha in PTS. Do you have a go-to plan for its calming effects? Please describe.
2. Name two other botanicals that are calming.
3. Name one activity from 'connecting with the earth' that can induce calm.

3. Hydrotherapy

Aah... the sound of water flowing, dripping, cascading down rocks; the feel of cold or warm or hot on the skin, down the throat; all conspiring to calm us, nourish and energize our body and mind. Water is so basic, it's hard to believe the depth of healing it can generate, but hydrotherapy, perhaps the simplest therapy of all, is not to be taken lightly or ignored in any type of anxiety or depression. It bolsters our inner resources by stimulating blood flow and blood pressure, whether through total immersion or specific application to a part of the body.

Water can do so much, not just physiologically, although that's where it starts, but in how it optimizes the workings of our brain and mind, encouraging any presentation of PTS/trauma to heal, through a natural, safe process, again not turning to pharmaceuticals.

It was the first modality I discovered at Bastyr, or more pointedly in the bathroom where I lived with three other older students! Over the years since, I have discovered how powerful hydrotherapy is for both physical aches and mental anguish, and for the latter its ability to soothe and regulate the nervous system makes it an ideal treatment if done with care for a person suffering from PTS, ACE or any of their comorbidities.

In this section, I focus on cold water, although hot mineral springs can feel fabulous. This is because, unless you are also countering the heat with cold, a person whose adrenal glands are already somewhat depleted, used up by anxiety and mental anguish, may feel more worn out than peacefully energized by adding more heat. Cold, on the other hand, settles our nerves (after the initial plunge or application), calming our anxiety. This mechanism starts by cold water constricting blood vessels; this stimulates our ANS (autonomic nervous system). This initially acts via the SNS (sympathetic nervous system), with its neurotransmitter, norepinephrine, and then is ultimately counteracted by the PNS (parasympathetic nervous system) via its ventral vagus nerve and its pacifying neurotransmitter, GABA. Implementing hydrotherapy, with at least part of the session using cold water, daily or weekly, is a huge boon to trauma survivors.

People have utilized the benefits of cold water, including improving mood, since time began. Lately I have noticed more naturopathic physicians and others (see the extreme athlete Wim

Hof below) have become keen participants in what was termed the 'cold-water cure' in the 1800s, a medical system of its own. And although I will discuss the diving reflex (page 132), I am not suggesting anyone with extreme anxiety start treatment by diving into and under cold water as so many northern Europeans do in winter as sport. The diving reflex has, however, given us an opportunity to see the impact cold water can have on our endocrine and neurological systems. Even if we simply put a cloth dipped in cold water on our face or slowly enter a cold swimming pool, lake or ocean, we get the benefit of this physiological magic.

Why do it

In a person suffering severe anxiety and any of its comorbidities, the cold-water cure can be a huge revelation as it opposes heat generated in the body by anxiety that increases inflammation, heart rate and blood pressure, and taxes our adrenal glands, often the bellringers of disease. Overall, and cheaply, with often the bonus of being in nature (see Chapter 5 for the benefits of forest bathing (page 123) or earthing (page xx) – the best is the ocean with its minerals) as well as offering an enclosure of soft-ness, cold water can act as a conduit to heal deeply and perma-nently. It may be the easiest action to do to soothe our nervous system and be of immediate help when we need something we can do right away.

A favorite of naturopathic medical students, at least at Bastyr, the 'wet socks treatment' (see page 137) is legendary in Naturopathic Medicine (if we can't get to nature, don't have a pool or don't have the cash for a $6 to $10, 000 ice machine for our daily plunge). The same goes for the 'wet sheet treatment' (page 136) where we can fall asleep afterwards, conceivably in our own bed. Both treatments allow our body to settle, coax our immune system by amplifying white blood cells if needed and call forward all the parts of the brain and body we have been discussing that lead to calming an agitated state.

A little history

Almost all cultures have used hydrotherapy (or hydropathy, as it was known in the 1800s) instead of pills to settle a rattled nervous system. Used by Indigenous people for spiritual and healing purposes for thousands of years, water in European traditions was attributed with supernatural powers: 'shed by nymphs and water gods well worship was practiced in ancient Babylon and modern Derbyshire'.[36]

As early as 1702 in England there were writings[37] of illnesses cured by cold water, including John Wesley's book *Primitive Physic, or an Easy and Natural Method of Curing Most Diseases*. He noted that, if conducted properly, cold water therapy could cure almost any condition or disease.

In 1826, Vincent Pressnitz opened Grafenberg (or 'Water University') in present day Poland and became famous for the cold-water cure. (He himself had used it to heal broken ribs.) By 1840, as royalty and commoners were in attendance to heal a myriad of ills (including success in epidemics) his theories and practices made it across the Atlantic where botanist and herbalist Samuel Thomson (1769-1843) was already popularizing techniques learned from the First Nations (Native Americans) who made particular use of steam to promote sweating as well as cold water immersion.

A medical system unto itself in America in the 1800s, the water-cure movement led to hydropathy becoming a prominent modality in naturopathic medicine. Americans embraced the application and immersion of water, particularly cold, mimicking cultures around the world who had access to hot springs or streams, rivers, even snow.

In her book *Wash and Be Healed, The Water Cure Movement and Women's Health*, Susan Cayleff wrote: '... [hydrotherapy] offered a group context in which personal improvement could serve as a model for societal reformation, focused not on its past connection of magic and faith healing, a "purification of souls" using hygiene to combat disease without resorting to drugs.'[2]

Mary Gove Nichols (1810-1884), said to have been one of the most influential women in America as a physician (hydropath), lecturer and American women's rights advocate, penned the classic book *Experience in Water Cure*.[38] A radical social reformer, she wrote of utopian communities and the diminishment of happiness by the injustice of poverty. Having experienced emotional and sexual abuse from her first husband, she lectured extensively on health reform that included promoting not just the cold-water cure but the right for every woman to have control over her own body. Yet history tells us that the trend toward self-reliance and community healing borne from taking charge of one's own healthcare, was short-lived. The 1851 *Water-Cure Journal*, the predominant hydropathy publication noted: 'The Hygienic physician soon teaches his patient to be independent of him, and so runs his own business down; while the Drug doctor leaves his patients more ignorant and more sickly than he finds him, and so works his own business up.'[39]

Taking the cure

The German hydropath, Father Kniepp (1821-1897), originator of the Kneipp water cure (he healed himself of tuberculosis) which involved applications of warm but primarily cold water, passed his knowledge onto Benedict Lust, who emigrated to America in the late 1800s. As reported earlier, after meeting Louisa Stroeble, together they founded the naturopathic medicine profession with hydrotherapy as a main modality.

Naturopathic pioneer Dr. Otis G. Carrol was pivotal in applying sine wave (an oscillating frequency in a sinusoidal pattern) to a hydrotherapy treatment (hot and cold packs) for a myriad of acute and chronic illnesses. This treatment was a favorite of Dr. John Bastyr, the university's namesake. This specific treatment became known as 'constitutional hydrotherapy', but I see most hydrotherapy treatments as bolstering the constitution. Now, in the 21st century, medical research[40, 41, 42, 43, 44, 45,46] has confirmed specific benefits from cold water for those suffering PTS, anxiety and depression, as hydrotherapy can relieve anxiety, neuro-endocrine excitement and pain, decrease cortisol, and manipulate neurotransmitters like norepinephrine.

Wim Hof, the Dutch extreme athlete and winner of many world records (barefoot on snow or diving under ice for protracted periods of time), along with the naturopathic profession, is reactivating the popularity of the cold-water cure today. As Hof says, 'It gives us energy and peace'. And as naturopathic physicians say, 'This is a cornerstone treatment of naturopathic medical history'. Simple, usually no charge and a great feeling, at least afterwards. It's no longer just the New Year's Day plunge; people are buying thousands of dollars of equipment to have their very own ice hole at home. And it doesn't need to be an icy temperature but a swimming pool that's unheated. Or maybe all you need to feel a little calmer is a cold shower. What could be better to recommend for someone with PTS/trauma?

The science

One study hypothesized that a lack of physiological stresses can in fact interfere with wellbeing as it leaves the body under-challenged and that a brief change in body temperature, such as a cold shower or cold swim, can affect the body and mind profoundly.[46] Even counteracting depression. This approach uses what is called 'hormetic stress': short, intermittent bursts of a certain stressor. 'Hormetic stress' indicates that sweet spot where stress is ideal, waking you up but not blasting you out of your seat. And not too little where nothing happens.

Immersion in cold water, even if only applied to the face, engages the bloodstream to amplify the transportation of oxygen and other nutrients to cells, specifically those in the endocrine system or neural pathways that are so important in calming the mind and emotions.[45] Basically, you want the cold to constrict blood vessels enough for norepinephrine to be triggered and then afterwards for vessels to expand, enabling the calming effect of GABA and serotonin while improving circulation and optimizing the lymph system.

Cold water constricts blood vessels and increases blood flow, triggering cellular mechanisms and signaling pathways that:

- fight inflammation and oxidative stress.
- make new mitochondria (mitochondrial biogenesis).
- repair DNA and cellular damage.
- increase detoxification and/or autophagy cellular responses that optimize metabolism and, ultimately, resilience while reducing inflammation, blood pressure, muscle soreness and chronic pain and generating sound sleep.

These are all positive benefits to someone suffering PTS/trauma to get them centered and back in charge. This makes hydrotherapy a no-brainer to build resilience, strength, and endurance, although caution must be exercised.

The diving reflex[47, 48, 49]

Cold water as a healing agent got a boost in 1870 with a publication that revived a 1786 study; it discussed the physiologic attributes of a person holding their breath underwater. It was determined that the primary role or function of the 'diving reflex' or 'diving response' is the preservation of oxygen while immersed, and resulted in:

1. The slowing down of the heart, labeled 'bradycardia'.
2. The temporary loss of breath, labeled apnea, due to increased vascular resistance.

The diving reflex is the body's innate, multi-organ physiologic response to cold water immersion that ultimately protects oxygen stores. This action redistributes blood to vital organs while limiting oxygen to muscle groups.

It would be another century before the diving reflex was understood to help PSVT (paroxysmal supraventricular tachycardia), a rapid heartbeat when electrical impulses have been disrupted. This may be helpful in a condition like Graves' disease (autoimmune hyperthyroidism) where the resting heart rate can go above 100 bpm.

We don't, however, have to activate the diving reflex to get similar results. A cold-water plunge without going fully underwater may be all we need as plunging into cold water also constricts blood vessels, shrinking them. This closes skin pores, shuts down sweat glands as muscles tense, while certain organs, such as the adrenal glands, become more active as does the parasympathetic nervous system, thereby increasing GABA, the calming neurotransmitter.

Action of cold water in more detail

Hydrotherapy works by changing temperature and pressure in the body. These changes are sensed by nerve endings in the skin and muscles and result in neural 'reflex effects' that are controlled by the brain and spinal cord. The most important of these are vasodilation and vasoconstriction that respectively relax or tense the blood vessels. This physical change causes changes in the rate of blood flow and then any metabolic functions related to blood flow. This can happen systemically (whole body) or locally (in one area of the body).

Hot and cold water act in different ways. Cold water and ice cause the body to try to conserve heat. Blood vessels constrict, decreasing the amount of blood that flows through them. Blood flow then is diverted from the extremities (less essential) to the core of the body and its organs (more essential to the body as a whole). The pores of the skin close, sweat glands shut down, muscles tense yet certain organs like the adrenal glands become more active. This can be useful for short periods of time.

Hormonally, cold water triggers the production of norepinephrine, a neurotransmitter that helps us focus and regulates energy. As noted, stimulation of our sympathetic nervous system will be countered by the relaxation of the parasympathetic nervous system by way of the frontal vagus nerve and the neurotransmitter GABA. Blood vessels dilate, boosting circulation, driving nutrients into cells and flushing out toxins.

Heat, on the other hand, increases blood flow through blood vessels, increasing blood flow to the extremities and skin as well as relaxing muscles. Many ailments will be helped by this change in blood flow, with the ability to flush the system of any toxins or inflammatory debris. Ultimately, in cold, this can have a similar effect. If you do an alternating hot and cold series, this process will act by a pumping action. The difference will be area of coverage of the body and the length of the procedure time.

The effect on mood and more

The fact that cold water causes the neurotransmitter norepinephrine to be released into the bloodstream and the locus coeruleus region of the brain[50] means hydrotherapy can improve a person's mood. This is because norepinephrine helps regulate mood, including depression and anxiety, and can improve energy and focus. It decreases neural (aka brain) inflammation,[51] countering inflammatory molecules (i.e., TNF alpha and E2 prostaglandins) that encourage anxiety and depression by inhibiting the neurotransmitter serotonin from being released from nerve cells. There are also cold shock proteins called RBM3 that, as a neuroprotective activated by cold,[52, 53] may have benefit in severe anxiety as well.

The heart rate slows quite quickly when the face meets cold water. The trigeminal facial nerves (the fifth cranial nerves) relay the information to the brain which harnesses the vagus nerve (the tenth cranial nerve), causing the slow heart rate and peripheral vasoconstriction mentioned above, and therefore calm. Temperature is paramount – the colder, the faster the reaction, with anything over 70°F (21°C) having no effect. Vasoconstriction away from the arms and legs is more gradual, allowing the most vital organs – the brain, heart, and lungs - to maintain dominance. Since the diving reflex involves our vagus nerve, if we cover our face – forehead and nose particularly – with a cold wet towel/cloth and hold our breath, we can activate this reflex, which is handy if you need almost instant relaxation.

And remember, you don't need to swim under snow and ice like Wim Hof to get benefit from cold water, although you will need to take an initial deep breath as you surmount the discomfort, depending on the temperature. As noted, the colder it is, the speedier the benefits. But again, be careful... there have been deaths by reckless people believing they were doing the right thing in terms of health.

Cold water treatments

The following are options for cold water treatment. *Always make sure to be well hydrated* when undertaking any of these.

Full immersion

Full immersion in lakes, rivers, oceans... a cold swimming pool or with buckets of ice is what works best to boost your immune system and parasympathetic nervous system and firm up your capillaries. Wim Hof recommends: 5 minutes with a water temperature of 59°C or less. If it's even colder, say 35°C, make it for 3 minutes.

If you can manage it, don't dry off. Put your clothes back on and let your body dry itself.

For a contrast plunge, sit in an infrared or other sauna for 5 to 15 minutes before going into the cold water for 3 minutes. Work up to 10 minutes or more when your body feels like that is a good idea.

Alternatives include:

1. Stand in cold water up to your ankles; splash up your legs for 20 seconds.
2. Immerse up to your thighs and splash water up to your belly button. Make sure to splash your face too. For 20 seconds.
3. Immerse up to your neck or all the way in. Twist and turn. For 20 seconds.
4. If you can manage it, don't dry off as above, but let your body dry itself.

Contrast shower

For those who shouldn't or who don't want full body immersion, try a simple hot and cold alternating shower. It can work wonders not just to boost the circulation and immune system but also to calm the mind. The procedure is:

• Go back and forth three times between hot and cold, or warm and cool if you are feeling weak.
• The idea is to alternate hot/cold...hot/cold...hot/cold, three times, taking three times as long for cold.

- Then change to 90 seconds hot, 30 seconds cold or 30 seconds hot and 10 seconds cold. Always finish with cold water.
- If you can manage it, don't dry off. Put your clothes back on and let your body dry itself.

Face dipping

For those who can't get to the needed cold water for immersion or don't have the stamina or desire, try this:

- Dip your face in a sink of cold water.
- Do this for up to 5 minutes, two to three times a week.
- The cold water sends a profusion of electrical impulses to the brain.
- This boosts alertness and energy and triggers calm.

Wet sheet treatment

For this you will need:

- a cotton sheet
- a bucket of ice water
- a wool blanket.

To explain the method, we will call the participant B, and the helper A.

- A soaks a cotton (preferably organic) sheet in a bucket of ice water and squeezes out as much water as possible before spreading it over the bed onto a thick wool blanket. (Put something waterproof under the blanket to protect the mattress.)
- B lies down on the wet sheet quickly and A wraps the sheet like a mummy tightly around B, leaving B's head out only.
- The wool blanket is then wrapped around B.

This treatment is done until the person's body warmth has dried the sheet. People often fall asleep, even for the entire night if done before bed.

Wet socks treatment

In this treatment, substitute organic cotton and heavy wool socks for sheet and blanket.

- Put the cotton socks in ice-cold water followed by the wool socks then put on first the cotton, then the wool.
- Lie back and enjoy your body heating the socks til they are dry... This allows for many of the benefits that enable relaxation and rejuvenation.

Balneotherapy

Hydrotherapy is termed 'balneotherapy' when the source is hot springs loaded with the following minerals, each with its own unique healing properties in varying amounts: sulfur, sodium bicarbonate, boron, calcium, chloride, lithium, potassium, magnesium, manganese, iron, silica, zinc, fluoride, phosphate, and nitrogen. If you can't get to a hot spring, make your own **mineral bath** as follows.

Add to your bath:

- 2-3 cups magnesium sulfate (Epsom salts) or Dead Sea salts
- 1 cup baking soda or sea salt
- Essential oils by drops singly or in combination:
  - lavender: helps alleviate anxiety, panic, depression, even nightmares
  - bergamot: relieves anxiety and fear
  - ylang ylang: helps to reduce anger and calm rage
  - clary sage: similar to ylang ylang
  - frankincense, chamomile, sandalwood and more.

Massage using water

This option includes body scrubs (see Korean spas – page xx) and waterfall. (Many spas have this.) The benefits include:

- mobilizes the lymph, hence improves detoxification.

- increases serotonin and dopamine levels and decreases cortisol levels.
- promotes release of oxytocin (through interaction with another person).

A NOTE TO THE CLINICIAN: Hydrotherapy

Treating disturbed emotion using water can easily be given as homework to regularly strengthen the ventral vagus nerve and/or cleanse cellular debris that inhibits cellular function.

A cold-water plunge is not for everyone, but it does get results we are looking for, especially in challenging cases, whether with autoimmune conditions like Graves' disease (see my story on my website and radio play on my podcast) or chronic insomnia or severe anxiety. It harnesses the ventral vagus nerve, releasing the neurotransmitter GABA. However, there are other methods that may not be as effective as a cold-water plunge but can be soothing. For instance, getting a massage with a warm rain shower cascading over you (popular at many spas now) can be greatly comforting. Sometimes just suggesting, especially to women, to take time and space with an application of water is met with a big smile. Though these treatments can be necessities, they are something we often put off yet may be all that is needed to reduce triggers and get back to center. Muscles relax, detox organs optimize, and the mind calms.

And for those who want to offer retreats, whatever your profession, the easiest way is to find a mineral-springs resort or accommodation by the ocean or a lake. You can build your workshops around the power of water. So

---

simple. Attendees will be relaxed and able to take in the information you want to share.

ASSIGNMENT #6C

1. Discuss the cold-water cure historically.
2. How does cold water generate calm?
3. What are the components of the diving reflex?

Chapter 7

Trauma-informed care

Shame. Triggers. Separation. Discrimination.
Injustice. Listening. The snowball effect.

Whatever the root and subsequent symptom picture, the core of PTS is chronic, and often debilitating, anxiety with the development of other distinctive symptoms tracked back to the initiating event(s) experienced by the individual. When PTS is experienced as a community, we, as both professionals and survivors, need to consider the possibility of resultant psychological trauma that may be the source of physiological symptoms; unlike the psychological, we can more easily quantify whether the trigger is an historical event such as the holocaust in World War II or an epidemic wiping out an entire First Nation village, or the cruel incarceration of refugees, or those repressed within or discriminated against by their neighbors because of the color of their skin, sexual orientation, being differently abled, demanding medical transparency and so on. This connection between the body's expression of physical symptoms and the mental/emotional source of behavior must be our focus.

Whatever we turn to in natural medicine or use in practice – nutrition, plant medicine, homeopathy, hydrotherapy, talk therapy, art therapy and so on – we must realize every person suffering a trauma will have a unique experience even though there will be similar changes in brain function, neurotransmitter levels, hormones (particularly the long-term levels of high or low cortisol) and many other metabolic factors we can, if we choose to, use as biomarkers to measure physiological damages and psychological presentations. Thus, whether PTS has been characterized as a normal stress response, acute stress lasting one to three months (see recommendations in Appendix 6, page 333), uncomplicated PTS, comorbid PTS (with another condition such as depression or heart disease) or complex-PTS (C-PTS), these definitions can be inadequate and mean little in terms of emotional healing. In fact, definitions may confuse treatment. This is the reason I steer away from labels and attempt to see each person with their own story and their own pathway to healing it.

Ultimately, what is needed is to create new neural circuits, ones where the cycle of hyper-vigilance and numbness step back, where triggers that have blasted their way to consciousness are, no matter how slowly, minimized over time.

You might not know exactly what the next step is but trust the direction that will ultimately lead not only to a greater freedom of expression but also to a throwing off of suffering, whatever that means individually. In this way, even if wobbly to begin with, the survivor starts to feel stronger emotionally, more empowered and can begin to embody parts of themselves that have not been revealed before.

This history might have remained hidden to the end of the survivor's days and may poke out slowly due to trust in the healing relationship that we, as clinicians, are creating, and the survivor is committed to. We may want our techniques to resolve any symptoms quickly, but remember, everyone has their own speed and time.

The goal is to assess the extent of the trauma and motivate the survivor to participate in a pathway to healing.

Suppression

The first step in treating trauma is recognizing that it is even there and causing distress, but it is also necessary to know what came before, to resolve conflicts that may have come from a more distant past – a childhood of abandonment, neglect, and abuse perhaps.

Ingrained patterns and habits as well as individual triggers may need to be probed; otherwise, psychological, and energetic disturbances can manifest in specific and non-specific physical and psychological conditions with no end in sight.

A person may continue to hold on, albeit unconsciously, to an emotional armor that is trapped in the body, resulting in contracted musculature that can interfere physiologically by decreasing oxygen perfusion and lymphatic function. This leads to toxic accumulation, and possibly health conditions and disease.

Suppression can be cultural and has roots in past injustice. One example is from Moayad Bani Younes in her master's thesis,[1] *History, Identity, Trauma and Narratives* which presents Toni Morrison's *Beloved* in relation to 'Black Lives Matter (BLM)', and concludes in part, '...both Morrison and BLM feel that narrating history, depicting traumas and remembering the past of African-Americans are needed for an identity construction. This process can emerge as a source for a true enrichment of identity and empowerment.' 'Can', however, does not mean a person is healing. Racism is a complicated affair 'and cannot be finished'. A prime example is intergenerational trauma.

Repression and suppression are thought to be different in that the former unconsciously pushes away thoughts and feelings while in the latter process, one is intentionally trying to forget. Either way, if a terrifying event (or events) has left a mark on the individual psychologically, affecting behavior, and is not interrupted, this can last to their dying breath.

It doesn't matter if the event was a rape, violence in war or peacetime, being bullied, an illness, or another shocking experience. Symptoms remain unresolved; each day some aspect of irresolution may manifest – an eating disorder, insomnia, or another manifestation of physical or mental imbalance. For example, it is common for women who have been raped to have a difficult time giving birth; men are more likely to attempt suppressing emotion, often leading to substance use disorders.

In the process of forming a relationship, the clinician may encounter several standard defenses in the survivor's response. Being aware of any resistance shines light on various factors that a difficult experience/s has intensified. The alternative, to continue suppressing post-traumatic stress, is to set the stage for ill health. Go slow.

Physician, know thy self

Note:This section is aimed at health professionals but if you are a carer for someone with PTS or ACE you may also find it relevant.

Whether a clinician or a carer, it is essential to observe ourselves, reflect on our own behavior, connect with our intuition, our heart, before connecting with someone who has experienced emotional devastation. This means being able to reflect on our own past traumatic events to access empathy for the other.

The best way to establish an honest and compassionate line of communication with a survivor means being dedicated and brave enough to know yourself, your weaknesses, especially so you know how to handle them when they are triggered.

- To be trustworthy, we need to allow a specific time for our own reflection, perhaps in early morning meditation or a walk in the park after work.
- Every day, work to let go of fears, anxieties, prejudices, judgments so our most centered self is available for those we intend to help.

- Make sure to take care to eat well, sleep well, move, have fun, be creative, get into nature.
- Surround yourself with inspiration, whatever that means to you, whether music or a bird warbling on a nearby branch. Take time, pause, inhale, exhale... center.... Then when you are needed to be a witness to another you aren't in a reactive mode from something – person or event – that needs to stay outside the room.
- This way we keep the person in the room front and center as we have taken care of our own needs and wants.

Listen to the story

Don't assume anything. The beauty of taking a case homeopathically, but without necessarily prescribing a homeopathic medicine, is that it allows questions to be asked in a way that is open and non-judgmental. You need to suss out what the survivor's support system is or the dysfunction they have been living with; this can come out slowly or quickly.

Today most people know a lot about why they are the way they are, including the family dynamic. They might simply need instruction on how to help their physiological makeup, or encouragement to express their deepest wounds in a place of trust and safety, Remember, this can take time.

From a gentle gesture or comforting remark to the power of a homeopathic medicine, to introducing food that nourishes, to suggesting an activity to promote empowerment, we all have our own way of helping survivors transform their lives to one of calmness and joy. Yet the route prescribed by practitioners of natural medicine in the telling of the story is often ignored. Using creativity to get the survivor to access their imagination, whether first by guided visualization and/or the expressive arts, the inner world can engage authenticity that may have been shut out due to societal constraints or expectations. It doesn't matter what class we were born into, or race, or height or weight we have become, or what language is spoken, now those under our care can use their imagination – even if at first just to brush into – to dig themselves out, making their way back to an empowered state of mind. And, as it turns out, it doesn't have to be difficult, as this book demonstrates.

Gently tracking the story of an adult with trauma is essential no matter what your treatment plan – biochemical balance, simple listening or more. If the survivor is a child:

- Let them be creative with crayons or stuffed animals.
- Being silly with children can work wonders.
- What they need from you, again at any age, is a safe space where they feel you are interested in them, are there for them, and will understand they may have certain triggers and won't freak out if their emotions become strong. They need to know you will advocate for them.

Don't judge or label

It is critical not to box your patient in by placing them in a preordained category. This is not always easy, especially when a person's behavior is criminal or borders on criminal, but if the doctor-patient relationship is going to remain sacrosanct you must try. This doesn't mean you don't report them to the author-ities; it means looking past the behavior and/or offense to see them deeper than their transgression(s).

One of the problems of reducing a person's health dynamic to a label is that, by classifying disease, creating subparts, we obscure our most important task and that is to seek a truth that is greater than the sum of the parts, incorporating that trusted holistic perspective. Therefore, it is imperative we tread lightly in terms of classification, until we feel we really 'see' the person in their true light, not in objective parts or with labels being superimposed.

This is not to say a diagnosis doesn't help; it can lead to specific labs and nutrients, but until the depth and possibly hidden reactions of the person's experience are probed in totality we are at a disadvantage. Therefore:

- No projections, no cookie-cutter treatment plan.
- The surest way to treat PTS/trauma successfully is to begin with the assumption that each person is unique.
- Being present to hear their story in all its dimensions may be the most important thing you can do. This way we don't assume anything.

Curiosity

It goes without saying that empathy must be the initiating connection but let yourself be curious: what makes this person tick? Dealing with people who are mentally imbalanced or on edge is akin to acting like a priest or spiritual advisor. You need to keep looking deeper into the why; demonstrate your curiosity:

- If they are crying, let them. Offer a tissue or handkerchief.
- Try not to pull them out of it as much as stay with them.
- Let them know emotion flowing is healing.
- If they are angry, don't react or try not to, unless of course there is potential harm.
- Ask them to follow your lead, to breathe, be still while you listen.
- Offer them a way to deal with the anger when it feels right.
- Was their childhood disrupted by abuse?
- Have they had one too many heartaches?
- Have they been playing too many video games?
- All the while, listen to their words, watching their face, posture, tone of voice.
- How do they express themselves?
- Are they shy? Or bold?

- Check the questions listed in Appendix 6.
- What could be their authentic route to expressing themselves?
- Are they deficient in zinc or other nutrients?
- Are they full of lead, arsenic, aluminum, or another neurotoxin that might be affecting their behavior?

Triggers

Triggers are anything that can re-stimulate terror as the person is reminded of the event(s). Or a trigger can bring out **delayed PTSD**, a suppressed or repressed response to a traumatic event that at the time evoked little reaction. In either case, a feeling of doom or dread can conspire with memory and bring out irrational behavior – anger or some type of upset – that has been generated.

Again, a trigger can be anything at all:

- Anything a person associates with the terror of the event(s). They may not know what the trigger might be until it happens as this reaction may be elicited by an impulse out of their range of awareness.
- Keep in mind there may be past events that have piled up on top of each other with their own lasting imprint, long before seeking treatment.
- The context and meaning of a specific event to the survivor will be influenced by all their senses, including smells, tastes, sounds, and images, as the memory of the tragedy refuses to abate.
- When this happens, even a very slight reminder of the traumatic event can trigger an automatic response, throwing the sympathetic nervous system into action: fight or flight or, as per the polyvagal theory (see page 83), the dorsal vagus; remember, the parasympathetic ventral pathway is what

we aim to access, increasing GABA, the calming chemical messenger in the brain.

- We can do this through various measurable means—breath work, food, supplements, botanicals, homeopathy, internal messaging (visualization, tracking) as will be discussed fully.
- Ehlers et al liken a traumatic memory to 'a cupboard in which many things have been thrown in quickly and in a disorganized fashion, so it is impossible to fully close the door and things fall out at unpredictable times.'[2]

The snowball effect

The clinician should be aware of the 'snowball effect', (a non-medical term). Once safety, security, and even survival feel under threat, whether suddenly or more slowly, the brain reacts by initiating changes in almost every system in the body. This cascading series of responses can be especially cruel. For example, the original fear or terror can cause lack of sleep, perhaps nightmares. Lack of sleep can bring on further anxiety or depression. Depression can bring on an eating disorder. Addiction may result from the desire to be free of psychic pain. The cycle continues – a continuous loop that won't shut off until a determined and motivated effort is made, an effort that will demand focused and loving support.

Active listening is essential: not being able to share anxiety or other psychic pain deepens the damage, heightening the feeling of shame and powerlessness. This then harnesses ongoing anguish, suicidal feelings, or actual suicide unless addressed.

Whether this 'stuckness' is tied to a historical past, a present condition or an already compromised state of health, we must consider everything as we attempt realignment in a holistic model – many parts of an actionable whole gaining strength and recovery to serve what many might call the soul's liberation from imprisonment.

To sum up, acquiring competent skill sets as a communicator begins with a willingness to examine, and reflect on, your own shortcomings so that you can show compassion for yourself and others who have survived excruciating experiences and help them move to a better place. To listen to the story without judgment gives us hope of finding the source of pain that can be freed.

Nonviolent Communication: A Language of Compassion by Marshall Rosenberg is an extraordinary book.[3] The author speaks about many things that block healing, including the blame game, and how: 'Violence comes from the belief that other people cause our pain and therefore deserve punishment.'

The community factor

Healing trauma also assumes a component of community (family, friends, coworkers, neighbors, and society at large), that social support is an essential ingredient to generate lasting healing. The physiological, the emotional, the bigger group we are part of... all are important to address with PTS/trauma. Being oppressed/targeted for skin color, gender, sexuality, religion and so on adds another layer that we must consider.

Sensitivity of the clinician

Note: Again, this section is aimed more at health professionals, and carers, than at survivors.

As caretakers of trauma survivors, we must be sensitive to the most tender of feelings, having taken the time to understand the sources and depth of lingering psychological trauma. If you are a survivor, you know what I am talking about. It can be very difficult to communicate our deepest and most sacred thoughts and feelings. Be aware that medical personnel may not be adequately trained in dealing with specific groups of people who have experienced trauma.

A few years ago, when murders of trans people first started breaking my heart, I asked a friend, a nurse, for a few words about transitioning and trauma. He wrote:

> *Most of us have considered suicide; a significant minority have attempted it; unknown (and uncounted) numbers are successful. High rates of violence, discrimination, abuse. Healthcare itself can be another location of trauma: discrimination, outright refusal of service, utter lack of understanding of trans beliefs, experiences, or concerns. Unwillingness to adapt healthcare behavior or strategies to a very different population. These experiences lead to decreased use of healthcare services, an increased rate of dropout from healthcare, poorer health outcomes, higher mortality, and more risky behavior (i.e., smoking, street drugs, unsafe living circumstances, poverty, etc.). Lack of access to safe work also means, in the US especially, inability to afford health care anyway.*
>
> *Also, healthcare workers generally have no understanding of what gender dysphoria — especially body dysphoria — actually consists of, both experientially for individuals or psychologically as a defining characteristic and experience. This in itself presents a huge barrier to accessing treatment in that for many trans people, there is trauma simply in naming body parts that are foreign to their own experience of gender, trauma in exposing these "impossible" body parts, trauma in being misgendered by healthcare professionals, and extreme trauma in not being believed or understood in a context of such bodily — AND existential — vulnerability already.*
>
> *Utter erasure on all levels of human meaning is a common and endlessly repeated experience for many trans people: we are always at risk of real erasure yet again (yet again).*

What might seem like a minor setback for a cis person – an unfortunate but easily dismissed encounter with a jerk – can be extremely destabilizing for a trans person and threatens erasure (one's literal existential demise). Very much traumatizing.[4]

Keys to treatment

Trust

My experience of treating PTS showed me repeatedly that, until a person can trust and tell their story, nothing else will resolve.

When you work with trauma survivors you embark on a sacred journey. A safe environment where they can share themselves without judgment sets the stage for the process of self-discovery and calming. Being caring will take you much further along the road of trust than wearing a white coat. Respect and kindness must be at the top of your intent.

Dignity

In his book, *Adults in the Room*, Yanis Varoufakis, a former Greek finance minister, recounts the story of a performance art piece by his partner, Danae Stratou, created during the midst of a national economic crisis. The art installation consisted of 100 black metal boxes (akin to a plane's black box), each of which required filling with a piece of paper that contained, in writing, a single-worded answer to the following question: 'What is the one thing a healthy person cannot do without other than food and shelter and love? What are you most afraid of, or what is the one thing you want to preserve?'[5]

The word was not one that was expected, like 'jobs', or 'security'. The word was **'dignity'**.

A sexual abuse survivor or anyone with PTS could very well have supplied the same answer and, in doing so, revealed what had been so violently taken away. Because if helplessness lies at the center of a person with PTS, then dignity, the feeling of being of worth, is what the mentally shifted person needs to rediscover: that they are respected and honored. We are seen, we are listened to, we are believed as we garner stability and love of ourselves, our being, of a life that was lost to the traumatic event.

And what more authentic and dignified way to recover, to regain our balance, than to connect with the muse, to use our own inherent imagination, to trust it, be motivated by it, to dip into creativity and create, using the expressive arts as a way home, to gain a sense of control and magic from the narrative that has exploded with the defining event or events that led to a diagnosis of PTS?

Resilience

While a difficult quality to define, it is our job in treatment to cultivate and nurture the patient's resilience in response to the event. Our goal is to facilitate a pathway for the person's recovery from trauma that, eventually, will create empowerment. This is especially important when a person has previously felt alienated in an unfriendly world; otherwise, the new trauma can simply amplify the feeling of isolation. It may sound counterintuitive, but the time and difficulty of trauma treatment and recovery do not necessarily reflect the intensity of the event. For instance, in terms of sexual abuse, someone who has experienced sex trafficking and all its accompanying horrors for a period may be able to recover more fully than someone who has been raped once.

Whether it be genetics, parental care, birth order, or astrological sign, each person has their own sensibility in recovery that lends itself or not to activating resilience and building back strength.

The response to a tragic event or an accumulation of trauma – the degree of emotional pain and possible physical pain, and the length of time to recover – is dependent on many aspects but no more so than on emotional support before and after the event. Therefore, community is so important and can alone make or break the healing process. If an individual doesn't feel they have people they can trust to reach out to to generate feelings of safety, they may continue to experience distress.

Interaction

As we encourage self-love and acceptance, helping to undo the damage of shame that may have led to isolation – turning away from a social support network, a prime factor in relapse – we feed the body (reduce inflammation), balance the mind (quiet the amygdala and restore the adrenals), finally exposing the underlying story (through imagination and the expressive arts) to re-ignite *la joie de vivre*, the passion for living an empowered life. This is the perfect prescription for a person with an addiction. Be aware that every person's story may have similar threads but, truly, each patient, each client, each person is unique with a unique story to be probed and/or narrated.

When interacting with a survivor, take the following into account, first and foremost:

- If sitting in an office proves too difficult, take them for a walk in the park or sit under a tree. Nature with compassion is the ultimate healer.
- Simply remind them to slow down:
  - Sit in silence, do nothing, listen to the birds or soothing music.
  - Remind them that these are imperative for their journey to wholeness and peace.

○ For some people who have guarded emotions, you might get them more involved in the process if you can put it in more scientific terms: to engage the parasympathetic nervous system with its wandering ventral vagus nerve and GABA, its prime neurotransmitter.

Although a terrifying event can wipe away all sense of empowerment, a person in optimal health has a better chance of a quicker recovery. Be careful, however; the most solid-seeming person can be devastated inside. It is imperative to remember that the person sitting in front of you is vulnerable. They need your respect, not pity, as you help them throw off the feeling of helplessness.

A NOTE TO THE CLINICIAN

You may be the first person to interact with the survivor. If you do nothing else, simply listen, and if you are met with silence, listen to their breathing, wait, offer tea or warm water to sip. Have it in the back of your mind to look beyond individual symptoms and diseases to a possible originating event. The symptoms that are causing the most emotional pain are not always obvious. Assume nothing.

At the same time, make sure you know the community of helpers – lay and professional – who are working in trauma recovery locally to you. Make their information, including brochures, visible and freely available in your waiting room.

For people suffering PTS/trauma, it is too easy for anxiety to create inner turmoil which can manifest outwardly as well. Being in control, feeling centered, can seem like a foreign concept to someone with chronic anxiety, but it is doable, in time and with determination. The

---

techniques of contemplation, spot-finding, different breathwork, meditation, sound-healing, and others discussed later will help the needed 'center' access solutions. They will calm the limbic system and may even change a perception of the world.

The first visit to you may be the first time they have ever shared their deepest and possibly most shameful thoughts. From where we stand, these techniques are essential in everyday practice. Yet, often, when suffering PTS and any of its comorbidities, this type of treatment may be insufficient to flush out and transform emotional pain. Therefore, whether you are working with an individual or a group, you must let go of all judgments and allow each person the dignity and respect any person deserves. I'll never forget having to swallow my resistance and judgment when I started treating male sex offenders. I had to see them, their heart and soul, not their crime, to help them heal. I believe, to a man, they had been abused themselves.

The goal is to decrease the reactivity of feelings and we can transform rage, confusion, shame, guilt, and any other feeling that gets in our way, with this two-pronged approach: balance the biochemistry naturally (what naturopathic physicians excel at) and tell or revise the story with added knowledge that neither we nor our patients may have considered or accessed before.

ASSIGNMENT #7

1. What is most important for a clinician to do in treating PTS/trauma?
2. Give three examples of triggers.
3. What is central to both a physiological and psychological presentation?
4. Give three examples of a positive interaction.

Part Three

Traversing the inner world

'Aah,' she sighed as light fell, holding onto the last book. 'Perhaps I'll meet Alice or the Little Prince. They have certainly been down this path.' She smiled and exhaled; she was in good company.

Chapter 8

A way in

*Breathe in and out. Nowhere to go,
nothing to do. The moment opens
and we are in it.*

Providing an entrance

Our inner universe may not be easy to access when we are in an aggravated state of mind... angry, fearful, depleted, desperate. But this is what we will need to do, somehow. Perhaps using sound to pull us forward, perhaps a towel that can be squeezed, or an inhale of lavender, or a hand held, a long hug. Soon, perhaps over time, we gently nod, perhaps blowing out that first bubble, committed to rising up... wonder returns, curiosity too, of what is, what could be, our center grounding, even miniscule, the earth holding us in an embrace that allows the exhale to elongate.

Post-traumatic stress means the body-mind is holding an immense level of fear from the original or ongoing events that have threatened our safety and created pandemonium in our brain. This disturbance lingers in our body and, often, worst of all, provokes our critical, inner judge, leaving us hampered by a continuous loop of thoughts and feelings that won't go away, at least easily. Even having helped ourselves physiologically (i.e., balancing cortisol, improving gut function), something is still not quite right. We may still feel unable to move forward, to recapture that old feeling of curiosity, awestruck by life's mysteries.

The primary effect of a traumatic experience is involuntary from primitive reflexes, the innocent emotions and accompanying thoughts. For the secondary effect we can choose to construct, using free will, a healing path based on motivation and attitude to create our way through our inner world that has been fraught with these foreboding emotions and debilitating thoughts.

To begin the journey of healing mind and body, the survivor requires access to the 'stillpoint', the centered part of the self that feels safe, calm, confident, and authentic enough to access the emotions frozen for so long and, having accessed them, use their imaginative powers to materialize some measure of release. This release can extend from a momentous exhalation of relief to a piece of expressive art in the form of writing, art, music, dance, or theatre, soon to be covered in the, perhaps, most unique section of my book (Part Four, page 225).

In treating someone with PTS we can turn to the five senses – sound, taste, sight, smell, and touch – to probe and penetrate the memory of the traumatic event. We absolutely need to take the crucial past events into account when healing PTS and/or its comorbidities. As the polyvagal theory (page 83) goes, we need to activate the ventral vagus nerve, the healthy pathway of the parasympathetic system, as opposed to staying stuck circling the drain of the sympathetic nervous system with its agitated fight or flight, or the dorsal vagal system of feeling numb, frozen emotion.[1] Whether a therapist or a friend is involved, the key to transforming trauma is to feel safe, when engaged with one another. The polyvagal theory confirms this by extending the understanding of both the benefit of true empathy from the health professional and the heightened need for safety that Stephen Porges (see page 83) terms the 'social engagement system'. The support of the community can, as well, make a huge difference to the outcome, as I have said many times.

Chapter 8

Once this is ensured, while balancing the biochemistry naturally, there are so many ways to bring the internal audio and visual into play to traverse the inner landscape to perceive and/or harness the energy of the event, engage the story so trauma no longer dictates every waking moment. I will only speak about the concepts and treatments I have personally experienced, that have worked in my practice and in my life. You may have guessed by now that my preference is for non-linear healing that comes through the right brain, exposing the body-mind connection. Talking can be extremely helpful but I believe 'the body never lies', and this is at the core of a non-linear approach. This is a place to hear and feel the reaction/response without the limitations of cognitive-induced thinking, that unified whole of all our senses, to a shocking event. This to me is a necessity to realize full trauma recovery.

If, after dialing down from being chronically wired with excess cortisol and adrenaline is achieved (through food etc.), how do we engage our inner world if emotions continue to jump up and bite us? How do we consciously leave helplessness behind by reshaping an event in our mind and body that has, over short or long periods of time, threatened our happiness and ability to enjoy life? How do we do this when the person we are helping feels miserable and barely has the strength to get up in the morning?

To address and understand the narrative creeping out from the shadow of memory, usually over time, is to deal with all the negative debris that became caught in a rat-wheel kind of spin. We don't swallow a pill... we must investigate symptoms, thoughts, feelings, and behavior.

Underlying our efforts is the intention to create a continual safe and interesting context where the pre-frontal cortex (the part of the brain central to cognitive control functions) can increasingly come online to regulate the amygdala, breaking the vicious cycle of primitive brain responses, and reducing the traumatic response. To achieve inner peace we must be ready to acknowledge something must be changed and are ready to do the work necessary to move through the moment or the energy when trauma slammed on the brakes of our happiness, our peace of mind gone, vaporized. We can begin to examine that hungry ghost that continues to linger, that has attempted to sabotage our efforts to become balanced, to regain a feeling of comfort, that feeling of being in control, and ultimately that *joie de vivre* we most likely felt as children. And all this requires the achievement of a 'still point'!

Find the still point

Stillness is the first step to creating a strong center. Letting senses fall away allows us to pause, to reflect, conjuring an initial stability that induces a positive environment for exploring, with the aim of deep psychological healing. This is the key to being in control enough to transform the defining event of PTS and is essential to being at one with oneself, if only later.

Mindfulness is a commonly accepted method to gather focus and observe thoughts. In a sense it is the opposite of dissociation, the protective reactivity that can happen in trauma. Mindfulness-based psychotherapist, Michael Shiffman PhD, says it best, describing it as 'the cultivation of moment-to-moment nonjudgmental awareness... (it) combines cognitive stability with emotional regulation to produce a stable awareness of experience and as such... reduces reactivity and increases openness.'[2]

Shiffman then goes on to succinctly explain the opposing state of mind: 'Dissociation is a protective response taking the form of disconnection, isolation and separation.' Both mindfulness and dissociation are 'relevant strategies for managing suffering; dissociation is a survival strategy arising from the context of threat, and mindfulness is a conscious strategy to eliminate the suffering of daily life.'[2]

To start accessing your still point, all you need to do is close your eyes. By creating a focus, you can draw into where you are as well as the lingering experience so you can transform it. But accessing your still point isn't nearly as easy as the word sounds. Daily, we have many distractions, and our mind easily becomes what is commonly referred to as 'monkey mind', swinging from one distraction to the next, filling our thoughts up while neglecting what we need to focus on.

Whether this is from being low in dopamine or low in serotonin doesn't matter, the fact remains we must be able to access our still point to heal, and the surefire, drugless way to do this is through breathwork during meditation. The reality is that we have had techniques for centuries to be able to do this, the chief among which is breathwork, the building block of meditation.

Breathwork

The main source for finding your still point is breathwork. Neuroscientist Candace Pert, who discovered the opiate receptor in the brain, wrote: 'Simply bringing awareness to the process of breathing initiates the release of peptide molecules from the hind brain to regulate breathing while unifying all systems.'[3]

The breath is physiologically dependent on feedback signals from the lungs as well as oxygen and carbon dioxide in the blood. Swami Rama, a spiritual adept who explored higher states of consciousness in India and Tibet, took this a step farther in *Science of Breath*, a book published by two medical doctors in 1972, when he observed: 'controlling the breath is a prerequisite to controlling the mind and body.'[4] The authors, Rudolph Ballentine MD and Alan Hymes MD, lauded the swami's acknowledgment that the breath is the link between body and mind, before adding this humorous description: 'People laughed at the image of pretzel-legged yogis focusing on the tip of their noses until Swami Rama walked into a laboratory and showed scientists what a yogi with control over his respiration can do. Before astonished researchers, he demonstrated perfect control over his heart rate and brain waves, control physiologists hadn't believed humans could possibly achieve.'

Again according to Stephen Porges, as we have discussed,[1] the dorsal vagus nerve can cause you to freeze, lowering the concentration of oxygen and the level of oxygen perfusion through organs, like the thyroid and adrenals, which is particularly detrimental to anyone experiencing stress. Deep or proper breathing, which can be learned, can be used to negate the 'fight or flight' response that follows a traumatic event and activates all systems to engage your foe by maximizing all the energy, oxygen, and nutrients available on the spot.

The optimal function of all our organs is, of course, always important, but these go out of balance quickly when they encounter stress and create symptoms that can sometimes take a long time to get back in sync. Whereas the ventral vagus nerve can act quickly, once engaged in favor of recovery. Knowing all this, we can simply put the vagus nerve to work for us in stressful situations, including long-term suffering of PTS, and need not be stuck in a vicious cycle where the prefrontal cortex has shrunk, and primitive circuits predominate. We can change this, with no need for sophisticated equipment. We simply observe our breath, our breathing. Through pause or expansion at the intersection of the inhale and exhale we can learn to influence not only the action of the lungs but even those metabolic processes, such as the secretion of digestive organs, reproductive organs and more. We don't have to worry about 'losing our breath' since there is an involuntary reflex activity that acts as a safeguard. The breath is the only physiological function that is both involuntary and voluntary for all of us.

Ultimately, by changing our pattern of breathing, we can improve our ability to evoke the relaxation response, the feeling of peace, and through this practice, which every person can do, initiate an impact on behavior. We need good breathwork for maintaining life but by manipulating its duration, and depth, we can use it to influence behavior.

Steps for finding your still point

1. Find a safe and quiet environment.
2. Practice breathwork with the following meditation techniques:
   a. Simple contemplation
   b. Beginning rhythm
   c. Diaphragmatic breathing
   d. Rhythmic breathing.
3. Sit quietly or move or dance in slow motion.
4. Go further into a system of movement such as t'ai chi or qi gong.

The aim of learning a healing art, not necessarily to become an expert, is to use the avenues of breathwork and meditation to take PTS survivors inside themselves, thereby enabling them to express those thoughts and feelings that have become roadblocks to optimal health and freedom. Then the five senses can be investigated, visualizing and tracking emotion back, uncovering the story and its stepping stones to healing the pieces in the puzzle.

Accessing a still point is the entry point to expand your access to your inner world and allow your creativity to flow in various artistic mediums. Making the decision to heal will involve reaching sufficient calmness to create intentions and set goals with a trustworthy guide; accessing the neural circuitry in the pre-frontal cortex (PFC) will reduce worry and anxiety. In this regard, you'll need to:

- Set a regular time and place for a continual, safe, and creative context for the session. Consider doing it first thing in the morning, especially if you have very little free time or you travel often, as that way you will make sure to include it in your day.
- Have a spot or area that you can go to every day, which will act as an anchor to a wandering mind, where you can sit or move undisturbed.
- Use a cushion or a chair; barefoot is preferable.
- Outdoors can be beneficial even if only weekly.
- Place objects that are dear to you close by to feel grounded, a means of reminding yourself this is your place for going within – anything at all that holds meaning: a stone, rock, leaf, a beautiful piece of fabric, or a photo of an ancestor or someone you love or have been inspired by.
- Do all this, when in treatment, with someone who can be trusted, so you can feel safe and sufficiently free to tell your story.
- Finding a friend or a group to work with may be very helpful.

Common meditation techniques

The meditation techniques outlined in this section can be used with patients in the office or clinic, individually or in a group setting (workshop or retreat), given as homework or used as an introduction to the meditative disciplines of yoga, t'ai chi, and so on. Or use them in the context of Physician Heal Thyself and learn more about your own obstacles and blocks. Whatever the modality, whatever the technique, the goal is the same – breaking through helplessness and growing stronger from within. Our internal voice with its wily judge can be accessed and re-taught.

To be clear, restlessness, nervousness is not to be shunned but mined for the messages it offers, but not to the point of being overwhelming. Again, it's all about balance. Once we pause and engage the breath, it becomes a friend that we feel safe and secure with, a place we can pivot to when needed.

Simple contemplation

- If meditation is new to you, start simply with a practice of contemplation.
- Sit somewhere quietly (perhaps in nature but anywhere you won't be interrupted) and let your quiet mind lead the way.
- If you're having trouble blocking out noise (in general or your own thoughts), or if it isn't quite enough:
  - imagine you are sitting on top of a mountain observing a lake and all its ripples or waves below, or
  - imagine being at the seaside with waves tickling your toes, or
  - listen for a simple jiggle of leaves on a tree.
- Just let yourself be taken, connecting to something in nature, or focus on the light.
- Of course, if you have religious deities you connect with, use your personal approach.

Beginning rhythm

One of the first things we can teach our patients (or ourselves) is to feel the pulse at the wrist or neck. Sometimes you'll have someone go: 'Yuck, that feels weird', but most people have already learned to trust you and love the feeling of tuning into their body's rhythm:
- Simply take your/have them take their own pulse – you can help them find it if necessary.
- Then count with them… 1, 2, 3 and so on…

- Once they feel it, ask them to breathe into this pulse… 1, 2, 3, 4 inhale, then 1, 2, 3, 4 exhale…
- Let them feel comfortable before activating the ventral vagus nerve (the PNS initial attempt for calm), inhale for four – 1, 2, 3, 4 – and exhale for eight – 1, 2, 3, 4, 5, 6, 7, 8.
- There are other patterns, but this is a good place to start.

Diaphragmatic breathing

By learning to use the diaphragm to breathe deeply and evenly, we may straightforwardly elicit the relaxation response. The two main synchronistic mechanisms that move air into the lungs and expand are through inhalation whereby the diaphragm moves downward while the ribs expand outward. This ongoing action pulls air into the lungs from the upper airways to the trachea and bronchial tree and then into the alveoli – the tiny air sacs where respiratory gases are exchanged into and out of pulmonary capillaries. This action:

- takes oxygen into the bloodstream and escorts carbon dioxide out.
- reduces any ventilation-perfusion irregularities.

To check out and/or practice what this two-part process feels like:
- Start by lying on your back.
- Place one palm on the center of your chest, the other on the lower border of your rib cage, at the top of the abdomen.
- Notice that as you inhale, your rib cage expands, and your abdomen rises.
- Upon exhalation, the opposite should happen.
- You should see little movement in your upper chest, which would otherwise indicate shallow breathing.
- While the goal is to use diaphragmatic breathing unconsciously, initially you must learn it consciously.

- It is like learning anything, such as playing an instrument or a child taking their first steps.

If you practice deep breathing until it becomes automatic:
- your oxygen perfusion-ventilation quotient will increase.
- your entire circulatory function will improve.
- the load on your heart will decrease.
- suction pressure created in the thoracic cavity by increasing its capacity will augment (a good thing for optimal lung function).
- the function of the venous return of blood to the heart will improve and this can help peripheral veins as well.

Rhythmic breathing

Once you are breathing from your diaphragm, apply it to the '1, 2, 3, 4 inhale, 1, 2, 3, 4, 5, 6, 7, 8 exhale' technique you learned in Beginning rhythm (page 169) and try engaging in rhythmic breathing.
- Your pulse will slow.
- Your blood pressure will fall to a safe level.
- Your oxygen concentrations will be optimal.
- Your still point (page xx) through the vagus nerve and parasympathetic nervous system will achieve a sense of calm.
- Your breath will become an entry point into a place of serenity, the achievement of a deeper consciousness of the inner world, and a possible creative reservoir on which your upcoming expressive art project can draw.

Recalling the ventral vagus nerve

The breath is intimately connected with the autonomic nervous system (ANS). The ANS is divided into the sympathetic and parasympathetic systems, as described in Chapter 4. Simply by observing your out-breath and lengthening it we engage the parasympathetic system, via the ventral vagus nerve, which then helps relieve anxiety and depression.

You can consciously make this happen (as well as increasing oxytocin and hormonal balance in most cases) with easily accessible activities such as:

- Singing (see the Expressive arts, page 243)
- Chanting
- Orgasm
- Loving touch
- Immersion in cold water or splashed on cheeks (see Hydrotherapy, page 128)
- Laughing
- Prayer
- Exercise
- Fasting
- Gargling
- Sleeping
- Other activities that indirectly stimulate your vagus nerve.

Yoga

Breathing, or *'prana'*, the Sanskrit word for universal energy, is the vital energy, and active force, underlying any physical organism. This concept has been handed down through various ancient traditions, in India and Tibet, as well as China, Japan and Egypt. It was Patanjali, an Indian sage, who, expounding on the science of yoga, circa 200 BCE, first observed that the control of *prana* is the regulation of inhalation and exhalation.

Meditation in yoga, beginning with breathwork or *prana*, is practiced with several other components, namely the chakras, mantras, bandhas and mudras described next.

Chapter 8

Chakras

- Translated from the Sanskrit for 'wheel', chakras are subtle energy centers that are positioned down the body.
- Each one can be seen as a spinning wheel of light energy. (See below)

Mantras

Derived from two Sanskrit roots, the word 'mantra' means 'mind' from *manas* and 'tool' from *tra*. It can be a sound, a word, or a phrase that helps to focus the mind through its tone or rhythm. When repeated it has the ability to influence consciousness.[5]

There are thousands of mantras that are used for various reasons, but, for our purposes as learners, we will use and interpret mantras as the repetition of the open vowels cited below, each of which is assigned a 'chakra' – a nexus of nerves up the spine, during meditation. I usually start to hum 'Oo' while mentally focusing on the first chakra, the point on the perineum between the vagina and anus, and then proceed as follows:

Oo – perineum
Oh – three fingers' below the navel
Aaah – solar plexus
Ahhh – heart
Eeee – throat
Ning – third eye (from Hinduism), a mystic point in the middle of the forehead said to connect with the pineal gland
Om – top of head.

We can use these sounds to usher us directly to our still point, to deepen it, and ground our meditation. We can then embrace it to expand our experience, and increase our sense of relaxation, helping us become more centered and attuned to the peaceful vibrations that run through a universe that is often difficult to get to in our distracted and hurried life. (A mantra can help induce sleep too.)

Mudras and bandhas

Two other important yoga-related concepts are mudras and bandhas. Mudras are the various seals mentioned in yoga texts. One common one is the *Jnana Mudra*, wherein the thumb and first finger form an O, while you rest your hands on your knees seated in a lotus or similar position.

Bandas represent energetic locks in yoga, a physical action that can be consciously released to direct and regulate the flow of *prana* (life force energy) to various areas of the body. For example, *jalandhara bandha* (the chin lock), or *uddiyana bandha* (the abdominal lock), or *mula bandha* (the anal lock). It is best to ask a yoga teacher how to do this properly (see Resources, page 349).

Humming bee breath (Bhramari)[6]

This is a simple technique, an easy and effortless prep for meditation. It quiets the mind quickly and is said to relieve sinus blockages, tinnitus and headaches. Simply follow these steps:
- In a meditation position, breathe normally while blocking your ears gently with your index fingers on the cartilage.
- Breathe out and hum.
- Repeat a few times.
- Feel the peace.

(This pose also dovetails with 'Humming', a song from our children's musical, *The Calling Hour*. Grace, the protagonist, is teaching the other children, or should I say chanimals, to hum to calm down; no fingers in ears, but perhaps we can add that the next time it is performed.)

174

The crocodile or makarasana pose

If diaphragmatic breathing proves elusive, try the crocodile or makarasana pose:
- Lying on your belly, position your legs comfortably apart, toes pointed out.
- Fold your arms under your head and rest your hands on your upper arms.
- Don't let your chest touch the floor as you rest your head on your arms.
- When you inhale you should feel your abdomen pressing against the floor.
- The exhale allows your abdominal muscles to relax.
- By exclusion you can observe your diaphragm.

A sample meditation

Understanding your breath and utilizing the bandhas and mudras will deepen your meditation practice. Here's a taste of how I do it.
- Start with the breath.
- Picture a beautiful spot in nature, or simply a bright light.
- Let your body breathe by itself, allowing the focus of the present moment to deepen.
- Imagine light coming through the top of your head and rich earth energy coming up through the bottom of your spinal cord.
- These energies meet in your heart space.
- Adding sounds as a centering tool, like a mantra or a few minutes of yoga or movement before you begin can allow you to relax into it until you are simply 'breath breathing itself'. This is a beautiful place to start catching and balancing restless energy that can distract from meditation or an impending visualization or tracking.

- Hum 'oo, oh, aaah, ahh, eee, ning, om...' with a hand following the vowels, touching the intended target – each chakra (see page 173).
- Listening to recorded or live music or chanting can also be useful in creating harmony within, a deeper center to reflect from.

Coming back to our still point is just that: a place to come back to, over and over again, whether for comfort and relaxation, or to move forward into the inner journey. As the creative work opens up our memories and experiences we come back to the breath and still point to fill ourselves up, to nourish agitation or 'uncomfortableness' as we dig deeper, casting a wide net to tell our story.

More disciplines

Consider these additional sources to reset your brain with slow and purposeful movement thereby reducing anxiety and physical pain.

- T'ai Chi: This ancient Taoist discipline involves a continuous series of controlled, usually slow movements designed to improve physical and mental wellbeing.
- Qi Gong: Another ancient Eastern practice that focuses on Qi (same Chi as in T'ai Chi), the life energy that flows through the body's energy pathways. Like T'ai Chi, it combines movement, breathing and meditation.
- Slow motion: If you can't do any of these, simply move your body slowly as follows:
  - First one arm and then the next, bring the legs into it.
  - Go as slowly as you possibly can.
  - Feel your breath moving with these very slow movements.

Our history, our healing

In whatever way, our inner world slowly becomes under our control as we learn to elucidate our story/stories with compassion and authenticity in the light of our muse. Breathwork, imagination, rhythm, and movement are stepping-stones to tell and share your factual story or to revising the energy of the experience. Either way, we free ourselves, unraveling trauma; we heal, creating true happiness, affecting neurological circuits like almost nothing else. No side effects, no after taste.

In approaching healing, some individuals want to explore the original event, while others prefer to take the energy of the trauma and create something new in the hope of experiencing that magical quality of empowerment once or while the biochemistry is being stabilized. That is not to say that telling the story of the event is not important, but it can be too traumatic. We do not need to return to the scene of the crime. Rather we can create something new. We transform panic attacks, anxiety, or other stuck emotions of PTS by working to move the energy, to 'change the channel' of our own DVD, through new imagery.

The bottom line is we can re-frame, re-create the event that will diminish powerlessness and increase our sense of being in control, employing our own creativity to activate our own recovery.

A NOTE TO THE CLINICIAN

My interest in cultivating focused attention came in the form of meditation as a teenager when I became interested in the concept of the mind and body as one, beginning to sense the fallacy of the West's split version, a disconnect that has driven Western medicine's understanding of

---

health and healing. (Remember the days when the doctor's diagnosis was 'It's all in her head'?)

My first direct experience with meditation came at 15 years old when a friend and I took a bus to downtown Montreal on a Sunday to be initiated into transcendental meditation. I was told to bring flowers, which I did, but was then told they were unacceptable (having wilted on the long bus ride) and, it being Sunday, I had to traipse all over to find a flower store open. (Nothing like a little feeling of shame to start a lifelong practice!) Finally initiated, I was given a mantra I use to this day, along with other words, visualizations and Buddhist and Hindu prayers I have added over the years.

It was a time of turning away from the growing prescription-drug cult of allopathic medicine, becoming a movement that turned to the East to glean spiritual acumen through its ancient wisdom while incorporating Western ideas of what is possible for us humans from visionaries like Wilhelm Reich MD, Richard Alpert PhD (Ram Dass), even the Beatles and Joni Mitchell. Going within was paramount to discovering the richness we are endowed with coming into this world.

The truth is, there are so many ways to meditate. As I discovered in my practice, and in my life, you don't need to be a swami to experience many of the great and lasting benefits of sitting on your tail and meditating for up to an hour or as long as it takes to restore your center and sanity.

Still, I must admit, being totally present or with another human is one of the hardest things a human can do, never mind after experiencing a tragic event. Our emotions want to spin us away as they call for attention. By engaging therapies that activate our still point, we help center ourselves while we attempt to slow down our mind. Once we are able to do this, we are better able to probe our emotions, whether sadness, rage or shame, see them and use them as guideposts to better understand our own truth, our own story. And this makes it easier, when ready, to reach out to another.

ASSIGNMENT #8

1. Describe a type of breath work you are drawn to.
2. What is the Butterfly pose?
3. What is your favorite still-point therapy?
4. What can regular still-point therapy do for a person's health?

Chapter 9

The mind–body connection

'Your body is your subconscious mind and you can't heal it by talk alone.'[1]

Pain in the gut connected to memories of alcoholic parents. Head pain sourced to sexual assault decades ago. Menorrhagia, the uterus weeping. Back pain every time there is a feeling of lack of emotional support. Graves' disease from grieving the murder of her sister. Inability to conceive, a legacy of rape. The distress of gender dysphoria.

We now take what we learned in the previous chapter, continuing our inner work through guided psychotherapeutic processes, to acknowledge and track the mind–body connection. The ability to express and free psychic pain begins with the foundational practice of a still-point therapy, moving forward into a discovery of the mind–body connection, from the physiological to the psychological, the brain's link to the somatic body, which can then lead, if desired, to the outward articulation of one of the expressive arts.

This affords us this confirmation that our bodies reveal the story that the mind has experienced in PTS/trauma. Pert suggested: 'neuropeptides and their receptors form an information network within the body.'[1] For your information, these neuropeptides can be in the nodes of the chakras. Pert believed: 'This was key to understanding how mind and body are interconnected and how emotions can be manifested throughout the body.' I'll go a bit further in saying that, in my experience, this leads to emotions being at the center of conditions and disease.

To this end, the discovery and messaging of why, where we're at and where we need to be emotionally or physiologically can be filtered through our imagination and five senses to access and probe our subconscious and ensure authentic, deep and long-lasting healing.

There are of course many variations on what I present. This pathway to empowered wholeness is what I have found to be profound and true, personally and with patients, to dissolve helplessness generated by a traumatized brain and its wayward physiological determinants, perhaps in a way never experienced.

Delving into the senses

Once any possible imbalance with a physiological origin – gut flora, food allergies, hormones and so on – has been addressed, we can be confident it is time to delve into the five senses for further information and guidance. Don't forget this takes an informed guide, doctor, or therapist, to lead us on this journey to engage our subconscious/unconscious – what lies behind the conscious mind – at least to start with.

Delving into our senses means we have gone beyond talking and are involved or immersed in an authentic inner experience. Sight, sound, touch, smell, and taste become gateways that connect us to our brain. What we see or have seen, hear or have heard, and so on, leads us to memories that can be instrumental to getting to our truth(s) behind the illness.

Ultimately, the five senses and our intuition are the basis for exploring the mind–body connection that holds on to the original trauma. This is how the memory of the event is activated and can be deactivated. The memory is still there; all we need to do is access it, though easier said than done. We need to go back in time to free ourselves up, to liberate past trauma, which without effective treatment could leave us in a perpetual state of triggers and misery. We change our future by consciously 'changing the channel'.

Therefore, with our guide and trusted advisors – our senses and emotions – we can access a journal of our experience... our body and brain were there... our senses and emotions know more than we have given them credit for. They can tell a truth, confirm the experience, and bring it right back to the 'now', right here, this moment, by pointing us to something under the surface of our consciousness that may have been buried for a very long time.

The mind–body split

The body–mind split was never scientific fact. At first more existential than real, later it was a medical bias stemming from the scientific inquiry of separating out parts to explore the truth. In the 1600s, French philosopher and mathematician René Descartes (1596–1650) developed the concept of 'dualism',[2] according to which the mind and body represent separate entities and should be treated as such. Renowned English philosopher John Locke (1632–1704 – founder of the school of thought, British Empiricism, that believed the origin of all knowledge was from the senses) vehemently disagreed, and instead, in his 1690 *An Essay Concerning Human Understanding*,[3] proposed a theory of the self as a blank page, with knowledge and identity arising only from accumulated experience. (This is termed *'tabula rasa'*.) He believed somatic sensations, images, feelings, and thoughts occurred in the brain where the mind was able to scrutinize, contrast, and integrate this information in various ways.

Western psychotherapy, almost exclusively, has relied on linear change, a Newtonian mindset in which every action has a reaction, every force a counterforce, with the stronger winning. Following the Flexner report (see page 50) as we have seen, the preferred experience of healthcare reflected this dualistic approach that was adapted by conventional medicine and is embedded in allopathy. We need to understand that this is false. Our healing process must include many levels: physical, psychological, and spiritual.

Remember from the previous chapter on still-point therapy, and as we will see in Part Four devoted to the expressive arts, all these approaches focus on the use of the imagination, creativity, and a sense of play – in other words, the world of the subjective.

Visionaries

A term first coined by the infamous genius, psychiatrist Wilhelm Reich (1897–1956) in the 1930s, the 'mind–body connection' has only been scientifically proven to exist in the last two decades. As we've seen throughout this book, medical history has often demonstrated an aversion to progressive ideas, methods, or even techniques. Reich, the one-time deputy director of Freud's Psychoanalytic Polyclinic, waged a constant battle with the status quo. His book *Character Analysis*, published in 1933, offered an organization of a person's ego or neurosis that unconsciously resists reality and then went on to argue for the treatment of the whole person rather than focusing on single symptoms. He expounded on the practice of vegetotherapy, a treatment based on the understanding of physiological symptoms resulting from psychological phenomena, a practice known today as 'body' or 'somatic psychotherapy'. *Character Analysis* introduced his theory of 'armoring'[4] that included blocked psychosexual energy that produces not only emotional illness but also physical diseases. This is not unlike the earlier concepts of 'hysteria', but it was not gender specific therefore without the original sexism.

Though Reich's ideas were truly radical, his influence was wide-ranging and can be viewed through the work of many mental health professionals' theories and techniques, including somatic psychotherapy, Gestalt therapy, and bioenergetics, to name a few. The Human Potential Movement reflects this great man.

In formulating our own mind–body approach, we can turn to founders like Sigmund Freud and Carl Jung, both of whom believed that our 'storage data' – that is, the pattern of disturbance in our story – will resurface over and over until we consciously bring it from the darkness into the light. Freud called this 'repetition compulsion', the event re-enacted until we see all its tendrils and own the original distress. They both saw that these suppressions would appear in gestures, as we shall see with Moreno's psychodrama (page 204),[5] words and behaviors. Although the speech center and prefrontal cortex might shut down during a trauma and reappear as changed thinking and verbal expression, the memory is in fact still there; it has simply been submerged until the brain regains full function and tells us it is safe to do so.

Looking at conditioning factors in rodents, Robert Ader MD (1932–2011), considered the founder of PNI (psychoneuroim-munology), or psychoneuroendocrinology (PNEI), was surprised to discover in the 1980s the bidirectional link between the brain and the body's innate immune system – the neurological circuits that link the immune and endocrine systems[6] – confirming what many of us, beginning with Reich, knew: we *can* heal our pain, whether psychological or physiological, by tapping into basic neurological and physiological realities (breath, rhythm, color, imagery) to optimize our metabolism, and hence our wellness. This scientific term, psychoneuroimmunology, confirms that the mind and body are one.

And then, as has been mentioned a few times, we have the work of neuroscientist and pharmacologist Candace Pert PhD (1948–2013) who, like Reich, was reviled by her fellow scientists for her work. (Among other advances in peptide research, she discovered the opiate receptor – the cell site for the endorphins in the brain.) She suffered a premature death, no doubt caused at least in part by the forces of ridicule and injustice.

Called both the 'Mother of PNI' and the 'Goddess of Neuroscience', Pert steadfastly believed in mind–body medicine and psychosomatic wellness. She wrote: 'Since emotions run every system in the body, don't underestimate their power to treat and heal.'[1]

The non-linear approach

Early naturopathic doctors, as well as some psychiatrists, psychologists and religious and spiritual people, have experimented, and continue to do so, with therapies that aim to heal mental disturbances or imbalances through the whole person, through the recognition that the body and mind are one, and to expand consciousness, to promote our human potential in healing PTS/trauma through non-linear means.[7]

There are perhaps as many techniques these days as health practitioners that engage what has been called 'the right brain', basically uncovering emotion that may have been sealed off from the initiating event, allowing our senses along a pathway for a deeper look into what needs to be healed, circumventing the left brain's more linear or 'rational' approach. Just remember the phrase 'the body never lies', and our old friend, the imagination, that can tap into our five senses to heal what ails us.

The non-linear theories that employ the mind–body connection have many names: complexity theory; PNI, PNEI; vegetotherapy (a form of Reichian psychotherapy); right brain, left brain theory; somatic psychotherapy; gestalt therapy; and bioenergetics. For the purpose of this book, delving into right brain, left brain theory can be particularly fruitful.

Chapter 9

'Right brain' versus 'left brain'

Everyone these days has heard of the 'right brain, left brain' concept and, despite its oversimplification, it still affords the opportunity to convey how the brain works to organize thoughts and access emotions. It gives us the needed handle to work toward empowered resolution. Although talking can be helpful, if we want to move the 'stuck' energy in our somatic body initiated by the traumatic event(s), what our thoughts and feelings continue to latch onto, we need to escape the linear process. Often, trauma survivors have difficulty putting words or logic in their explanation of what happened to them, due to the diminished activity of the mPFC (medial pre-frontal cortex) leading to the loss of their executive functioning. Therefore, the use of non-linear processes is much more suited in trauma recovery and can lend itself to non-verbal communication. The world is dominated by logic, reason, 'left brain' functioning. By bringing in the imagination, integrating our mind and body to share the story that is communicated from survivor to listener, sometimes coming from a place that has been almost 'nailed shut', improves the chance of success in healing more completely.

The 'right brain' examines experiences, memories (conscious and subconscious), timelines, and attitudes, wherein curiosity can be brought forward. As such, it gives us access to our creative side, and feels safer, (even more fun), and the ability to connect holistically, by non-linear means, and engage not just the past but what is around us, what is meaningful. This can make all the difference in a survivor's world and cements the importance of creativity from a health perspective.

Ian McGilchrist, psychiatrist and author of *The Master and his Emissary*,[8] believes our right brain is what identifies us as human. We need both sides or our brain to survive, but the left brain, with its need for structure, can rob us of our ability to uncover what needs to be explored. Established society is left-brain dominant and that can cause all sorts of problems, especially in any type of relationship. When we can produce or at least appreciate music and the arts, the brain can steer us to what makes us happy.

We can go as far as to say that the 'right brain', our non-logical, creative side, is able to see the big picture, and to connect the dots toward healing, while the 'left brain', structured and analytic, takes its sweet time, waiting to clean up the mess and reorganize. It is an interesting process to watch, when a person is in their body, in their world, responding to 'right brain' activities, using story, the five senses and/or intuition, hunches, gut feelings, to evolve, to resolve trauma in a dynamic, organic flow with its own inherent order.

This brings in the concept of fractal geometry and chaos theory. A fractal is a never-ending pattern, infinitely complex, that is self-similar across different scales (sizes). Fractals are most evident in nature – trees, seashells and the like, with their repeating feedback loop. Coupled with chaos theory, with chaos being viewed more as an interruption rather than disorder, we can better comprehend that a human being is comprised of many layers with a central core of authenticity that is disrupted by the traumatic experience which shapes us and, by allowing the process to continue, we keep growing from who we are – our inner Self.

Thus, fractals and chaos theory are a means of grasping more inclusively the infinite complexity of our minds and memories and bring the full spectrum of mental healthcare into view by engaging our subjective reality and interpretations during the process of healing as we sort through our inner world. In fact, fractals[9] and chaos theory have been implicated in almost every system and discipline, and healing is no different. These seemingly endless patterns, interrupted by chaos, by unintended or unpredictable disruptions, are our natural rhythm, replicate our intimate experience with life. This is how our life goes: patterns that grow from the interruption, changing flow and pace as we accommodate them. We aren't strange or freaks because our pattern is disrupted. This is our chance to grow; it is the natural way of things. This allows us to feel confident of the process of healing. It lessens the chance of becoming so afraid of the process to center and get back on our feet that we are willing to poison ourselves with pills.

Toward the mind–body connection

I believe there is nothing more important to our planet's well-being than individual growth – mentally and spiritually – as it feeds into community and a healthy society. But how does this knowledge help us practically in PTS/trauma? How do we understand rage or another emotion that simply won't go away and is triggered continually? The answer to this is by learning what is operating, seemingly on autopilot, in our mind and is expressed by emotions and symptoms in our body. It is here we can identify the positive intent of any physical or psychological symptom, understanding why and/or how our subconscious has retained this expression. This means we dig in, to reframe the subconscious holding pattern (tense muscles, stomach aches, headaches, frequent outbursts and so on) and redesign the reactive response to this. (And yes, more conventional psychotherapies can influence these as well; this simply has been my path and what I know will heal.)

The use of non-linear, holistic therapies that have emerged in practical application over the past three quarters of a century prepares a person to locate a sense of calm and to tell their story, and with proper guidance or witnessing, endows them with the ability to revise the traumatic event by visualizing and tracking physical symptoms, to link them to emotions conjuring images, and to tap into the other senses that will facilitate healing by excavating and owning the damaging history. By learning simple techniques, we can elicit the deepest level of healing through the patient's narrative, which, no matter how nasty and disabling, can be weakened simply by discovery, focus and personal work. And this all begins with and pertains to probing the mind–body connection.

Through a non-linear approach, we can uncover our story going through either the emotion or the physiological symptom. And we have the option to track trauma either way. Sometimes when we don't know we have had a trauma, or have suppressed it, physical symptoms will show us the way into what is true, the deepest level of our pain that has been expressed on the physical level.

However, because the body 'tells our story', coming from our unconscious or subconscious where memories are stored, the five senses, by tapping into our psyche, can provide a reliable means to make sense of the survivor's reality. Without taking the time and trouble to investigate, we are often unable to see the connection. The story, whether hidden or in need of being revised, without intervention is probably too painful to recount. Yet therapists, with the mind–body approach, can use the energy of the experience to change an internal world that has been stuck, is damaged and needs repair. Ideas rely on intuition and the fact the autonomic nervous system can be calmed, first through safety and then connection to a deeper truth.

Whatever techniques we choose whether auditory, imaginative, expressive, or manipulating biochemistry, they will affect the emotions and physiology to elicit a change of consciousness, an awareness that can offer a new understanding of reality. We are always creating something with our thoughts which will manifest in an activity, whether behavior (sometimes negative) or something creative which is mostly positive due to the fact the act of creating is interesting, exciting, even exhilarating.

Yet never forget the most important activity of working with people who have experienced trauma: listen well, respect their experience... This is the first step in finding their unique path that will allow them, through their five senses and their intuition, to navigate through lingering trauma, coming out the other side with triggers reduced and hopefully at some point a smile on their face and a renewed heart....

Don't limit yourself to what I say or even what you may read about. Experiment. I was thrown into treating trauma from sexual abuse when virtually no one else felt competent; it was new territory. I tried out ideas and concepts within my clinic and retreat space which turned out to be extraordinarily effective for people with unresolved psychological trauma; we can heal through imagery, sound, and the other senses or, as in the next section, by creating stories through writing, drama, comedy, dramedy, dance, singing, or playing music. Patients, especially children, were open to calling on their imagination, using their senses to explore the mind–body connection.

Whether a person chooses to reduce their medications or not, it is my belief that reflection through psychotherapies or mind–body techniques is essential to heal the brain from a traumatic event[10] as we work to free up metabolic pathways through natural medicine. Through balancing biochemistry, we can set aside a hormonal or allergic imbalance that is simply a reflection of the actual traumatic event, and then proceed to treat the actual event that has defined the root of the PTS/trauma diagnosis.

If you believe an emotional dynamic precedes or accompanies almost every pathological physiological presentation, which I do, we can trace physical symptoms to psychological trauma as part of our case-taking or treatments. In Chinese medicine, and in homeopathy, organs and emotions are matched: grief with the lungs, anger with the liver, fretfulness with the heart or stomach, and fear with the kidneys. Even if you don't use these modalities in your practice, you can use these pairings to dig deeper, to target a disease by the entirety of symptoms the body and mind have aroused and then provide a treatment with a specific remedy. All the non-linear theories use the body to indicate distress signals relayed to the brain, and all rely on a connection to the five senses and the imagination.

The techniques or activities on which I shall expand in the following sections include Visualization, Tracking, Psychodrama (for community therapy), Playback theatre, Dream Revision, and my Womb exercise.

Visualization

Shakti Gawain's book, *Creative Visualization*, published in 1978, was the first book on the subject to open my eyes to the power of conscious imagination.[11] A true visionary, Gawain also advocated intuition as a healing force and to be careful not to ignore that voice deep within at the cost of your spiritual and physical wellbeing.

Visualization can lead to deep awareness as we make friends with our emotions. And normally, in my experience, we don't need to worry. Even if the mind is in a depressed state, it will take you to a good place as long as that informed guide is on hand. Using the senses to visualize our inner world will give us only what we can bear, or process. It acts as a guidepost to where we've been, where we are or where we are going.

Visualization begins with engaging what the mind's eye sees and layering it with the other four senses to get an even more 3-D experience. This then begins our journey, giving us a guidepost, a roadmap to our inner world. It has so many uses, from helping us set goals or cajoling us to stay present to removing an impediment like an inner judge, as we bear difficult feelings. It holds our hand as we traverse our inner world. And it is ours; we don't need to copy anyone else's. We can be inspired by others but for our truth to come forward, to heal our deepest wounds, we embrace our inner reality with intuition and imagination, feeling renewed confidence with feelings of empowerment. Helplessness, be gone!

Gawain believed that we need to listen to our bodies since they have a lot to say. By our bodies, she was referring to our brains, which, if we open ourselves to that inner, deeper voice, and learn to trust, will guide us along the healing path.[11]

Research supports the following:[12]

- The visual cortex in the occipital lobe is the visualizing processing area of the brain and includes visuospatial processing, depth perception and memory.[13]
- Through brain scans we know that a thought triggers a cascade of neurochemicals, mostly neurotransmitters, regardless of if we are thinking about the past, the present, or the future.
- That thought(s) is connected to a feeling, to memory, and many parts of the brain such as the prefrontal cortex, hippocampus, and neurons. These become stimulated in the same way whether we physically perform an action or simply visualize it to happen in our mind's eye.
- When a thought or image is focused and repeated, it is an extremely direct way of using thought to stimulate neurons aka neurostimulation.
- By using the technique of visualization and understanding that thought is a physical part of our brain, we can have a powerful lever to visualize (like an athlete in a competition) success in the future or to probe our past.
- Once we know how our thoughts are triggered, we can interject positive images and ultimately change our emotions and therefore behavior.

Tracking

Vernon Woolf, PhD FM, wrote the book *The Holodynamic State of Being*,[14] another pivotal moment for me as a naturopathic physician. (I had to stop using 'physician' in California, now 'naturopathic medical doctor'.) I discovered it at the home of my colleague, Dr. Sheila Dunn, in the late '80s and couldn't put it down.

Woolf's concept of tracking back to an initiating event is akin to following tracks in the snow, albeit in Technicolor. Tracking a symptom back to the event that has been suppressed is especially helpful in treating headaches or gut symptoms that haven't resolved by changing the diet, addressing the adrenals, or increasing hydration and minerals.

Using the imagery from the five senses held the key for me to unlocking the subconscious of many patients with physiological distress that had arisen from psychological trauma. Having attended many of Woolf's courses, I began practicing a form of non-authoritarian hypnosis on adults and children who had been sexually, ritually, or medically abused.

Being able to root out negative thoughts, feelings, and behaviors at the points of origin, pole-vaulted me to a new dimension in my practice. I now had a way to traverse the minds and hearts that were stuck in suffering chronic physical and/or emotional symptoms.

One of Woolf's major ideas is to track generations back, bringing to light messages that may have come down to us through our families as seen in intergenerational trauma, noted in Chapter 1 (see page 8). A form of Psychodrama, this led me to offering retreats where I developed the Womb exercise (see Appendix 4).

To start

Tracking can start with physical symptoms or, alternatively, negative emotions. For example, chronic headaches as mentioned earlier, may lead us to the origin that may turn out to be a trauma like sexual abuse. At the core of it all, and in accordance with this technique:

- When the person under treatment visualizes the emotional or physical pain (with all the senses), it allows images, sounds etc. to come forward to tell the story and unveil the root cause.
- The initiating event will come up from the subconscious, slowly or almost instantly.

Another way is to bring up the anxiety that you already know represents the cause:
- See the anxiety, thank it for helping to protect…
- Bring flowers or other beautiful meaningful objects to it…
- You are focusing on the psychic pain, loving it…

There are so many ways to use this paramount technique, starting with visualization, and this connection is what heals. Remember, the right side of the brain is what lets you observe the connections and gather the whole picture. It will enable you to experience your body's sensations and use them to change. The left brain is great at organization, but you can't just think away psychological trauma, you must feel it if only to see, hear or taste it at a distance and bring it a beautiful object. This is your way in, no matter what technique we talk about; the right brain is the way to get information and heal.

While every person's story is unique, the method to access it can be universal. Then, as we gain access to the story of the initiating event and find out the intent of emotions in it, we can determine several aspects. Were they protective? Usually. Is this protective seal damaging us now? So many questions, universal and individual. So many answers, universal and individual.

Universal tracking steps

1. Begin by having the person visualize the five senses: smell, taste, touch, sight, and hearing. For instance:

- Sight – seeing a place, as on a mountain top or in a meadow.
- Sound – add the sound of branches in a breeze.
- Touch – feel the soft earth or a flower.
- Smell – smell the forest.
- Taste – this is often a taste from an enjoyable memory.

2. Taking all five senses we create a place of peace where we can begin to discover what else is there.
   - Create a safe space in the mind's eye – beach, mountain top…
   - If the person can't imagine it, tell them to pretend… it works every time.

3. Call forward to your full potential.
   - Have the person see or feel that part of themselves that is behind the conscious mind, the healer or wise person within.
   - Some religious people will use their symbolism or people.

4. Make sure the person is committed to the process.
   - Have them say, 'I am committed to this process of healing'.

Tracking tips for the clinician

- The essence of tracking is to keep probing using the five senses.
- You can employ each sense as an actual character; for example, dressed up in fun hat and clothes, and perhaps given an accent.
- Encouraging creativity can give a health professional a lot of information.
- Sometimes it can be very quick, or you may have to keep going until something significant emerges. I find it fascinating how much is on the surface of the subconscious, ready to be told…

- As the tracking continues, you and the survivor will become increasingly adept at using the five senses as guides to what's deeper, to what the subconscious will share. It's like painting a picture, or writing a song, you keep going with color and texture, sound, taste. If you hit a wall that there is nothing, just wait and if there is still nothing apparent as a response, ask them to gently rock or you rock them. Something will come.

Examples of treating PTS/trauma — Symptoms and comorbidities

Headaches

If someone has a recurring headache and our initial naturopathic treatments are not having the expected effect, we can, with a simple mind–body technique, attempt to track it to unresolved emotional trauma.

This happened in my practice time and time again as I worked with those suffering from PTS/trauma. With a woman who had suffered migraines from the time she was 9 years old:

I simply asked, 'What was going on when you were 9?'

She wasted no time in telling me her family had been living in a foreign country where her siblings and other children attended a school.

Then came the clue: one by one the head teacher had taken a child into a room and abused them sexually.

Once we had identified the cause of her upset, she was able to deal with her feelings anchored in the past event.

Having confronted the suppressed emotion through guided visualization, her body relaxed, and the migraines resolved.

Fibromyalgia

Fibromyalgia provides us with an example of using tracking and the mind–body connection to successfully treat a concurrence or comorbidity of PTS.

When the term surfaced in the '80s, it wasn't long before female health therapists using this technique were able to connect the unexplained pain to sexual abuse; i.e., the body was holding on to the suppressed emotion and in doing so had created a pain pathway to the brain.

Other symptomatic presentations

I was able to apply this same technique to a great many of my patients: men, women, and children, who came in with such diverse presentations as:

- temporomandibular joint problems (TMJ)
- digestive disorders
- panic attacks
- cystitis
- irritable bowel syndrome (IBS)
- heart palpitations
- hypertension (high blood pressure)
- chronic back pain
- any uterine presentation
- vaginismus.†

Any of these can present, unconsciously manifesting as a reaction to fear or terror or other strong emotion. The techniques offered here are tremendously helpful.

---

† Vaginismus presents when vaginal muscles contract automatically when penetrated and not just from a penis. Tampons are a big issue, with the first onset of a menstrual cycle. I remember one workshop participant who had this condition and had been traumatized further by having a group of young interns surround her, staring at her and her vagina, as a doctor attempted to use pencil-like objects to expand her vagina. Sometimes it just takes plain common sense and empathy not to use patients as guinea pigs.

The good news is that all the above can be linked, tracked back to negative emotions (anxiety, anger, grief) manifested after a traumatic incident. Remember, these emotions can be triggered over and over, and they can accumulate... sometimes leading to an autoimmune disorder, as they did with me with Graves' disease.

A sample session
Tracking can combine with another natural medical modality to offer closure. I offer you the following demonstration:

Homeopathy plus tracking for depression

A 32-year-old woman with depression who responded to homeopathic *Staphysagria* is, after a few months of treatment, able to articulate her feelings more accurately, but she still feels not quite right. Acting as her guide (G) this is how the tracking might proceed with the patient (P):

G: 'It is time to engage your five senses, to tap into your imagination, to uncover your narrative. Breathe slowly in and out.' After a few moments, I would say 'Continuing to visualize your senses, try to "see, taste, hear, smell, or touch" the depression.'

P: 'I see only black.'

G: 'Is the blackness making a sound or does the blackness have a taste or an odor?'

G: While she is searching... 'Is there a texture to it?' As she continues to search inside her still point, I suggest 'Keep using the five senses until one of them emerges.'

P: 'The black is swirling.'

G: 'What does it want you to know? What is its positive intent?'

P: 'It's angry. No, it's afraid.'

G: 'Of what?'

P: A big sigh, followed by 'I don't know'.

G: I wait patiently... if nothing comes after a few minutes, I ask her to rock with extremely small movements to see if an image will emerge. 'What does the anger or fear look like? What does it want you to know?'

P: 'I see a little girl on a swing.'

G: 'Can she tell you anything?'

P: 'She was happy but then she says...' suddenly a very sad voice 'I was molested'.

P: Her voice is stronger... 'The little girl had a lot more to say'.

G: 'What would she say to the adult today about feeling depressed?'

P: She pounds her hands. 'I don't need to be helpless anymore. I'm strong.'

This session shows how well using homeopathy to balance the biochemistry, in this case *Staphysagria*, a remedy for suppressed emotion (usually anger), combined with tracking, can provide closure. Truth to tell, some homeopaths have become psychotherapists and some psychotherapists have become homeopaths; it's a powerful combo.

Going further

You can keep tracking, to a deeper layer, back to an event or a deeper emotion as in from depression to shame, a surefire indicator of a past traumatic encounter. To an experienced therapist, depression is an easier, less taxing emotion for the victim to express, and hence more difficult to deal with as a trusted guide, but, having brought shame, so common in sexual abuse, to the surface of the response, you can first ask:

'What would shame say if she could speak?'

'What does it/she/he need to know to move forward?'

Shame's positive intent is to protect the sufferer, to keep, in the sample session, the person safe.

Once exposed, shame is guilty of thwarting the PTS survivor from disclosing the traumatic event, and so, in the final analysis, has done more harm than good. Moreover, once the shame is revealed and treated with respect, it loses its power. Feeling safe, you/your patient may own the fact from a completely different emotion that they were sexually abused. In the end, the act of uncovering and illuminating what was a horrific event has freed them from this conflicting emotion, setting them on their way to letting go of the negative emotions associated with shame and ultimately moving them into an empowered state where further healing can occur.

To sum up:

- You can use a present physical symptom or emotion as a way in.
- You keep going, asking for more through the five senses or treating either as a character who can speak or show in some way what it knows.
- You do this until you have something that makes sense, that can mean something to the patient.
- It takes time to learn this, and you do need to access or feel comfortable with your intuition (but not pounce from your intuition).
- Go slowly.
- See how the person feels afterwards – ask them:

'Did it give you something you can work with?'

> 'Is there a deeper understanding of the situation, the initiating trauma?'

The womb exercise

During my first year of practice in 1988, I started the retreat *Moving to Healing* after being contracted by the Archdiocese of Vancouver to treat sexual abuse. This exercise is intended particularly for survivors of sexual, medical, or ritual abuse. Although a combination of clinical nutrition, botanical medicine, detoxification, and homeopathy had a dramatic effect on patients, I sensed the tools I personally relied on to de-stress would be perfect for their healing as well. In my spare moments I had read a study on the importance of community support in breast cancer, and when the idea of a retreat at a waterfront home presented itself, I jumped at it. What could be better, I thought, than being surrounded by the sea in a forest setting, eating homemade organic food, dancing, singing, and playing with a group of women.

I then set out to create exercises to help women with pelvic pain, whether it came from sexual, medical, or ritual abuse and/or pelvic conditions like PID (pelvic inflammatory disease). I don't know what I expected but I was thrilled when I realized the depth of healing generated, especially from an exercise I call 'The Womb' (see Appendix 4, page 321).

A form of psychodrama, the Womb Exercise is a perfect example of using visualization (imagery based on the five senses combined with intuition) to enter our subconscious, to build trust with ourselves, to let our unique story emerge.

It is also a way to feel community, create social support, build trust with others as we connect the dots with our physiological and psychological states.

Examining what has hindered our psycho-spiritual growth gives us material for our story to be told. If desired, this can be the writing material that leads to us incorporating our voice, movement/dance and/or theatre with our healing, as outlined in the next section, The expressive arts.

Sound frequencies

The goal of any breath or sound work is a sophisticated form of movement re-education that retrains the brain and the nervous system. Sounds can create healing simply through their frequency. Jonathan Goldman, adept in sound healing, explains the concept as the whole universe is vibrating.[15] His ideas include:

- When we are in a state of health, all our bodily parts are working together in harmony, creating an overall harmonic of health.
- If one of these parts begins to vibrate at a different rate, this is what we call disease.

One way to see what is happening in the body as we heal is to understand that everything in life vibrates at a certain energy or frequency, including our cells, our emotions, our thoughts, plants, trees; even rocks have a frequency. As feelings or thoughts change, we change our cellular vibration to a higher or lower frequency. If we have negative emotions such as anger, sadness and so on, these wreak havoc by being stored, resulting in blockages of energy throughout the body. These then manifest as physical symptoms, such as headache or pain, and may grow into a disease. By blowing out these blockages through understanding, tracking and so on, we can elicit a higher frequency. It's like cleaning out debris and, as we heal, we learn to bring in light and joy and the body will naturally raise its vibration. My way has always been to understand the emotions first through tracking and the five senses, never to suppress our journey. This is why I love sound healing: it can raise the vibration of our turmoil, lightening the load. But we still, in my view, must track what's there. Once we have done this and going forward, when we are triggered, sound therapy can bring us back to our center with little effort.

One of the basic concepts of healing with sound on the physical body is to project the correct resonant frequency of the organ, or whatever is out of balance, back into the body. Echoing the finding of epigenetics, Goldman adds that neuroscience has confirmed the mind–body connection, that the physiological and psychological are tied together and will inevitably affect each other.[15] Key concepts here are:

- Different brain wave patterns affect emotions, including lowering our anxiety, simply by tuning in to sound.
- This brings up the famous droning of Tibetan bowls that have no beat or melody but a pulsing tone that can evoke healing.

Jeffrey Thompson, founder of the Center for Neuroacoustic Research, acknowledges the relationship between the density of tissue and its susceptibility to a specific sound frequency and subsequent rebuilding, adding that penetration of the body's cellular structure can both improve and elevate healing.[16]

Joshua Leeds, in his book *Power of Sound*, recalls a review of 20 studies published in the 2008 journal *Alternative Therapies in Health and Medicine*, that concludes brainwave entrainment is an effective tool to treat cognitive functioning deficits, stress, pain, headaches and premenstrual syndrome (PMS), hence PTS/trauma.[17]

Psychodrama

As an introduction to the next section, the Expressive arts, I'd like to add Psychodrama to the fold. Viennese psychiatrist Jacob Moreno (1889-1974)[5] developed this activity by combining his interests in philosophy, theatre, and mysticism.

Psychodrama places itself in the center of a group that by necessity is both safe and ongoing, and uses role theory to evoke cognitive, emotional, and behavioral responses through dramatic action, while encouraging intuition and creativity to explore personal issues that inhibit our life experience. Like any therapy, its goal is to resolve challenges or difficulties that are often rooted in past situations, in this case, focusing on the expression of strong emotion to facilitate balance and calm.

Moreno came to America in 1925 and in the '30s founded Beacon Hospital which had a therapeutic theater for psychodrama. Through a study from 1932 to 1938 at the New York State Training School for Girls in Hudson NY, Moreno became convinced this method significantly reduced runaways. By 1942 he had established the American Society of Group Psychotherapy and Psychodrama. Moreno succinctly described psychodrama as the 'scientific exploration of truth through dramatic method'.[5]

At the center of his theoretical framework is spirituality, believing everyone had a 'Godhead', a divine light within, from which creativity and spontaneity flowed. Most personal issues arose from a blockage of these two active qualities.

A psychodrama session

A typical session consists of six to eight people as the **warm-up phase** for trust and group cohesion.

The **action phase** involves a single participant who creates a scene based on their life. The other participants follow the lead of the facilitator as helpers.

The **sharing phase** returns to the group context in which the facilitator processes the scene.

Techniques in the action phase include:
- Role reversal: the person working (protagonist) enacts someone who has been significant in their lives which can

bring understanding of the dynamics of the relationship and empathy.

- Mirroring: the protagonist is an observer while the others act out an event.
- Doubling: further to mirroring, a group member adopts the person working's behavior and movements, expressing aloud any emotions or thoughts they believe the protagonist might have.
- Soliloquy: the protagonist expresses inner thoughts and feelings to the audience... they can do this speaking to the double or to the facilitator/director.

Playback theatre

Playback Theatre[18] is improvisational theatre, developed by Jonathan Fox in 1975, which, like Moreno's psychodrama, honors personal story through acting out an event in one's own life. Often a musician is present, and the actors can use dance, mime, sound, or puppetry, even costumes and props, to create the 'playback'.

Dream revision

Dreams also uncover our truth and can play a huge role in accessing our subconscious, what we really think and feel, helping us to clarify problems and find solutions. It is a fact that many cultures get up in the morning and discuss dreams. (What a concept!)

As Dr. Frank Lawless says in *PTSD Breakthrough*: 'When dream revision works, it goes right to the site of the traumatic injury in the brain, like a magic bullet. In contrast the medications seem to act only at the edge of the trauma.'[19]

A technique that concentrates on the individual, I learned dream revision at Yasodhara Ashram in British Columbia when I was recovering from Graves' disease. Here are the steps:

- Write down your dream in the present tense in its entirety.
- Circle a significant event or person or thing.
- For each circle, write out what that means to you and then read the passage back.

This will make so much more sense and be far more personal in meaning than delving into books, which you can also do if desired.

A NOTE TO THE CLINICIAN

Visualization, tracking, and my own 'psychodrama' Womb Exercise in sexual abuse survivors are all excellent techniques to explore the mind–body connection when the circumstances – respect, safe space, right timing and so on – are right. I may use concepts that originated with Freud's psychoanalysis, the most popular psychotherapy of the last century, or other psychotherapists or scientists' concepts, such as chaos or complexity theory, but I didn't have formal training in these when I first started practice. I simply relied on what I had been taught at naturopathic medical school, and before attending Bastyr, what I learned during summers as a counselor at Camp Discovery in Nova Scotia with people like Eleanor Hamilton, PhD, and Gina Ogden, PhD, who were pioneers in the Human Potential Movement, and had been friends and trained with Wilhelm Reich, MD. More than anyone, my patients, particularly in Kitsilano, British Columbia, helped form my method.

Non-linear therapies tap into the right brain, our senses, and move us forward in a way that left-brain talking therapies, including cognitive behavioral therapy (CBT) can't, in my experience. Of course, CBT is a wonderful method and is needed, even in minute amounts, for

---

awareness, but I believe trauma recovery must venture further than CBT, a left-brain approach, to truly heal.

Until the Archdiocese and other health professionals sent me patients who had been abused or were experiencing trauma, I hadn't realized how valuable a Doctor of Naturopathic Medicine could be in addressing mental health through a non-linear approach, after biochemistry for optimal physiology had been supported. Unresolved psychological trauma is often hidden and can be accessed through physiological symptoms as is explored in this chapter. I am grateful that so many naturopathic physicians now are specializing in mental health, primarily balancing biochemistry through the scientific understanding of a stress response through food and so on.

For instance, a woman comes in with a lifelong migraine and you wonder why. Or bad digestion and no diet or probiotic is changing the picture to the degree you'd like... or a woman is bleeding profusely on her period, it's gone on for months and she is exhausted from iron depletion and nothing mechanical or chemical is alleviating this... what is really going on? Trained as a sleuth to discover the cause of an illness, we turn to story and, lo and behold, it's not diet or even an herb or a homeopathic treatment that is needed. There is a deeper story that needs to be told, expressed, or simply affirmed before true healing can be generated. The menorrhagia turns out to be the pain of never having children – the uterus is weeping; or the digestive disturbance dates to an alcoholic parent who made the person feel 'sick to your stomach'; the lifelong migraine originated when living overseas with her missionary family and a teacher sexually abused her.

ASSIGNMENT #9

1. Who first coined the term body–mind connection? What do you know about him?
2. The five senses and intuition begin the adventure of traversing the inner world. How might this fit into your work if you are a health professional? Or if a lay person or other type of professional, what might you recommend to a survivor of PTS/trauma?
3. Describe a session using Tracking.
4. Describe one of the other therapies mentioned.

Chapter 10

The arts as refuge

Description. Angle. Hand stretched 'No'. A crack in the sidewalk. Dissolution, stage gone quiet. Curved shoulder. Melody. Color splashed across a canvas. Manuscript torn. A row of short eees.

The second part of my two-pronged approach in trauma recovery is the telling or revising of one's own story through the expressive arts. A journey that is drug free, a force to be reckoned with, is a perfect addition to any treatment without turning to a pill – in other words, a completely natural modality to heal disturbed emotion.

The arts and the imagination have been a refuge to relieve stress since the time of cave paintings, or a song sung to offer comfort to our inner or outer child. In most ancient cultures, music was magical and mystical and considered a necessary part of life, even daily, a way to bring the community together. Music is a universal healer, noted all the way back to ancient China in which a treatise was written of music's influence on health and morality. According to Plato, 'Music is a moral law. It gives soul to the universe, wings to the mind, flight to the imagination, and charm and gaiety to life and to everything.'[1] (The Greeks even used music as a treatment for a hangover.[2])

Shamanic rituals of Indigenous peoples include drums and chanting to heal the sick, ward off evil spirits or connect with the Earth and these continue around the world in present time. In scientific speak, music is a stimulus, modifies our emotional affect with a neurological basis that can be measured subjectively as well as objectively with biomarkers and physiological measurements.

So, what's not to like about music or any of the expressive arts? How do we include them to let go of trauma in our individual story? What can get in our way? Judgment? Shyness? A perception of lack of talent?

Channelling authentic emotion

There is an indispensable lesson to be learned by recognized 'artistes', those talented humans who forged their reputations as being brilliant in their field of choice, though most, it should be mentioned, were wealthy enough to practice it as a hobby. But let's not forget that these same artists also sought to express themselves as a means of coming to terms with reality, often painful and full of emotional suffering. What is of great importance to anyone who creates an original work based on their own personal history is not only the expert way in which it is conveyed but the source of energy it rides throughout the process of expression. The piece must emanate from the individual's own soul to possess the credence to heal its creator and impact the viewer or listener. What is interesting to me is the people who create or created real or authentic art may have had an intended audience in mind, but their purpose was to reach down into the depths of their consciousness to produce it.

There is a history we can trace that led to this state of mind among the artists of today. While artists through to the Baroque and Renaissance periods were told by their private patrons or the church what to conceive, beginning in the nineteenth century there was a growing awareness among them to infuse their work with a more relatable or genuine form of emotion, one generated from the depths of the artist's need, not merely calculated to get a laugh or angry retort, despite the imaginary realm from which it was conveyed. This is what we want to encourage as clinicians or guides, what is behind the effort to get the survivor to reveal their inner story.

This increased focus in the 1800s on being more 'natural', or aligned with one's own 'natural' self, was a time filled with discoveries that elbowed in on our natural, inherent senses coupled with an acute awareness of the natural world. An example is François Delsarte (1811–1871), a French musician, singer, composer, and, most importantly, the founder of modern or contemporary dance, who was a major contributor to the movement. In his words: 'The object of art is to crystallize emotion into thought and give it form.'[3] He inspired Isadora Duncan and other modern dancers and actors by investing their work with heightened emotional meaning and expression. To the eclectic Delsarte, the style of acting at the time was likewise 'unnatural and unconnected to reality'.

Although his work has been altered and shanghaied, sometimes seen as a parody, his influence, to this day, is huge. In the 1930s, the esteemed acting teacher Konstantin Stanislawski saw the emotional being as the actor's primal force, espousing Delsarte's Method of Physical Actions at the end of his tenure, something we will pursue later. What is important is that Delsarte, like the early naturopathic doctors, turned to nature, to the performers' own natural makeup, to express an authentic experience through dance and other mediums.

The origins of art therapy

As things progressed during the 20th century, it was only a matter of time before the idea or notion that art could heal worked its way into the psychology profession. Music therapy, most probably because of its capacity to bypass left brain activity, emerged as the forerunner of the arts used in therapy, and initiated the transition to professional help through the arts.

In his book, *This Is Your Brain on Music*, scholar and musician Daniel J. Levitin describes music as the most prominent among all art forms since it's been around in every culture from the beginning of time.[4] To make his point, Levitin brings back the idea that the benefits and practice of art needn't be restricted to professionals. He is distressed by the tendency of American culture to place the great artists and performers on a god-like level to the detriment of arts practice by us ordinary humans.

As a result of this, many people shy away from taking advantage of how music or any of the arts can heal. Yet music, an improvised rhythm, is in fact primal, a tool to use in discovery of our shadowed stories, begging to be brought into the light.

Turning to another contemporary figure, psychologist Arthur Robbins believed the search for authentic emotional expression could be adapted to the treatment of an emotionally damaged patient. A pioneer in the therapeutic creative process, Robbins in his book *The Psycho Aesthetic Experience – An Approach to Depth-Oriented Treatment*, published in 1989, makes the point that psychotherapy, like the creation of an art piece, needn't always be linear. Considering the aesthetic value of non-verbal communication, the strict confines of the scientific approach, in his view, are not easily adaptable to the therapeutic context, wherein patient and clinician must be able to interact freely for true healing to occur. As a side comment, he reminds us that those we anoint as true artists have used their creativity to heal themselves.[5]

Treating the soldier

In the pages ahead, we will focus on the 'active' aspect of writing, singing, drawing, dancing, and acting. However, healing can also take place in the more 'passive' realm of reading. One of the greatest needs of a survivor is to break out of that confined space the trauma has created as a safety net, by keeping history, so to speak, at bay.

Many of us became acquainted with the acronym PTSD through its relation to veterans scarred by their wartime experience. Beginning in the early 1990s, a reading program generated by the US military reached out to soldiers to spirit them out of depression. Ancient Greek tragedy, including Homer's *The Iliad*[6] and *The Odyssey*,[7] that recorded 80 years of battles and engaged over 17,000 citizen-soldiers, became a form of 'relatable' storytelling for present day war veterans. Jonathan Shay[8] among others recognized the need for reading books that 'communalized' the experience of battle, becoming a popular activity for healing trauma.

The plays of the ancient Greek philosopher, Sophocles, which mirrored the experience of damaged American troops, were also popular. It is easy to see why wounded vets could identify with his fallen heroes, like Ajax, who suffers a shameful death. Clearly, no one wins in war but Americans who have survived the battlefield, according to Tess Banko, director of the UCLA Veteran Family Wellness Center and a Marine Corps veteran and sexual assault survivor, can now pick up a pen or enroll in art or music courses as a means of dealing with trauma, and lessening suffering.[9]

The threat of celebrity culture

Just as the 'superior' standard posed by 'professionals' in their field is shackled and still impedes the free expression of emotion through an art form, celebrity culture has thwarted the need for self-expression among the American public. As a health professional, beware of the popularly held notion that the realm of the artist is reserved for the 'elite' lest it infringe on your effort to get the PTS survivor to reveal their story.

Living in a society where certain people are regarded as 'better' or more empowered than others, more talented, more glamorous, with the sanctioning of the gifted as being apart from the ordinary, it may be difficult for many to feel they have the wherewithal to embrace the magic of the muse, and to express themselves from an authentic, honest position. But the truth is, almost everyone can close their eyes and imagine scenes filled with images, color, texture, sounds, and smells. Connect this to trapped or disturbing emotion, begging to tell its tale or revision, and you will feel your soul embarking eagerly (albeit perhaps with some trepidation) on a journey to write, paint, sing, dance, or act. Whatever the lingering physicality, condition, or disease, the hungry ghost is waiting to create an experience that will most likely be nothing short of transformational.

Approaching healing

The purpose of this chapter is to encourage anyone with PTS/ trauma to reach out to the expressive arts as a vehicle for excreting toxic emotions and getting out of the frozen state that has kept them sheltered from the originating event. One needn't study psychoanalysis or go to a psychoanalyst to use or access an artistic or creative approach to healing.

In the Still point and Mind–body chapters, visualization was shown as a tool to calm the brain and emotions. To take the still point a step farther, while accessing it to feel grounded, the process of expression through an art form can be amplified in clarity while guided by feelings and imagination to produce something uniquely our own. As we continue to learn to express our psychological wounding in its totality, imagery, color, sound, texture, and/or rhythm, we move into more elaborate work, a long form with the goal to manifest a more fully empowered state of being.

It's your choice

Perhaps a survivor will ask, 'How do you expect me to do anything when all I want to do is stay warm under my blankets, eat my favorite comfort foods, and run as far away as possible from memories and triggers? C'mon, how can I create something when I can barely get off my butt to do the things I need to do to survive? Never mind buying into all your fancy words like 'creativity' and how dare you call me disempowered when I am the victim here?' Perhaps adding, 'Is it really necessary to take back control of my life from an event that has trampled me, squashing my life force into defeat without a whit of control?'

Good point. Well, here's my answer. How awful is it to feel disempowered, to always respond from a 'victim' perspective, when you can practice self-care and feel connected to what lies inside for your own peace of mind? How is your behavior affecting your life, your goals, your every moment, or someone you love, and what about the world? Because you, my friend, are precious and the world, the planet, needs you. It needs your experience, your healing, your wisdom. By deepening your truth, surrendering to the forces that are driving to make you whole again, transforming the feeling of disempowerment and reaching out, you can experience healing, joy, and empowerment.

Consider, again, what it might mean to be a candidate for neurotransmitter balance, your amygdala, hippocampus, prefrontal cortex, vagus nerve, mitochondria no longer in an agitated state. What might happen, for example, to your thyroid when you sing or what happens in your brain when writing down feelings that may turn into a story, or scribble color on a sheet of paper? Our health can't help but improve as primal forces engage us in an interesting, and often exhilarating fashion.

For the clinician or helper, don't worry if you feel you can't string a few words together or hold a paintbrush or are pitch deaf. You will find something that works to nudge the survivor's creativity. In practice, I didn't care that I didn't have the talent of Van Gogh or thought I stunk at drawing; that didn't stop me from prescribing art to a 17–year-old who was determined to give up her pharmaceuticals. After the simple suggestion of focusing on artwork, I became the one she wanted to see, not her two psychiatrists. I saw her, dignified her by helping her tap into her creativity, her healing muse, helped her, as beautifully described by writer/playwright, James Baldwin, in a testimony to the arts, find her inner 'truth'.[10]

Donald W. MacKinnon, in his 1966 article, 'What Makes a Person Creative?'[11] writes about the scope of the journey those who partake of the arts can travel to discover themselves. Having found, or in the case of therapy, having been shown the way, they can draw on a wealth of experience, which, despite being initially daunting, once surmounted will enable them to pursue their path to healing.

So, even if we have no experience in writing or another art, if we can own and have feelings for an experience in life, we can create, and that is the second part of my two-pronged approach to healing trauma: tell the story or revise it with the energy endowed to it.

A soprano can send shivers through the listeners' spines, but while being an observer can certainly inspire, the process of accessing our own emotional being as an active participant, linking our emotions and our energy, and exposing our psyches to an ongoing natural process to wellness, as I have witnessed and experienced, can be transformative. In fact, all creative expressions, whether writing, poetry, music, or dance, let our souls sing out our pain.

And don't be deterred by the term 'therapy', which has a similar ring to it as the 'disorder' in 'PTSD', and why 'PTS' is preferred. Art therapy, music therapy, etc. are simply established modalities, but the truth is one need only show up with a pen and paper, art supplies, a sheet of music, a tune to dance to, to tap into the profound force of our imagination. Depending on your state of mind or heart, having a guide, a teacher may be a better choice in the beginning, if one can afford it. However, the journey can be initiated alone. It is up to you. How far one wants to go is a matter of choice, whether in the hope of subduing the initial insult and injury to your brain and body or proceeding to create an entire piece of art. And no need to start big or have a big idea.

The goal

Breaking open to tell our story and then using its energy in a completely unexpected way allows us to mine our experiences to heal as deeply as our psyche permits, showing the world, the truth of our soul, of our life. Treading the path of the five senses, using our intuition, and freeing up our thoughts and feelings, we can move into our story, ready, knowing we have the tools to do so as the muse, our spirit and heart, and artistic guide, point the way to creation in what is called the expressive or healing arts. This is the next step to shedding emotional pain.

Also referred to as the 'psycho-aesthetic experience' or 'depth-oriented treatment', any of the individual modalities of the expressive arts are an extraordinary healing tool when experiencing psychological trauma. It can put you in the driver's seat in a way not thought possible when you feel you are being dragged behind a runaway vehicle and are especially apt for those who are having difficulty verbalizing what has occurred. As we turn now to our muse in healing, bringing the inside out to shed our emotional pain, we lean into our imagination, and authentic emotion to soothe and repair a fractured spirit.

In writing or performing an original piece, we'll need to wander along the path of the five senses coupled with intuition and thoughts and feelings, to devise a storyboard for the telling (and revising) of our authentic story. By moving into our individual story, we will need to utilize the muse, our spirit and heart, and artistic guide, to point the way to creation. With creative expression as our companion, we traverse our innermost being, illuminating the story that is begging to be told. Be rest assured there is a formidable history of people who've embraced an artistic discipline and emerged from a dark and extremely challenging morass, their stories a vindication of recovery, a healing journey that guides the path to wellness.

If we believe we are one in body and mind, and are willing to deepen our experience through creativity, we can push a traumatic experience into a form that can intrigue and delight us as much as it heals. We can choose to write about our trauma; we can create art and music based on the rhythms and textures that have ensnared us; we can dance it or act it out. By expressing ourselves, telling our story in whatever form, we feel most comfortable if we free ourselves of the damning emotions that seem to want to bring us further down. Telling our story frees us: it loosens the stranglehold of guilt, shame, self-loathing, or any of the myriad of other destructive reactions that can ensnare. This journey of discovery can empower us in a way we may never have imagined.

As a survivor of trauma, we are endowed with the canvas of our choice to be an artist. To speak from the heart and mind, whatever it wants to express. Remember, it's not about how fabulous the piece, it's about accessing the authenticity of emotion inside that has been twisted in on itself, an expression of tragedy that struggles to be whole, to be set free, no matter how often we push it down, shoo it away for another day. And we have the say whether we share it or not.

This culture has created the haters, but really they are people who are acting out from their own suffering, a long trail of trauma that has buttoned on to criticizing others for release, making themselves feel superior while generating untenable emotions for others. Here is a perfect example of why we need to promote music and the arts in school... we can get at trauma early by helping children (who as we saw are the highest number with PTS) explore their creativity, communicating their feelings, their stories, so that the difficult experiences don't end up stuffed down and will someday erupt in rage and/or hate.

A NOTE TO THE CLINICIAN

Whatever the lingering emotion, practicing the arts can free up the professional or survivor alike, giving access to the inner artist. This activity need not remain the exclusive domain of acclaimed artists. I don't mean a person in this program cannot be an artist after years of hard work. It simply means an exploration through creativity is measured by the freedom it evokes. This is what we are after as clinicians. Therefore, it must be consciously made available for all as I, along with many others, firmly believe it is imperative to find a way to tell or revise the story of a traumatic memory with people suffering PTS.

However, while it is not easy, remember, the piece created need not be an accurate recapturing or retelling of the event; only the energy and emotion surrounding it needs to be explored. And it never needs to be shown to anyone else. Either way, this can lead to positive transformation, the feeling of liberation emerging.

Always make sure that this process is understood to go as slowly as one needs to, that it is of course necessary to see what works without eliciting further difficult emotion, keeping triggers at a minimum.

You will be practicing in the face of most professionals who refuse to employ the easily accessible tools of imagination or creative expression and will refer out. But don't let their attitude deter you. Know that it may be very valuable for the survivor that you understand this process, that what they are doing is helpful to their recovery, that you are able and perhaps eager to keep abreast of this in an informed manner.

You may want to run a retreat so that your patients or clients can immerse themselves in their emotional and creative process without distraction. Plus, the support of others can be invaluable to the healing process, allowing freedom and affirmation of what the survivor is going through.

When I offered Moving to Healing to women in my practice, I felt it was what was needed, that sitting one to one in a clinic office was limiting their potential (and mine). They were all sexual abuse survivors and all eager to connect with each other. I absolutely loved facilitating these retreats and was so grateful for the Womb Exercise I created to address the organs and limbs and heart of the experience of sexual abuse that led to their presentation of PTS/trauma.

The bottom line is that, however we want to explore creativity, singly, as a survivor or guide, in the city or wilderness, whatever the modality we choose in exploring various forms of expression, by utilizing imagination we can harness an easier pathway to express difficult emotions including despair and loneliness that can lead to deep depression and possible suicide. This pathway grows in the doing, confidence building through associations of the five senses, utilizing characters and story. It may even, at some point, allow the possibility of learning to find humor in oneself or one's journey, a possibility I discuss in the next part of this book.

If we are to be whole, we can't underestimate the value of art and its effect on the architecture of our soul. Not only has healthcare in America been perverted and the offerings of the earth scoffed at, but the world we live in has been exploited, so obvious in the cities but also the countryside, highways, and small towns where the cheapest substances and materials are used leading to a bleakness of vision. This book can't address this in the fullness it deserves but as we talk about restoring wholeness to our lives, remember to look around and appreciate the beauty in nature, and still standing architecture and art that humans create. We need more of both to be truly socially engaged and connected to each other and the world we live in. What we choose to surround ourselves with is as important as who.

Each of the expressive arts in the following chapters have common elements along with a particular strength or area of interest to draw on. Any one of them will provide a means of access otherwise denied to the conventional approach. You will learn why each discipline is useful as a healing tool, what it offers specifically in terms of how it affects the brain and learn the steps that will enable you to traverse the process of materializing a piece of art from beginning to end.

And for those of you wanting to create workshops or retreats, adding a creative aspect will bring out so much emotion, depth, and authenticity to the experience. Also fun, laughter, and curiosity! Because, as difficult as moments in trauma recovery might be, expressing ourselves with the muse at our shoulder can make the journey truly enjoyable!

ASSIGNMENT #10

1. How do you express yourself when feeling anxious?
2. How would you define creativity?
3. Discuss the threat of celebrity culture.
4. Discuss François Delsarte or Isadora Duncan's contribution to the arts.

Part Four

The expressive arts

*The little girl lost no time. She spread her arms wide,
reaching past a thousand stars. And twirled and twirled.*

Chapter 11

Writing and visual art

Nouns, verbs, adjectives... Journaling, short stories, long stories, essays, poetry, scripts for radio, theatre, stage, or screen.

Writing, for most of us, is the most easily accessible of the expressive arts. Even writing a list is telling a story. In the old days all you needed was a pencil, preferably a sharp one, and a piece of paper, and an eraser. Now all you need is an inexpensive computer. Of paramount importance is that you write in a space in which you feel comfortable and safe.

To be sure, writing can take many forms: And, as emphasized throughout this book, the healing of PTS is based and focused on the telling of the survivor's story, the unique tale that has real life characters with real emotion, bad and good, that has commanded your attention sufficiently to get it out of your head and onto paper or a computer screen. Maybe it's a story that can be transformed into a drama or maybe it can't. It really doesn't matter how it ends up. The point is to be on the journey. 'Open a vein and start writing', as the saying goes.

Studies

More and more research is confirming the fact that writing can help reduce anxiety even though it may increase uncomfortable feelings in the beginning. In 1986, psychologist James Pennebaker was the first to correlate the effect of writing on health.[1] He had students write about a trauma they had had or a difficult time, encouraging them to dig into their deepest thoughts while another group wrote about a tree, nothing that sparked emotion. They wrote for 15 minutes a day for four days. Pennebaker then waited six months, noting that those who had written their deepest thoughts had significantly fewer visits to the health center. L.K. Rose, in a literature review, confirmed Pennebaker's findings, and concluded that writing out one's thoughts about a traumatic event can reduce the conflicting thoughts and emotions surrounding it.[2]

Another study sheds light on the effects of expressive writing as an intervention with women who had a history of childhood sexual abuse, high rates of depression, posttraumatic stress disorder, and sexual problems in adulthood for its effects on psychopathology, sexual function, satisfaction, and distress. Results showed: 'women in both writing interventions exhibited improved symptoms of depression and posttraumatic stress disorder. It concluded that women who were instructed to write about the impact of the abuse on their sexual schema were significantly more likely to recover from sexual dysfunction.'[3]

And then there are groups that came together to share their experience, such as in Born in Slavery: Slave Narratives from the Federal Writers' Project from 1938-1939.[4] Or trauma and injustice written through novels like *Ramona* by Helen Hunt Jackson who wrote a romance so more people would be drawn to her attempt to share the tragedy of Native Americans in southern California. The list of course goes on and on.

The artist's model

To help you, especially if you are shy, or are not used to expressing deeper emotions, we've designed a model with steps to follow for each subject area. You can access them in any order you like, putting pen to paper or finger to iPad.

1. Why we write

I started writing to stem burnout from treating sexual abuse survivors for over a decade. Henry Beston wrote lyrical stories and faerie tales to ease his traumatic experiences in World War I in the United States Navy where he served with the volunteer ambulance corps. At a time when emergency medicine would have been rather primitive, he must have witnessed tremendous agony. His books, *The Outermost House*[5] and *Firelight Faerie*,[6] relied on both his observations of nature and his imagined faeries to heal his lingering psychic wounds.

Recording his thoughts longhand, he stared out at the Atlantic Ocean from his desert encampment on the African dunes which always seemed to evoke 'a poetic, perceptive chronicle of nature's year, and our place within it'. The rhythmic sweep and flux of the tides, the migrations of shorebirds, the shimmer of August heat and the fury of February storms, the march of constellations across the night sky: all were caught in the net of his senses and transmuted, indelibly, through the poetic power of his pen.

Beston considered himself a poet of landscape, bearing witness to the cycles and recurrences, great and small, of nature. *The Outermost House* can be read as a single, sustained song, a lyrical meditation on the cycling pageant of the seasons.

This is a wonderful example of connecting to something other, something as mysterious and magical as nature. Perhaps it was Beston's war experiences that heightened his observations of nature and his insight into, even reverence for, other life forms as exemplified in the following passage: 'We need another and a wiser and perhaps a more mystical concept of animals. Remote from universal nature, and living by complicated artifice, man in civilization surveys the creature... a bird perhaps... through the glass of his knowledge and sees thereby a feather magnified and the whole image in distortion. We patronize them for their incompleteness, for their tragic fate of having taken form so far below ourselves. And therein we err, and greatly err. For the animal shall not be measured by man. In a world older and more complete than ours they move finished and complete, gifted with extensions of the senses we have lost or never attained; living by voices we shall never hear. They are not brethren, they are not underlings; they are other nations, caught with ourselves in the net of life and time, fellow prisoners of the splendor and travail of the earth.'

To me, this is an example of opportunity; this fragile state forced a new perception of reality, of animals as beings. We become victors through new insight, leaving the hurt victim behind. The possibility to see into life in a new way, and if shaped from an honest place within, this new perspective may allow a survivor to crack the shell of isolation, begin to reach out to others, even align with goals and ideals that lead us to be better humans, better citizens, and caretakers of our planet. We rediscover what is important in life.

Remember, the beauty of this journey is that you own it, you know your story like no one else. You can choose to tell it to one person or one hundred, or to no one at all except perhaps your therapist. I *had* to tell my story, even if only to myself. I could no longer be a vessel for people to transfer emotional suffering. Yet at that point, I wasn't reflecting on my own childhood traumas. I was simply following directions from books that contained easy exercises such as *The Artist's Way*[7] by Julia Cameron or, as mentioned, books by Natalie Goldberg, in particular *Writing Down the Bones*.[8] These 'bones' may reflect our inner sinew (our stories), pumping blood and renewal into our heart daily through our five senses. We can't forget to honor this and the further extension of the planet that holds us up with no action of our own.

One caution comes from Professor, Marianne Hirsch, a woman who grew up in a family who experienced the Holocaust. She writes, 'The challenge for us in the next generation is to acknowledge and to signal our own distance from the traumatic events that preceded us and not to appropriate them for ourselves.'[9]

2. The starting point

This is a helpful way to proceed:

- Find a safe, secure space.
- Get out paper and pen or your computer and start writing.
- Write for 15, 20, 30 minutes to 3 hours a day... whatever length of time fits best.
- You can embark on a 'stream of consciousness', i.e., automatic writing.
- It can be a page, a short haiku written on a napkin, an idea for a screenplay, anything that takes you out of yourself, allowing your imagination to make it fun, interesting, engaging.
- Be consistent; if only 5 minutes is available, do that; the threads of your subconscious need the prodding to stay open and on track.
- Give yourself permission to take one or two days off a week.
- Don't worry about spelling and grammar and punctuation; you can go back later and correct it if needed.
- Remember, you don't have to have the goal of writing a novel or even a short story.
  - The essence is to first claim the experience that harmed you, and that you are committed to expressing it in a way that decontaminates its negative effect.
  - Journaling can be profound, eliciting information as to where you are, removing masks you might have put on to cover up suppressed feelings or traumatic events.
  - The advantage of reading your personal journal later – actual events and emotions that have been recorded – is that over time you see trends.

- ○ Sometimes false fronts are layered over trauma and reflecting on the journal entries can help you confront inaccuracies and unconscious sugar-coated expressions.
- Letter-writing can likewise have profound results, even if not sent.

3. *Target the trauma*

- What do you feel compelled to write about? You don't have to jump into the traumatic event or a lifetime of trauma. You can start with anything at all: what the sky looks like, the sound of your child playing, an argument with your spouse, a trigger of a terrible event such as the marking of the Tulsa Massacre or the finding of a mass grave in Mexico or at a First Nation residential school – whatever is engaging your emotions now, fear or sadness; stay with the emotion.
- Then when you are ready and this can be a slow process: days, months, years, begin to target the traumatic event that you've personally experienced, one that threw you off-course and is still getting in the way of your life. For some people there will be many traumas, others perhaps only one that changed their life's direction significantly as happened to me. To whatever degree, your emotions act as the driving force in its unraveling. Let them guide you in the safe space and time you have created.
- Stand or sit back and get a sense about the feelings you need to exhume. Are you aware of them often? Are they creeping up only now? I have often had to teach patients what a feeling is. There is no shame in that. Reach out for help whenever needed.
- The most important thing is being involved in what you're writing about. This is the best way to avoid that abstract state where your muse won't show, perhaps fear

dominating. This is why doing work in the body-mind connection can be essential.

- Yet, all it really takes is the commitment to be present, to show up consistently.
- You don't need to always hold onto the pen or type at the computer. You can close your eyes (I prefer lying on the floor), letting your breath deepen and explore what is there.
- Ask yourself: 'Do I know my story? Do I care enough about it to unlock the emotion and set it free?' Whichever way you choose to, begin. Anywhere. This is why a designated space and time can help as support with you simply showing up.
- My advice is to pay attention to feelings rather than an event or characters in the beginning. Let them guide you so the focus is on expressing your emotion, on especially getting those negative feelings out that, in time, will move through you into an empowered story.
- It may seem chaotic at first but as the peaks and valleys of emotion are expressed, a story will come through.
- Patience can be a real virtue... breathe into the moment: something will show up that you can hang your hat or beret on.

4. Telling your story

- You'll need to be brave 'to break open that vein' and confront what life has thrown at you by expressing your unique experience.
- For some, rendering an accurate account of what happened in order to understand the circumstances, to spell out the experience, and gain all we can from it, is what is needed. But this may simply be augmenting the original trauma.
- For many, revision is a better choice: changing a story rather than reliving horror. As Avi says: 'Don't underestimate

your imagination as a means of unraveling what is real and true.'[10]

- For others, telling the story as truthfully as possible and within a designated community works its magic, as seen in the writing project from the 1930s, the Slave Narratives.[4]
- Moving the energy of the event through to something newly created, to overcome feelings of helplessness, is often not only more manageable but also allows an element of fun to emerge.
- We change the story to help us gain perspective and distance ourselves from difficult feelings, emotions that were set in motion from the experience.
- We don't stay 'stuck'; we create a new plot where victim becomes victor, in a safe setting where joy rises.
- While writing, don't imagine anyone else reading it or making sense of it. Wait until your emotion feels poured into the ether.
- If the emotion feels too strong, at any point, go for a walk, sing, dance.
- Don't force it and don't feel further traumatized. Writing may not be for you.
- We are in control of how the story ends.
- Final note: The saying 'Nothing bad ever happens to a writer', can be comforting in the sense that this poison, our experience of memories of harm, that are stuck inside with the potential to be triggered, can be accessed and mobilized.

5. Shaping the plot

- You can embark on a 'stream of consciousness', i.e., automatic writing, until called to organize what you have written.
- Or in shaping your plot, you can use the beginning, middle and end prototype.

- Usually, it's better to allow yourself the freedom and hence opportunity to work backwards; most often, writers need to realize the conclusion before rendering the final draft of their opening since, during the journey, one is never sure where, how or when the story ends.
- It will have to end sometime, and when it does you'll have a much better idea of what it's about and may very well find yourself editing the beginning or even the title.

6. Adding characters

- Once you get a sense of the story, you can use characters to populate your setting, though be careful at first not to use too many.
- Begin to endow them with specific personalities and roles to express your main themes, adding conflict and color as you go along.
- Again use your senses and, to begin with, don't worry about any particular order.
  - Hear the voice of the protagonist – is there a discernible accent?
  - Are they wearing a coat, a scarf, what color?
  - What does their clothing say about their personality?
  - How does that lead to their behavior, their motivation?
  - Have fun creating them.
- Think of their voices, clothing, speech patterns, their primary mood... act them out... make them ugly or awful, have them say mean things... the erase function is there if you need it later.

7. Accessibility

- In all these endeavors you can draw on past models, and the stories of past writers for inspiration and clues, to authors like Beston (see page 229), who have suffered a traumatic event and survived, in part, by turning it into art.

- There are numerous books on how to write, and you might want to take a look at those recommended by your friends or guide or therapist. Julia Cameron and Natalie Goldberg were my go-to guides.
- At some point you might want to study technique with one-on-one sessions with a writing teacher or in a group class.
- In the case of choosing to recall your story in a group, be sure the leader is well-trained and versed in trauma, and isn't simply projecting a professional demeanor which can often, even unconsciously, be abusive or at the least lacking in sensitivity, and risk a return to square one.
- Try not to get too distracted or caught up in the process; the important thing is to start, write, and finish the job as it comes together. Ultimately, writing out my trauma was something I needed to do alone.

Poetry

And what about poetry, a genre that bypasses the rational and evokes fragile beauty mixed with raw emotion? You can use the same models while taking the following into account.

- It isn't as easy to write.
- On the other hand, it provides a more direct route than prose for accessing emotion with the capacity to dance along a feeling and to express a deeper reality.
- It needn't rhyme but that can be fun as well as challenging.
- As an advantage, it's a seedbed for song lyrics if you wish to enter the music realm, next on the list.
- To me, poetry adds an etheric emotional dimension, closely akin to instrumental music.

I am grateful for a poem, written upon the death of poet Jim Natal's father,[11] that he passed on to me during a funeral at sea. See Appendix 5, Writing.

Visual art

While writing and the visual arts have a lot in common, as will be noted below, both may heal in different ways. The release of expression is similar, but the application of different colors is reputed to facilitate a more primal form of expression, and hence may affect neural pathways differently. Color may evoke freedom in a way words can't. Painting or sculpting is perhaps more like writing poetry by the way it conveys raw emotion in a condensed form. Children, as one might expect, are extremely open to doing art as a way in, as therapy, and in the direst of circumstances. An extraordinary example lies with an impromptu art teacher, imprisoned in a German concentration camp during World War II. The book, *I Never Saw Another Butterfly... Children's Drawings and Poems from Terezin Concentration Camp* 1942–1944 edited by Y. Volavkova, recounts the story of Freidl Dicker-Brandeis, a camp inmate, who took on the role of art teacher.[12] As a former Viennese art student, she showed the children prisoners how to transport themselves from their horrifying reality to nature and playgrounds they could access though their imagination.

This rendering of an unimaginable time may be one of the most profound in clarifying what the expressive arts are able to accomplish in transcending moments of despair. As the Holocaust Museum in its final sentence in the preface of this book so poignantly adds: 'Through their artistic expressions, the voices of these children, each unique and individual, reach across the abyss of the greatest crime in human history, allow us to touch them, and restore our own humanity in doing so.'[12]

Yes, it is truly both heartbreaking and awe-inspiring to see what the arts can do.

1. Why we draw

It wasn't until the 1940s, during World War II, that psychotherapists and artists began collaborating in the treatment of severely disturbed clients, discovering non-verbal modes of communication can be much easier than verbal. Art therapy pioneer, Charles Anderson ATR-BC, avowed that his role as a therapist is related to his own need for emotional healing. By tracing the progress of his drawing or artwork, he was able to identify his inner conflict and express how it affected him out into the open.

Anderson offered as an example a technique he often used with a group of people who had attempted suicide. He broke down a common exercise into four phases:

1. Rapport-building for preparation for tasks and functions.
2. Drawing the suicidal object or situation.
3. Art therapy interaction and group support by redrawing the objects to make them safe.
4. Writing by patients sharing three written paragraphs about themes of hope, danger, and change.

Anderson also specialized in arts and crafts and drew a distinction between art therapists and talk therapists: 'Art therapists use media as the focus, while many others may use art, but focus on talk therapy.' He clarified, 'Everyone is having people make art, but art therapists bring a different level of training and understand art as a medium.'[13]

Art therapy has made huge inroads over the last 30 years, validated now to be a very important form that reveals information that allows an integration of seeing. This is especially important when trauma survivors cannot verbally express the trauma they experienced. We know children's art holds and reveals so much about the creator's personality or psyche that can't or wouldn't be known otherwise.

More and more artists and art therapists, whether at home or in schools, hospitals, nursing homes or counseling centers, are using art to heal each day.

2. The starting point

- Find a safe and secure place where you will not be disturbed.
- Don't procrastinate.
- You have lots to choose:
  - From crayons to splashes across a canvas.
  - Dabbling with a lump of clay could be your thing.
  - Drawings in a notebook may suit you better.
- Again, don't procrastinate!
- Simply go to a paint store and roam through color swatches or get a color wheel and play with color with no goal in mind.
- Slowly see what may emerge.
- Or travel to a forest or ocean and watch leaves tremble or the waves fall onto the beach.
  - What colors do you see?
  - What shapes are you drawn to?
- Is there an overall rhythm you connect to?
- Sketching the piece may be likened to a writer's first draft, and may employ a 'stream of consciousness'.

3. Target the trauma

- Make sure you choose to portray a subject that has deeply affected you.
- See writing steps in Chapter 11 (page 231).

4. Handling your emotions/shaping the plot

- As in writing prose or poetry, your art piece will tell a story using a setting, and characters or still objects driven by emotion, while filtered through your imagination.
- While the setting is likewise present, it differs by being both 'timeless' and event specific, like a poem.
- Whatever the medium, a visual piece differs in form from its writing counterpart by the expectation of an immediate response, i.e., the audience views all the components of the piece simultaneously and needn't fully understand the intention of the piece upon first viewing to get something from it, again, similar to poetry.
- Similarly, take the precautions necessary to protect yourself or your patient from negative exposure.

5. Accessibility

- There is an abundance of accessible art on the internet for inspiration.
- There are also plenty of good 'how to' books available at your local library or art store.
- Check out organizations like We Rise, an initiative of the Los Angeles County of Mental Health, that exist to promote 'wellbeing and healing through art, music and creative expression to help the entire Los Angeles County community. We are stronger together. And, together, we are building a community where everyone feels a sense of belonging, connection, meaning and purpose'.[14]

A NOTE TO THE CLINICIAN

Using the expressive arts may be a completely different way to assess a patient/client if you are not a therapist trained in the field. Delving into your own personal pain may be something you'll need to do to work with people who have experienced tragedy and are in the process of working to heal the after-effects. Taking time to familiarize yourself with this field may not prove as difficult as you think and could add a huge mode of application when working with trauma survivors. As I said before, if doing retreats, in the wilderness especially, attendees will be far from distraction and much more able to get into a natural flow as you and they immerse both in nature and the muse.

However, before giving simple writing or art homework to your patient or client, try writing a short piece or taking some colored pencils or watercolors to a large piece of paper yourself and see how that feels. Open to the energy, the feeling of expansion, perhaps a sense of *joie de vivre* to the point of a giggle. Or perhaps a meaningful reflection creeps in. Whatever it is, your mind has opened to a new experience of what is possible, most likely changing the biochemistry in your brain (and heart) for the better. Then when you ask the survivor to write down or draw their story, you will be far more aligned with their discovery, understand more fully whatever they are drawn to, be more aware of whatever feelings are twisting on them now, and encourage them to bring the writing or art into the next visit.

ASSIGNMENT #11

1. What story do you yourself, as the clinician or survivor, want or need to tell?
2. In a writing exercise, what part of the story do you think would be a good place to start for those in trauma recovery: character, thoughts, setting, emotions, landscape? There is no wrong answer but please explain why.
3. Get out some colors – pencils or felt pens or paints – and splash color on a sheet of paper or a canvas. Draw or finger paint some shapes. Do the colors or shapes hold any meaning for you?
4. Do you have a sense of what you would like to create?

Chapter 12

Music and vocalization

Sound. A melody streaming through the windows of the piano player above. Rhythm of an African Cuban band urging your feet to move. Pitch pouring forth, up and down: keening at the loss of a loved one.

There is so much to say about music but, again, Candace Pert puts it succinctly: 'Music, like emotions, seems to bridge the gap between the material and spiritual realms. But how does music heal? In short, by eliciting resonance in the bodymind.'[1]

Eliciting resonance or accessing different frequencies or vibrations in the body and mind is so much fun. We see this all the time, on the streets and in living rooms all over the world, with elderly people in nursing homes and with our children in so many wonderful ways, including singing lullabies to our babies. Yet we prefer a computer or a television these days to input information or to soothe or wile away our time. What has happened to us?

The Ancient Greeks and Indigenous peoples all over the world seemed to know something we no longer want to consider – namely, music's ability to transform negative emotions and behaviors, the 'secret power' that music unleashes within our deepest vibration.

Did you know that the Ancient Greeks had one God for both music and health? In Plato's *Republic*, Socrates points out to his interlocutor, Glaucon: 'Musical training is a more potent instrument than any other, because rhythm and harmony find their way into the inward places of the soul, on which they mightily fasten.'[2]

Music was pronounced the 'physics of the soul' and believed to be able to heal to the extent there were healing shrines. Those in a manic state could be encouraged to listen to the flute, while dulcimer music was prescribed for those with depression.[3]

Our middle ear evolved from the jaw bones of early reptiles and carried sound at particular frequencies, and none is more endearing than the 'overemphasized intonation and rhythm' between mother and child, the baby having grown in time to the mother's heartbeat.[4]

American philosopher Susanne Langer made many wonderful observations on speech and music in the mid-20th century, noting: 'Music reveals the nature of feelings with a detail and truth that language cannot approach. Adding voices soon made patterns and the long endearing melodies of primitive song became a part of communal celebration.'[5]

Beloved vocal coach Florence Mercurio Riggs shares her thoughts from her experience of how the voice can calm the storm and set the stage for growing peace inside the body: 'There is no need to be an accomplished singer in order to "tone" with the voice. We create various tones and pitches when we speak. Sustaining a tone or pitch on a certain vowel sound will bring one into a state of "sound healing", whether it is intentional or not, that can release stress, calm anxiety, lower blood pressure, and commonly facilitate mediation.'[6]

Until recently traditional neurology has been uninterested in prosody (emotional intonations of speech) and for our purposes in the earlier section, ruled by the right brain. Yet if music is a language of feeling, what might that mean to those overwrought by a tragic experience?

Studies of music's effect on our psyche are growing. Neuroscientist, Shantala Hegde, studies Indian Classical Music, one of the oldest forms of music (5000–2000 BCE). From her studies, she has come to believe that the structured improvisation of Ragas (Sanskrit for 'one which induces emotion in the mind') can heal mental imbalance and, by evoking various emotions such as sadness, romance, peace, courage, anger and so on, serve as a channel for recovery in the listener.[7] Music, in its simplest or most complicated form, like art and dance, allows trauma survivors to express themselves without being linear or verbal, encouraging all memories to be integrated using both pitch and rhythmic influences to transform and heal.

The basic elements of any sound include loudness, pitch, contour, duration (rhythm), tempo, timbre, spatial location, and reverberation. Clearly, human beings respond to pitch and these other characteristics whether amplified with major or minor keys, crescendos, decrescendos, intervals, or pauses, and tensions, all ways a composer uses to express and engage our senses engendering positive benefits for our cognitive, emotional, physiological, and social wellbeing. Because really, who doesn't respond to certain favorite melodies?

Along with the prescribed 'steps' as guides, this chapter highlights music's function as a neuroplasticity tool along with studies and anecdotes that demonstrate that, of all the expressive arts, music can heal trauma most swiftly. Our ears are always open, unlike our eyes, where we can decline a sensory input by closing them. Singing is something we can do by simply breathing in and adjusting our vocal cords to pitches well within the speaking range of most humans. As many vocal experts put it, singing is just talking in tune. With music as accompaniment, we touch a part of our deepest selves.

We will focus on vocalization (acquiring an instrumental skill requires a lot of time and effort, not to mention the cost), and we don't have to play an instrument or sing as humming and chanting can change brain frequencies too. We simply need to listen, to move to it, to let it move us, allowing joy and connection to tumble out.

1. Why we sing and play

- The healing power of music has been shown in research, time and again, to affect emotions and hence behavior through sensory or motor function, language and cognitive functions: its importance in trauma recovery is clearer than ever before.
- Music therapists have praised music and singing for generations. For example, for singer, composer, educator, and trauma survivor Maya Rogers, music, specifically vocalization, serves as a means to probe the more profound parts of her personality and consciousness – the parts which we tend to neglect due to their daunting nature.[8]
- Music, whether singing, playing, or listening, helps in the development and expression of the limbic system and the prefrontal cortex, involved in emotional processing.[9]
- Areas of the brain (prefrontal cortex, hippocampus, and amygdala) damaged by severe stress, with reduction of new neuron production, are involved in the response to music, an activity that has been shown to lower blood pressure, slow heart rate and decrease stress hormones.[10, 11]
- Healing trauma requires increased production of neurons in the hippocampus and, since music increases neurons in the hippocampus, it seems a no-brainer (pardon the pun) to include it in any treatment plan.
- Neuropsychiatrist Jon Leiff, author of *The Secret Language of Cells*, comments on how music and the brain (amygdala, hippocampus and HPA system) function to bring people together through public and private activities and celebrations, essential to human survival.[3]
- Singing increases oxygenation, improves the thyroid gland whether normal, hypo or hyper, and contributes to feelings of happiness and wellbeing. So much so that we should all do it.

- Yet there is a relative dearth of research into singing. My own experience with Graves' disease showed me how much this is needed, to heal dysregulated thyroid glands, particularly.

- A prime example of Porges' polyvagal theory (page 88), the social engagement system activates the calming ventral vagus nerve with music. When we are desperately locked in a limbic state of anxiety and distress, we peel the door open, caressed by melody, whatever genre of music that melody may be, as long as we find it pleasurable.

- Therefore, music is a drug-free way to stimulate the brain in PTS, directly implicating some of the main hormones activated in the body's direct response to stress, such as cortisol, corticotropin-releasing hormone (CRH) and adrenocorticotropic hormone (ACTH), serotonin, and oxytocin.[9]

- Tapping along with music engages the cerebellum and will result in new connections between neurons. This may be wholly or largely due to the hormone, oxytocin, that is involved in relaxation, trust, and psychological stability. It regulates nonsocial behavior such as anxiety and depression and social behavior like aggression and bonding.[12] Synthesized in the hypothalamus (and supra-optic nuclei), this neuropeptide is released into general circulation through the pituitary and then via axons to brain regions, again including the hippocampus and amygdala, regulating neurotransmitters in these regions. The hippocampus has oxytocin receptors which may mean it helps regulate oxytocin release.[9] This increased activity of the social engagement nervous system increases production by our calming neurotransmitter GABA.

2. The starting point

- Candace Pert said: 'Surrendering to music may be the ultimate meditation. ...Music directly vibrates cellular receptors, each of which operates an ion channel or controls a cellular signal. Thus you "hear" music with every cell of the body. As you are a field of information and energy, your receptors "hear" in the same frequency range as your ears, 20-2000 Hertz. Your receptors resonate with harmonics of the eliciting musical frequencies.'[1]
- According to 'rocker turned neurosciencist' Daniel Levitin, the elements of pitch, rhythm (meter), and harmony allow the brain to create form out of sound.[13]
- Musical rhythms appear to be coordinated through the cerebellum, the part of the brain that underlies the occipital and temporal lobes. With 10% of the brain's volume but with over half of the brain's neurons, the cerebellum is important for motor learning as well as voluntary activities such as posture and balance and can be elicited by tapping your knee, or clapping your hands.
- Frank Lawlis, author of *The PTSD Breakthrough*, contends: 'Gospel music seems to trigger hopeful emotions that stimulate the amygdala.'[14] He has drum rhythm CDs that start with a 'basic heartbeat and progress in complexity, much like the brain increases in complex patterning'.[15]
- Singing allows for the free flow of emotions without relying on words alone to carry feelings forward, accessing areas of the brain perhaps denied to the other disciplines.

3. Target the trauma

We can find joy in simply singing along with our favorite artist on our electronic device. Or we can hum or chant along with our chakras that act as hotspots for the neuropeptides, according to

Pert, where emotions and biochemistry come together. Here are some examples:

- Chanting during meditation elicits calm. Go one step further and imagine your favorite color surrounding you.
- Listen to music you feel connected to. Sing along.
- If you decide to make singing a daily activity to help heal, like meditating, have a special spot and time for regularity. This can be after your meditation or during it. Learn some chants or simply make sounds. You can go up and down the scale feeling the higher notes in your head grow stronger.
- Find a teacher if music becomes your main path to healing unless of course you are a singer or play an instrument. (Then you won't need this section).
- If one day you want to compose your own song, here are some tips:
  - It's always useful to have a recording device for your musical thoughts – melodies.
  - This can range from the app on your smartphone to just using the microphone on your laptop or computer.
  - Popular advice among musicians is that you can come up with either the music first or the lyrics.
  - You don't have to do it all by yourself.
  - You can write your lyrics and find someone to compose the music.
  - Or, like my singing teacher, the late Laura Manning, you can simply substitute your own lyrics into a familiar musical standard. (Do be aware of copyright issues there, though, if you want to record and broadcast this.)
  - The tips in the writing section will be helpful.
  - Title: Coming up with a title that captures the main idea or theme for your tune is a good idea. You can always change the title at any point and often, as in writing, you'll find that the journey you thought you

were embarking on and was your original intention, has changed during the process.[15]

○ Lyrics: Poetry to music. You are writing a story and the lyrics can rhyme or not. Don't get bogged down by attending to too much detail along the way. This is a story, whatever one you want to tell.

○ The most easily accessed topics involve relationships or a social issue but stay away from preaching. Think about what you have experienced, and what still affects you.

○ Love or the lack of it tends to be high on the list since it engages deep emotion.

○ Compose something about a person or idea you care for or about or have a beef with. Where your emotion lies is where the energy is.

○ With that said, when it pertains to lyrics, you can find a composer who can put your words and ideas to music.

4. Telling your story

• Again, as in writing, you don't have to initially write about a real event or person.

• Don't be afraid or hesitate to fantasize.

• Don't try to say too much; instead do your best to come up with a musical theme that can undergo adaptation throughout; in music lingo, you'll want to get a hook and then continue to write variations on it in terms of form and melody as you go along.

• You'll need a beginning, middle, and end. Music, of course, has its own terminology but you get the idea.

Music therapy

It was in the last century that music became a therapy, a recognized profession as an outgrowth of occupational therapy

(OT) after World War I, when it had success in veterans' hospitals. However, as far back as Benjamin Rush in the 1700s and Adolf Meyer (1866–1950), a psychiatrist at the New York State Psychiatric Hospital, early clinicians believed music to be beneficial for mental health. The first academic training course in the United States was in 1944 at the University of Michigan, with professional organizations following in the 1950s. In 1959 the first European music therapy training program was initiated at the former Academy of Music and Performing Arts in Vienna.

Research overflows with music helping various clinical conditions (except perhaps singing and the thyroid) and has 'emerged as a specialized branch of cognitive neuroscience and psychology, variously referred to as neuromusicology, music cognition or music psychology'.[16]

A qualified music therapist can design a recovery plan for trauma perhaps in a way no other kind of therapist can because music taps into areas of the brain that both are primal (brainstem, cerebellum, parts of the limbic system) and respond to the elements of pitch and rhythm. Therapists Landis-Shack et al support the rise of music therapy and its use to treat those suffering from PTS and encourage further studies in the field.[17] Whether with an individual or in a group, a music therapist can guide those needing release and connection by promoting expression and communication to meet emotional needs. This will encompass a multitude of areas that promote optimal health and quality of life.

I attribute one reason I was able to heal from a serious case of Graves' disease (autoimmune hyperthyroidism as mentioned before) to vocalizing every day. According to Drs. Graves and Perry who first named this disease in the 1800s, a profound grief is at its root. Music can tap into this fifth chakra and amplify the thyroid's potential. We need studies to show this, as so many people, particularly women, have a dysregulated thyroid gland.

I am happy to have found someone else who agrees: Russian doctor, Dr. Oleg Torsunov below.

More studies

- A 1999 landmark study,[18] with postdoc fellows Anne Blood and Robert Zatorre at the Montreal Neurological Institute, examined the intensity and depth of pleasurable emotion evoked by music in certain individuals and contexts and showed they were associated with particular brain regions, including the nucleus accumbens (NAc), amygdala, and frontal cortex that could lead to addiction. A cascade of brain regulation seems to be mediated by increased dopamine levels in the NAc and by connections to the frontal lobe and limbic system, organs we know originate the stress response. Music clearly improves a person's mood.
- In 1979, Israel Zwerling MD PhD concluded that music was the ideal tool to further the social connection between patients introduced in therapy.[19]
- A review of a paper by Nigel Osborne[20] in *Neuroscience: Music* as a therapeutic resource for children in zones of conflict by the Institute for Music in Human and Social Development (IMHSD), Reid School of Music, University of Edinburgh concluded: 'Osborne skillfully supports the claim of music's regulating effect on the respiratory system … [and] the bi-directional relationship between PTSD and abnormal endocrine production, and then affirms with four additional papers supporting the beneficial effect of music on the hypothalamic–pituitary–adrenal (HPA) axis, the system responsible for hormone regulation.'
- Russian doctor Oleg Torsunov agrees with me that singing (his preference is happy songs) can directly affect the thyroid and excrete any embedded negativity in the gland.[21]

- A study on PTS pertaining to the U.S. military found that drumming, in addition to inspiring a sense of connectedness among the soldiers involved, was an excellent activity to channel, expel, and reduce anger and low self-esteem, and could improve emotional balance in the participants.[22]
- In another paper,[23] adult refugees diagnosed with PTS showed that both guided imagery and music (GIM) improved psychological health for trauma survivors.
- Researchers continue to study the mechanism leading to neural and behavioral changes through music, measuring heart rate, blood pressure, and respiratory, rate yielding a sense of relaxation and calm after the activity. They analyze blood samples to measure levels of cortisol, the bonding hormone, oxytocin, and changes in inflammation and neuroplasticity to determine if these factors can explain the benefits.[24, 25]
- With studies showing the benefit of music and Langer, more than half a century ago, believing the aim of art is insight and understanding of the essential life of feeling, what are we waiting for?

Anecdote from Avi

Just a moment ago, I witnessed an autistic student at the high school where I earn my living, combine with another student to give a rousing, tuneful performance of the US national anthem after which special ed kids from different neighborhood schools competed in a basketball game before the entire student population. The participation by both these groups will do wonders for confidence while expanding their love for their fellow humanity.

However the dominance of the capitalistic based music industry, our consumer society, and its love affair with celebrity culture, coupled with the multitudinous distractions of social media, has the vast majority of us far removed from the days when families used to play music together, though those from the upper echelons can still afford their children having piano and/or dance lessons. Therefore, it is of paramount importance for health professionals not to lose sight of how something as simple as singing or vocalizing can profoundly affect the brain and the neurological system in a positive way and how needed that is in schools. That music class in most schools takes a backseat to computer or math class is a real disservice to our children, many of whom have been sexually or otherwise abused, as it can fend off anxiety, depression and so many other conditions. Not only has music been lopped off school curriculums like a moldy piece of bread, its beneficial effects mere crumbs to be wiped away, but it is not taken seriously as a modality to heal deep anxiety, depression and the like.

A NOTE TO THE CLINICIAN

It seems we are ultimately and intimately a rhythmic entity commanded by our breath (in and out, in and out), our heartbeat (lub dub, lub dub), and our brain waves, vibrations that affect the cycles of our metabolic processes. And what better way to heal an event that has thrown us so far off center that triggers it has caused pummel our psyches like rocks pelting down – or maybe they feel more like boulders – and we are helpless in their trajectory. Music can help lift this weight, swinging us back into inherent rhythms we may not have felt since the womb. Rocking ourselves back into place through melody affects our deepest sense of wellbeing; it can change our mood and our physiological expression too. Ultimately, we are vibrations, a resonance that can be stirred, soothed and smoothed, healing us one frequency or melody at a time.

So how can it not be a good thing to encourage survivors to listen to music, or hum along with a song? Whatever our talent, we can all benefit from the simple act of opening our mouths and engaging our larynx, whether singing or chanting.

Writing lyrics or learning an instrument will also add to exercising the brain and encourage calm. Singing and drumming encapsulate the ageless communal experience we all so desperately need in our isolated lives. Yet instead of offering these precious ways to express themselves, we drug adults and children with unnecessary pharmaceuticals (I include most vaccines) that not only hinder curiosity and learning but also play havoc with their nutritional status and detoxification pathways. Therefore, now that research shows how music affects the hippocampus which plays a crucial role in PTS, we must, as a society, reconsider abandoning the creative tools humans need to beat out a rhythm. We must stop disabling the music and arts programs in schools. Boston is the one city in the US I know of that is reversing that trend. How much does education's declining emphasis on music for our children contribute to the declining GABA and dopamine in their brains that leads to addiction, to violence, to suicide?

At the very least, those in need should be encouraged to hum or sing a tune, move their bodies, until their brains respond... Vocalizing can generate healing, and the studies prove it!

And again, music is a 'must have' in any retreat. Humming, chanting, simple songs can start the process of opening up to feeling the power of rhythm and a harmonious melody that sinks into muscles and bones while lifting spirits high.

ASSIGNMENT #12

1. What are the brain areas involved in emotional processing?
2. What can you do today to help someone tap into the power of music?
3. How does music offer an empowering experience to an individual as well as communal experience?
4. What do you personally get out of music?

Chapter 13

Movement and dance

Rhythm. Sound. Our feet tap, we turn, our arms extended reaching, reaching. Fingers straight, suddenly curled. We hunch, we stride, we leap, feeling that primal rhythm within.

The bodily expression of emotions

In the 1800s, François Delsarte,[1] a French singer and coach to performing artists, developed a system of calisthenics for improving 'bodily grace and poise', believing in the 'bodily expression of emotions' that were natural, not the stylized dance of the time. He had a very strong impact on Interpretative aka Modern dance, influencing Isadora Duncan (1877–1927) and other dancers such as Ted Shawn and Ruth St. Denis.

Duncan changed dance forever by creating her own style, saying she wanted to express 'the feelings and emotions of humanity', that her goal was to manifest 'the highest intelligence in the freeset body'. She also said: 'If I could tell you what it meant, there would be no point in dancing it.'[2] And as a point of contact for life's moments: 'I have only danced my life.' Then from the opposite pole, she confessed: 'It has taken me years of struggle, hard work, and research to learn to make one simple gesture....' This embodies this moment, acknowledging our depth of experience holds tremendous power. Duncan lost two children who drowned as the car they were in rolled away;

you can read more about how dancing helped her deal with this insufferable grief in her 1927 book, *My Life*.[3]

Daria Halprin, daughter of pioneering dance therapist Anna Halprin, and a dance therapist herself, has relied on dance to connect with the beauty in life, and separate her from its inherent ugliness.[4] Another dancer, dance advocate Bonnie Bernstein, in her essay *Dancing beyond Trauma: Women Survivors of Sexual Abuse*, observed that the body is scarred by the experience of a traumatic event and holds on to it. Dance, she had discovered, provides an excellent means of lifting a damaged being out of the past and replacing it with a new way of acting and moving, while, in the process, uprooting the negativity that has for so long festered within.[5]

1. Why we dance

Getting back into our body is essential when we have experienced any type of abuse but especially sexual abuse. Just as the subtitle of Fran Levy's book *Dance and Other Expressive Therapies, When Words are Not Enough* says, we dance to bypass the rational and regain our center from a damaged shell. Negative experiences hold our bodies in a constricted state until we can make our way in and free muscle memory. Eating disorders are often a consequence of shame or self-hate or feeling disempowered.[5] I have treated many women who wanted to not be seen and became large enough to repel people in order to avoid intimacy and on the other hand, women who wanted to be large enough to hold the energy and power they couldn't quite materialize otherwise.

This said, how might simple movement, dance alone, or dance coupled with psychoanalysis, help someone afflicted with chronic anxiety or one of PTS's many accompanying conditions? It brings us home, it gives us control to transform the physical and frees the psychological at the same time.

Talk to any child who is skipping home or into the car after dance class and you'll witness euphoria. This is what we want to get back to. And by becoming more in tune with our inherent rhythms and gestures, what can that be doing to the brain, the amygdala and prefrontal cortex? Think about it.

- As clinicians we know now that suggesting a patient move at home regularly to their favorite music will positively affect their brain and therefore attitude and behavior.
- If nothing else, dance or simple movement can generate body awareness.
- Calming our intellectual or cognitive self by rocking, moving back and forth, we can dip into emotion more easily.
- We sense or feel the inflexibility of our spine and muscles, work with them through playfulness to press or squeeze our discomfort from ourselves.
- We work to stay open to what 'is' while moving forward to a greater freedom of living.
- And from the perspective of a naturopathic or integrative doctor, this movement can move the lymph, release toxins, increase wellbeing while being fun and eliciting curiosity.

2. The starting point

Metaphorically, stepping back into a body that has taken a beating psychically can be pivotal to letting go, to surrendering to what is.

Even with absolutely no understanding of anything but feeling the basic pulse and overriding rhythms – a simple step forward and back, rocking – is a movement or dance that can soothe and hence influence trauma recovery.

Using our whole self, our body connecting directly to thoughts and feelings, shakes up our neurobiology with a somatic response whether to an inherent inner rhythm or to an outer melody. Allow access to this healing power as it moves us.

If the desire is to go deeper into interpretation, there are trained therapists, people who can explain dysfunctional movement and phases of behavior, as in Freud's original psychoanalysis.

3. Your first step

Try it now – just move, no particular steps, even if you are sitting, simply move back and forth or with your sitz bones (your sitting bones at the bottom of the pelvis) as the pivot, move around in a circle. It feels good, right?

Studies show certain people need more structure in dance-movement and that improvising is not secure enough for them; for detailed indications and contradictions we can look to Sabine Koch's work.[6]

4. Telling your story

Take these steps to guide you:

- Isadora Duncan's credo boiled down to generating authentic movement through authentic emotion. Look to the moment, where you are right now. Breathe into it. If you are feeling anxious, start moving – a great way to release this energy and tap into who you are, what you want or need to express. And if you feel depressed, allow your body to begin with very small movements; let yourself feel it. Studies show healing through movement can do wonders.[7]
- Much can be gained by encouraging a survivor to explore movement on their own, tapping into emotion slowly with your encouragement, or in many of the groups that are out there that add dance to workouts or use improvisation to connect more deeply with others.
- Clearly dance, combining rigorous exercise with emotionally vital activity, can be an ideal method of healing for a variety of conditions that so often accompany PTS, but perhaps most particularly sexual abuse.

- Or add dance – a brief segment could be sufficient – to a solo show or ensemble piece that tells or revises the original event.
- Or a Dance Movement therapist might be the ticket if you want to go deeper with a witness and guide, allowing for psychoanalytic work. According to Levy, a psychotherapist and creative arts therapist, dance is chief among a wide spectrum of the arts that unveils both the subconscious and conscious mental and emotional forces to understand behavior while meeting nonverbal needs. 'The most important ingredient is the therapist's openness to, and empathy with, the patient. Through empathy, individuals receive the message that they are not alone but are traveling with the therapist in a joint journey of self-examination. It is within this empathy and spontaneous dance between therapist and patient that healing occurs.'[5]

5. Accessibility

There is a lot of useful information out there with regard to the natural ability to heal, beginning with French philosopher, M. Merleau-Ponty (1908–1961). He was concerned with the embodied human experience without theories or preconceptions and famously asked: 'Why is our body for us the mirror of our being unless it is a natural self?'[8] I take this to mean: Why look anywhere else?

Child-prodigy tap dancer Lynne Jassem told me: 'Surfing is the only thing that equals dance in terms of a feeling of transcendence. It is a completely present activity, a meditation. Everyone should put on some music and dance.'[9]

Dance therapy

Research and anecdotal observations show dance therapy to be a powerful therapeutic as well as a performing art.

- The American Dance Therapy Association (ADTA) defines Dance Movement Therapy (DMT) as: 'The psychotherapeutic use of movement to promote emotional, social, cognitive, and physical integration of the individual, for the purpose of improving health and wellbeing.'[10] The European Association adds the word 'spiritual'.[11]
- Elaine Siegel, another pioneer in dance-movement therapy, reasons: 'Most psychic phenomena have their residue in our bodies to be used and translated.'[12] There are studies that show dancing or DMT improves quality of life, sleep, blood pressure, psycho-motor and cognitive skills, and reduces cardiovascular problems, depression and other comorbidities of PTS, including in veterans.[13]
- So many dancers followed Duncan in understanding the depth of dance in healing mental states. For example, Gabrielle Roth, who said: 'Put your psyche into motion and it will heal itself', was a dancer who used trance dance and shamanism, designing *5 Rhythms*, 'a movement practice of being in the body, that ignites creativity, connection and community'.[14] And then there is Margie Gillis, an award-winning dancer, choreographer and social activist who has developed a 'powerful method of Conflict Transformation, conflict, movement and neuroscience'[15] with dancers who are committed to social change, and has been involved in the making of the book, *The Choreography of Resolution*.[16]
- Taking personal action into the political arena may be a way for many to understand the far-reaching effects of dance and communication, what is possible beyond our own story to help communities and our planet to heal.

A personal story of grief

Marianna, a former dancer,[17] shared an excerpt from her essay about dance after experiencing profound grief:

Chapter 13

When one of my children died in a tragic accident at an early age, my wonderful dance teacher called me and urged me to come to class and dance, that it was very important for me to do that. I felt extreme sadness and longing for my daughter which my body reflected, and a separateness from others, an overwhelming need to withdraw and grieve, which I now identify as part of the healing process in mourning a loved one's death. Although I felt set apart from everyone else as if no one could ever understand what I alone was going through, dance was the way by which I could begin relating to myself, and then the world in my own way and at my own speed. 'If I could only remember how to move again!' I thought.

It took first being able to relate to my own body and then gradually to the movement it was making and much later to the movement of the group. I began to be in touch with how it feels to stretch and contract my muscles, and then again, to release them. It felt very healing to do this. A familiar feeling was coming back to me without planning any particular movement – muscle memory.

These rich life experiences and my innate human desire to unify the whole of my life and bring all the parts to order, to involve myself in the movement of life rather than to separate myself from it, served as a catalyst to use dance and regard my training and this experience as a motivating force in my life. My inner self, as well as my outer one, preferred to move and not to be paralyzed.

The way I look at it, the awakening came after Marianna was able to access her mind–body connection and feel the grief in her body. This depth of emotion then triggered her original love of dance and movement and helped her assuage the trauma. She fed on that to heal. She was able to get back into her body, to free frozen emotions through movement and dance. This then is addressing the more primitive dorsal vagus nerve of the parasympathetic nervous system that can be stuck in grief, inexpression, and encouraged by her teacher and her classmates she was able to reach through the grief to tap into the memory of muscles and an earlier elated state of being to consciously move herself to healing.

There are so many ways to use dance-movement. Remember Isadora Duncan: you do it for the freedom, for movements and gestures that put you in touch with yourself (perhaps more than anything else other than vocalizing/singing). Or you can do it as a form of psychoanalysis to heal deep psychic wounds. Or you can simply put on some music and dance.

A NOTE TO THE CLINICIAN

From my experience with my own sexual abuse, I realized getting back in the body after sexual assault is akin to getting back on a horse after being thrown. But it is not easy. I had taken dance classes before my rape, but it took me years to feel anywhere near comfortable afterwards. I started dancing at home so no one could see me make mistakes as I had become so self-conscious, not knowing as a 16-year-old that the emotions I was experiencing were completely normal and were not something to feel ashamed of. (I love to dance so much I almost quit naturopathic medical school to train as a dancer and a movement therapist.)

I think for any clinician or helper, an encouragement to dance or move is always going to be met with a benefit. Even if someone is in a wheelchair. I remember the first time I saw a woman do wheelies on the dance floor of women's night, it was my second year at naturopathic medical school, and I will never forget my awe of this woman's courage and determination.

If you are doing retreats, start off with simple walking around the room, asking participants what they are feeling, who or what they are thinking about, and slowly come back to the room, connecting to each other. Once they feel they have arrived and are comfortable you can ask them to crawl around the room... this can lead to rocking on their backs or sides and finally standing up to begin a dance of their own creation. This process can take two hours or days.

The bottom line is that people are moving, letting their intentions flow into a long moment of being that can't be captured any other way than by what our limbs can create.

ASSIGNMENT #13

1. What is the difference between regular exercise and dance or movement?
2. How can dance–movement help someone with PTS or its comorbidities? What conditions could it help?
3. What concept did Isadora Duncan add to dance history?
4. Who was Delsarte and what did he contribute to dance therapy?

Chapter 14

Acting

On the retirement of the English actor, John Philip Kemble, the 19th century English poet, Thomas Campbell, composed his *Valedictory Stanzas*,[1] thereby appointing acting to the top of the list of the expressive arts. I pass this on with sincere apologies to the other expressive arts!

...His was the spell o'er hearts
Which only acting lends—
The youngest of the sister arts,
Where all their beauty blends;
For ill can Poetry express
Full many a tone or thought
*　　sublime,*

And Painting, mute and
*　　motionless,*
Steals but a glance of time.
But by the mighty actor brought,
Illusion's perfect triumphs
*　　come—*
Verse ceases to be airy thought
And sculpture to be dumb.

Whether on stage in theatre or in film or animation, acting can combine writing, art, music, vocalization, and movement to create an experience both for the audience member and the performer. It holds many pathways and genres to tell the story in trauma recovery, the 'spell o'er hearts' that allows our voice, our painful experience, to be heard, to be witnessed. Finally.

Witnessing

Theatre's healing function goes all the way back to BCE. Aristotle acknowledged that Greek drama could purge or purify emotions – that is, experience a 'catharsis'[2] (meaning purification in the Greek language) simply by becoming immersed as an audience member.

The ancient Theatre of Epidaurus, built on a mountainside by the architect Polykleitos in the late 4th century BCE, near the center honoring Asclepius, the god of healing, is still verdant with greenery and, with its extraordinary acoustics, once again home to 15,000 spectators, basking in the starry night, soaking up all the good vibes.

And the audience can be anywhere, including refugee camps.

I appreciate the work and words of Clowns Without Borders. Tim Cunningham, founder of the clowning group, writes: 'As professional actors, dancers and clowns, we do not claim to be specialists in trauma or psychosocial support of children. What we can speak to, as it arises from consistent experiences in places around the globe, is that when clowns are invited to perform for a community, we see people come together. We witness children laughing at us and parents laughing with the children. We see people holding hands and pointing towards the stage and at what the clowns are doing. After our shows, we have mothers come up to us and say things like: "I haven't seen my child smile since we left Syria months ago." The clowns are abnormal in completely abnormal settings. Perhaps two *abnormals* can make a normal, perhaps the absurdity of clowns in absurd settings caused by human greed, war, and natural disaster, can bring a brief sense of normalcy. That normalcy comes through laughter when people feel human again. We're not therapists, but I believe that sense of normalcy, even in a fleeting moment, can prove therapeutic.'[3]

In this work lies the confirmation of silliness and absurdity as truly healing, as play that generates a different point of view, shooing the mind toward pleasure and wholeness, an activity that reverberates throughout the body, and can allow informal theatrical improvisation to take over.

A word on humor

Let me add a word or two about the role humor can play when approaching your piece. Humor or a comedic work can help us laugh with others, or whenever possible, at ourselves, and open up to that 'bigger picture'. Placing a character in humorous situations and dressing them up with a sense of the ridiculous is very freeing. It presents us with another perspective, particularly when bringing out the absurd. It can break down the shell around the part of our psyche that keeps us isolated and stuck in the falsehood that we are undeserving of a better life, that there is no way through the morass of our mind. At the very least, a sense, if only a little bitty sense of humor, can calm us during the process of creation by nudging us to be silly, to play.

Living through a comic character, the world isn't as lonely or as small as it might have become. You begin to smile as you see other ways to be, to respond, by letting your inner child into the mix, to run off the rational track so your mind has no choice but to fall into the carefree, the unexpected, even silliness or absurdity, unafraid of landing on the completely irrational. This can be a huge relief... we are taken by surprise, allowing linear thinking to fall away. And as serious as the traumatizing event is, expressing this tragedy artistically does not mean (when you are ready) that a sense of humor cannot be employed. It doesn't necessarily detract from the seriousness of the situation or deny that an event was horrific. The truth is, if executed with the underlying commitment to dignity and respect, humor can deepen the impact of your message while lightening your own psychic holding. Most importantly, it can provide a foundation that allows us to breathe, to let go, to feel alive and connected, or at the very least, be the icing on the cake.

I have always admired the Japanese who, when missing a bus and feeling embarrassed, can start laughing. It's an accomplishment in a culture where, when shame looms, a person has the wherewithal to make fun of the scariest notions. Japanese horror films of the '60s and '70s are a perfect example. Similarly, First Nation tribes attack serious issues with humor, basing some of their finest stories on characters like the Trickster. And what about the Jews, truly experts in comedy beginning with Yiddish theatre, the hallmark of which is to deflect pain. In his book *From Age-ing to Sage-ing*, Rabbi Zalman Schachter-Shalomi, founder of the progressive Jewish Renewal Movement, offers anyone stuck in negativity the following advice: 'We need to re-learn how to play and let silly out so that we can simply have fun.'[4]

While helping edit *Meshugeneh, The Musical*, I took a course in Yiddish that deepened my belief that humor was originally constructed to dissipate terrible emotional pain. To me, Avi's songs such as *Don't Marry a Shiksah* (his mother's earlier advice to me before she confided I had become her fourth child) and *No More Jewish Princess* are genuinely hysterical and truly liberating. Sometimes it's just so important to laugh at ourselves. (I was brought up as a princess, albeit Presbyterian, even with my own pink telephone in my bedroom.)

And yes, it must be gauged correctly. Yet remembering the adage 'people don't stop playing because they get old, people get old because they stop playing', we can safely add it to our work, knowing the immune system responds positively to play, to music when the prefrontal cortex has gone offline, and the amygdala is continually reacting to triggers. As survivors, we need to find ways not just to relax but to play. The expressive arts are perfect for this.

Humor can also generate community, a tribe that can 'see' you as never before allows for a special kind of social engagement, as in Porges' polyvagal theory (see page 83).

The solo performer

Being the performer of course is structured and for a survivor can be a form that brings life events into a timeline or dramatizes the traumatic event in full view of an audience. In this chapter I will direct my words to the individual experience of performance because, although being a part of a cast may also be beneficial to a survivor, a solo show has a form that uniquely presents itself for the performer/survivor to stand on stage or in front of a camera, emotionally naked and alone. It seems this can be a most terrifying event for the beginner actor as for the seasoned pro. But what can be gained from such risk? Namely extraordinary completion of lingering psychological trauma through facing the deepest wound of a traumatic experience or lifetime of trauma by putting oneself in the spotlight of creative expression and here is why.

1. Why we act

- Any type of dramatic and/or comedic expression can be helpful to take back power, to own an emotion that may come from a prior experience.
- Theatre's most outstanding therapeutic quality lies in its capacity to transform or transport through the direct expression of emotion.
- Playing a character on stage or on screen can be the ultimate playground for expressing any mood or emotion, albeit while not revealing your own true identity.
- While the stage can be intimidating, once over the fright you can get outside of your old self, and not be limited by a lifetime of baggage you've accrued along the way.
- Though some may view the process as escapist, getting to be someone else can be tremendously freeing.

- As solo theatre director Jessica Johnson says: 'The miraculous aspect of this work is the incredible freedom of expression and radical transformation it provides to the Solo Artist. Through this expression and transformation come powerful paradigm shifts and deep healing.'[409]

2. Telling your story – Solo theatre

- Solo theatre is a performance in front of an audience, 'entertainment' that can be a cross between psychotherapy and theatre. Psychodrama for a party of one, it can tackle the psychological residue of a traumatic event.
- Beginning with breath and imagery, we tap into our five senses, taking the experience outside of ourselves.
- We write our own story based on facts or, alternatively, revise the event(s).
- Like psychodrama, solo theatre can make us aware of that deeper source, the hiding place that has affected the trauma from a subconscious state.
- By creating something of our very own we can free ourselves of crippling patterns that have been held in our bodies, often for a very long time, and can help us take healing one step further, linking the psychological to the physical, and then sharing it with the world.
- This can be the ultimate healer in trauma recovery and can be especially effective in recovery from a comorbidity such as addiction that usually has PTS at the core.
- With the source of most PTS/trauma being from childhood sexual abuse, the further the time from the event, the easier or safer it is to perform…usually.
- Places can take on character traits. What you have experienced in a certain setting can give you an extension of your feelings that are, if you are doing the work, transforming over time. What might have been a comforting

room or cabin may now hold memories of terror. As we begin to own a traumatic experience, our feelings will change. Once comforting, now terrifying, theatre (like writing a novel) can allow us to manipulate settings so they can be comforting once again. Refocusing our energy and empowering our settings, those rooms or buildings or even countries we walk into, are no longer charged with danger.

3. Shaping the plot

- This is your story to tell, and solo theatre can be a therapeutic method to resolve challenges coming from a traumatic event.
- Remember, this is *your* story, don't let anyone hijack it.
- If you choose to express different aspects of your personality, remember they are your characters and emotions coming from hurt. Honor and respect them, give them room to speak, to express themselves, all the while creating and remaining in a safe space for yourself.
- Whether you tell the original story or revise the event is up to you. Speaking from experience, I would say creating a new story from the original emotion it has provoked can be more manageable and perhaps more beneficial than simply retelling the event, especially if you plan to stage your play on a regular basis. It can still have the effect of transforming your negative experience into something that inspires you. You will maintain that pride of ownership and empowered discovery you can gain by cavorting with your muse.
- The characters you create may come from your dysfunctional family or from personified emotions within that have been spinning their wheels for years waiting to be released.

- The one component that seems to rise to the surface first is shame.
  - The important thing to remember is that you needn't be paralyzed by shame any longer.
  - You can personify shame, for example, by making it a comic character and imbuing it with a cartoon voice to pop its stranglehold on your psyche and soul.
- These characters may come from your body's muscle memory.
- As you delve into unknown levels of conscious and subconscious reality, they can take on a life of their own based on your truth.
- Humor can be an intrinsic element in relieving the overall tension for both the audience and the performer.
- Clowning is an excellent pursuit and allows the safety of comedy/absurdity, having the added advantage of engaging the community in a pleasant and salubrious enterprise.
- Your solo theatre piece will be limited to one character, but you do have the option of involving someone close to you, as I did with my husband, who, as a musician, wrote four songs for me, and played piano on stage.
- You always have the option of expanding your work into a fully-fledged drama, with a full score as in musical theater, as I am working on now.

Steve's experience

Steve staged his solo show after mine, and his view of the experience, a bit different from mine, is so important:

> *I have never been diagnosed with PTSD. It never occurred to me to ask about it until you asked me. Being raped was something that, as a man, I was never comfortable talking to other people about, but eventually through performing,*

I was finally able to talk about it in front of people. Solo theater started out to promote myself as an actor. I was inspired, however, by a few solo performers to push through it. A friend of mine put together a very successful solo show about coming out and having his partner pass away. It was beautiful. He described it as far more cathartic than going through actual therapy.

When I decided to put my assault on stage, I thought it was the most impactful way that I could connect to my audience. What it became was so much more. I was hoping to connect, but now I hope to educate about the challenges of masculinity and sexual assault. That hope arose from the connection that I was able to accomplish. Also, it put my story in the framework of the #metoo movement and in the minds of the largely female audience who saw my show alongside yours. In fact, I thank you for that opportunity, Heather. Solo theater is both theater and therapy. Any time you can put your own feelings out in a performance, it turns into catharsis. This includes improvisation and stand-up comedy. Some of the most tragic people can often be the best comedians.

Dramatizing a trauma can be good therapy for nearly everyone. Often, strangers can be the safest space you can be in. Perhaps taking a writing class is the best first step. Start with baby steps. Talk about your childhood. Bring up funny moments from your life. Starting this way and swerving into your traumatic experience allows the audience to first identify with you. Then you can take them on a ride into your trauma. They will follow you. They may have questions. Be prepared to answer them if you can. Sometimes the best teacher starts off as a new student.[5]

The potential downside of a solo show

Solo shows are tremendously popular these days. For the participant and close associates, it has the potential for deep healing, empowerment, and discovery. But performing one comes with this bundle of caveats:

- It is paramount to consider the danger of expressing yourself to an audience of strangers when your emotions are raw, and your state of being vulnerable.
- Creating a solo show can bring up old feelings that may not feel very good at all. If it is a specialized group, people you know who value what you're up to, being vulnerable may be no problem. But others may trigger you and make you feel worse than when you started.
- Be cognizant of where you are in recovery. I suggest not doing solo theatre until you know how to express the relevant emotions without falling back into that deep well of fear and loneliness. because you don't want to re-trigger the shame and anxiety from the original event(s).
- Make sure to have a director and/or class who can help with these pitfalls if you choose to go forward.
- Be aware that theatre-goers who are not family or friends buy tickets to an advertised show to be entertained in accordance with live theatre as they know it, and can invite an adverse response.
- Some promoters, directors or coaches may not understand the pitfalls or nuances of a solo performance.
- Make sure to have a support system from beginning to end, whether a class or friends or family, people who can be there for you as you relive your traumatic experience while you write, rehearse and perform your show.
- Once a survivor feels ready to do this, consider the audience as it is of tantamount importance. These are your witnesses. You want them to be there for you.

So, again, be careful. Unfortunately, the assumption that everyone should be interested in what happened to you and how you dealt with it will get you in trouble, bad reviews, and essentially undermine or even negate why you got involved in solo theatre in the first place. Instead, you must use all available theatrical devices to get them interested and hold them there throughout the event.

Solo shows can convey a healing experience for the survivor in a way that is incomparable. I love going to solo shows, but it is true that 'solo' theatre can elicit a bad opinion among the theatre community in general or in the audience if they become uncomfortable, and don't understand what they are experiencing. If it is judged on the grounds of bona fide theatre, of a performer who has had years of study and experience, then the possibility of a negative review can be disheartening to the performer who has not developed a thick skin or is, in fact, a beginner. It can be grueling. I once heard a neighbor, a performer herself, compare solo theatre to an extended 12 Step AA Alcoholic or NA Narcotic Anonymous Meeting and was grateful to my husband who was adamant that my show was entertaining as well as authentic.

Chat show, 12 Step meetings, psychotherapy, unrewarding pursuit? Yes, it can be entertainment that has the audience gasping, laughing, and crying. But it can be boring. From my own personal experience, it can be liberating beyond imagination, and I am grateful I took the risk and thankfully, received a good review.

And while solo theatre is not for everyone, those who are brave enough to go on the journey of the solo artist may experience a creativity and catharsis unlike any other they have experienced in any other art form. So if all the above doesn't scare you off, begin with your biological narrative, your life's timeline and take tips throughout this section. This gives you an idea if you want to tackle it all or focus on one event.

Tread lightly, love yourself greatly.

Have fun, just don't hurt yourself further.

A NOTE TO THE CLINICIAN

Many health professionals are also survivors. They have gone into a health profession wanting to help because they have experienced trauma themselves. Many professionals are triggered when they see clients who are rape or war or domestic violence survivors as a result of an experience of loss themselves. If this is the case, no matter what type of professional you are, I encourage you to write and perform your own solo show. The reason for this is that you will learn about yourself in a way that psychotherapy can't reach. It will give you priceless information. That said, check the caveats earlier. And remember you can always perform your piece with your spouse or your best friend. Or your dog. (Cats usually aren't interested!) It's up to you.

When I was growing up and an avid reader, one of my mother's greatest gifts to me was letting me know (as I didn't do it consciously) that I would embody the main character of a book over the course of a few days. Not much has changed as creating characters with the accent and personality and envisioning clothes and so on are one of my favorite moments. It takes me out of me and allows me feelings and thoughts I might never have had. It is such fun and so liberating.

I have loved solo theater since watching Margo Kane in *Moonlodge* in 1990. Margo gave so much in this performance, exhibiting her courage to identify with her character's journey through the barrenness of western culture to rediscover her native roots. This character is Agnes, someone we can laugh and cry with while understanding the deeper community trauma of what Indigenous people have gone through.[6]

It wasn't until a few years ago I finally summoned my nerve to reveal my own story. The events surrounding my own rape as a teenager became my solo show, *Hidden*, with music written by Avi, my husband and creative partner.

I have found out the hard way that a few acting teachers can be cruel. It has never deterred me but as someone who had to take the Hippocratic Oath as a doctor, I have had to hold my tongue at times at their lack of sensitivity and awareness. That said, there are also acting teachers who are better than any psychotherapist. Bottom line, make sure you know who you are working with, whether coach or director. You might want to check out psychodrama (Chapter 9), its roots and role in individual and community healing. Or take an Improv group, just have fun letting your expression lighten. Only you know if you are ready to expose yourself to people you may not know and will have difficulty trusting. If that is a possibility, joining a psychodrama group may be a better choice at this point, at least for now.

That said, my experience of performing my second solo show (after many years) created such healing because I had never told my story of rape to anyone. It was the audience, my social engagement party (remember the polyvagal theory – page 83), who rose up with love and acclaim that allowed me confirmation that my story was heard, was appreciated and supported. Without them it would have been (almost) meaningless.

Then, if you choose to engage survivors in a retreat setting, you can pull from your own experience which will certainly embody more compassion and insight. Whatever you are teaching will benefit survivors by acting out their own story, their own pain. It doesn't matter if it's art therapy or a writing class, or other, by learning to express ourselves through an embodied character with voice and gestures will deepen what is being taught and allow for a level of fun and discovery, enabling unconscious feelings to surface safely.

For PTS from sexual or medical or ritual abuse, my Womb Exercise (page 321), a psychodrama-type exercise, is a terrific event for a retreat. It can shorten trauma recovery significantly as it combines community and deep healing in a focused, contracted period of time.

ASSIGNMENT #14

1. What is a personal story you might want to tell, even if you don't?
2. Can you imagine costumes and, if so, what styles, colors and textures would they be?
3. Have any emotions come up for you with these two first questions?
4. If you, survivor or not, could share one thing on a stage with an audience, what would it be?

Part Five

The path forward

She held onto the bear, searching for the light to open the right door. She had fallen back into confusion, the sight of another sadness triggering. 'This might do,' she cried, pushing past the shadows.

Chapter 15

Putting it all together

Moving forward. Discovery. Empowerment.
Trust. Synthesis. Laughter. Joy. At last.

To heal the core disturbance that has been pushed off a natural flow, spun into a reality never asked for in a thousand ways, is the work that must be done. To let go of emotional pain, to transform it. Even if this is scary and it seems undoable. And that goes for helpers too, of whatever kind... doctor, lawyer, Indian chief.... Start slow, breathe into what is, and go from there.

Whatever way we come to the work of trauma recovery, it's important to acknowledge that trauma is best not treated with pharmaceuticals, but that recovery lies in quelling inflammation through cellular pathways in the brain and body naturally; we are then able to rein in symptoms more directly and more safely by using our still point and imagination to tell the story.

I think it's clear by now that trauma affects professionals as well. And that non-professionals are searching for more drugless approaches to inform their own trauma recovery. So, although this section is targeted at professionals, it should prove beneficial for all readers.

As professionals, we each have our own way of taking a case or helping. We have our own way of practicing what we have been trained to do, whether we are a health professional, lawyer, dance therapist, social worker, or government official. And we may have been doing it for years before we realize it's time to find new ways to help survivors (or ourselves) resolve a traumatizing event or a lifetime of abuse.

For some it may take years of treatment to correct the dysregulation of the stress axis – increased sympathetic and diminished ventral parasympathetic tone – that was generated from one event or over a longer period or was inherited. Others may need one or two appointments, enough to 'pick themselves up, dust themselves off' and get back on track, no longer defined by a moment or years of smashed boundaries that have dictated mood, behavior, and actions.

The fact is, people with PTS – and there is such a wide range of suffering and comorbidity – have journeyed through the human experience in ways some of us as clinicians or helpers can never ever imagine, never ever have dreamed of. Be sensitive to perceptions, to feelings. Be aware of triggers – theirs, and yours. It's not the linguistic and cognitive function that is as important initially as connecting emotionally with who is sitting across from you or wandering around the room.

Discover what makes you (or them) curious, what sparks the creative juices… and let the story roll out like a red carpet. Let all colors, images, textures, sounds, smells, intuitions rise up and delight in the telling to set you (or them) free. Let expression rule. Patience can be truly a virtue. It may take time… but it's there… in every human being…

The vagus nerve, the social engagement system that Porges (page 83) links to the human brainstem, regulates muscles of the face and head and can prove interesting in treatment for a clinician. In homeopathy we are trained to look at the facial expression and other gestures or characteristics of the person. I find myself most drawn to the sound of a voice if it is stuck and so on.

Knowing something about Porges' theory can give you a lot of information as a clinician, although, as stated throughout, the first action is to create a safe environment so that the ventral vagus is stimulated. Helping your patients become aware that their lingering emotions from the event(s), as well as any possible triggers (such as an image or tone of voice that compound these emotions), can stimulate curiosity on their part and help them engage further in their own healing. Making them aware that involuntary reactions from the sympathetic nervous system whether increased heart rate, sweating, nervousness and so on can increase conscious awareness of their process of recovery and help chart progress. You don't have to say what this translates to scientifically, i.e., as humans, we have lost regulation of this newer mammalian circuit (ventral vagus), but you could have a conversation that goes into this theory so that the patient/client/survivor/sufferer knows they are not alone in their therapeutic context. We all are participants in this struggle for peace and harmony.

In my estimation, Porges' polyvagal theory (page 83) can be of benefit in the following ways:

1. Knowing there are things survivors can think or do to become less calm or jump on the agitation back to fight or flight, or move to an immobile or freeze response, gives us concrete choices, generating empowerment.

2. If we offer a person with PTS something as simple as breathing in for a count of 4 and out for 8, we engage the vagus nerve positively while in the safe environment.

3. The hypervigilant state can be altered by 'safe' actions, such as smiling, music, intimate gestures or looks, and so on. And we can also add pleasing colors, sound, texture, smells (perhaps lavender oil from an aromatherapy diffuser), bringing distress back to the healing by the ventral vagus nerve. This may take time but knowing also that this neuroception of picking up prompts unconsciously can come from early maladaptive experiences, we can be patient, allowing the process and the survivor's story slowly come to light.

If nothing else, OBSERVE: In the clinic or office setting, asking people to stand tall can give you a lot of information. Are they comfortable in their body? Is their breathing shallow? When they speak, is their voice high pitched and squeaky? Do you get the sense they'd rather be curled up in a ball on the floor? What is their spine saying? Are shoulders rounded, the spine hunched? If you ask them to take a step, is the movement awkward? Do they seem willing to explore their trauma with physical movement, to get inside their body? Or is their breathing growing rapid and ragged?

Fear and humiliation have a profound effect on the muscles and limbs and, perhaps most telling, the spine. Everyone is different but encouraging anyone, especially a relative stranger, to express their emotions, to tell their story without boundaries or judgment, must start somewhere. A good way to break the ice is to start at home by rocking; dancing is even better. (At a retreat you could further this by seeing if they can make silly sounds, perhaps a yodel or imitations of sirens etc).

From the beginning of my naturopathic medical practice, my first visit has been a homeopathic case-taking. This allows for an open-ended and in-depth understanding of the person without yes or no answers. It's a great way to take a case even if you are not planning to prescribe a homeopathic medicine. I'm not trying to reinvent the wheel or your education; this book is simply an accumulation of what I have learned working with trauma survivors.

Once you get the biochemistry balanced or on the way to being balanced (see Chapter 5), encourage the survivor to continue telling the story, the traumatic experience that has sent them to you for help. It may not be about taking your dietary recommendations at first at all. They may need their imagination tweaked and be open to the expressive arts to feel happy and then be able to make changes. My suggestion with people who don't want to or can't is to nudge them to connect with music of their choice and use it with imagery. Then you may be able to get them to a farmer's market or health food store or section of a grocery store. You want to make this an easy transition to balancing the biochemistry and remember, balancing the biochemistry can come from many directions.

Generational codes

There are many 'filters' that can define a person, whether you use birth signs, political views, religious orientation, a member of the LGBTQ community, or a myriad of other groups, we may belong to, whether a conscious choice or not. Understanding the era a person was born and raised in is no exception.

According to Anna Liotta, former Vice President of the National Speakers Association, who grew up with 18 siblings, different age groups have different concerns and different ways of approaching and talking about them.[1] She believes people belong to one of five generational codes, ranging from Traditionalists, Baby Boomers, and Gen X, to Gen Y and what she calls the Globals, often the grandchildren of Baby Boomers who are here to 'save the world'.

One example I have been familiar with for a long time is that older women often have a strong need to share their story about sexual abuse before they die. They have been holding this pain in all those years since the event, or a lifetime of abuse, whereas younger people don't have the same level of shame and secrecy. (Sometimes the world really is getting better!)

In terms of the Globals, my time spent in my youngest grandson's classroom, many born in 2010, showed me how strong and fearless and community-minded these children are. My grandson would much rather share than have a treat all to himself.

Both examples give us hope that we may really be moving into better times despite so many other tragic realities.

Elderly considerations

A lifetime of experience and wisdom in the elderly can be sabotaged by memories of trauma that have been squirreled away or, more aptly, suppressed or repressed. Yet, in my experience those heading to life's finish line can become desperate to share their feelings resulting from the event. They need resolution, almost desperately.

Once you have ascertained that the source of their anxiety or discomfort is not coming from dehydration or lack of minerals or food allergies and so on, consider their symptom, condition or disease is erupting from years of pushing it away, from shame storming their PFC and amygdala.

Give them the space to tell their story, to trust you. Reassure them this is common; their story is unique but terror to tell it is not.

Recommendations for treatment as noted previously in children can be applicable for elderly people as well.

Children

Children are the most precious and the most vulnerable part of society. As a health professional, we have stopped doing our job by continuing to rely on pharmaceuticals, including vaccines, that can have disastrous effects. Now with COVID-19 there are so many wrongs we need to help put right. A difficult time for everyone but it is especially children and teenagers who are/ were affected by lockdowns, isolation, being kept apart from their friends.

The most important thing for children is to know and feel they are first and foremost loved. Whoever you are to a child with ACE or PTS, or any of its comorbidities, if you are honest and gentle and 'see' them, really listen and/or observe, you will be able to offer them a way forward. Whoever we are, we must take the time to consider what has been perhaps hidden from view or left out of our education, training or life experience. There are some issues you will know less of and those more of. The bottom line is to keep an open mind.

I have always maintained that treating or helping children is no different than treating an adult, even a teenager, yet the massive level of societal fear and untruths generated during the Covid-19 pandemic means we really need to listen to our young ones, and yes, advocate for them. Research shows clearly that forcing children (or adults) to wear masks or take a vaccine is a breach of individual rights, of our autonomy. Yet as I write (February 2022), public health officials were still considering mandated vaccinations for all children aged 5 to 11 in California. This is so wrong. Our children don't need it; we are poisoning them. And what about masks? Did you know studies are now showing that a mother who wears a mask will cause true harm to her child, decreasing their IQ by 20 %!

I am particularly sensitive to parents who have put their trust in allopathic medicine and their child has been harmed in some way. My first goal as a doctor was to get children off antibiotics; now it is off psychotropics. Pre-Covid-type vaccines have left children with a lifetime of seizures and/or autism. (Check out my podcast Dr. Heather Uncensored for the tragic stories of severe mismanagement.) Or perhaps a teenager was given pain medications that have left them with an opioid addiction or thoughts of suicide or of killing other children.)

Another concern is gender dysphoria (GD). (Again, see my podcast with Walt Heyer, a GD survivor.) The fact that GD has become so common leads to questions by health professionals, particularly of government regulation (see Canadian Bill C-6). As a health professional, you are there for your patients, that's your job, but this doesn't preclude you from encouraging them to do their own research, to see what others have gone through before enduring what will be irreversible. This in no way takes the power or truth away from the one with GD but it does bring in the fact we know more than we did 30 years ago.

These are two issues – gender dysphoria and pharmaceuticals – that professionals and parents and children are grappling with today in a time of uncertainty. Both can generate a lot of trauma and confusion. The need for open discussions without judgment has never been greater.

Keep in mind our children are bearing the brunt of the chaos and misinformation. What does forced masking all day long in the classroom mean now and what will it mean in the future? Brains are very sensitive to a lack of oxygen; what will society's ignorance of healthier ways to fight off a virus mean over time? Epidemiologist Paul E. Alexander PhD titles one of his research papers: 'Masking Children: Tragic, Unscientific and Damaging'.[2] We know children have an extremely low risk of even contracting SARS-CoV-2 as they have no ACE receptors in their nasal passages, have high levels of melatonin, and a positive Covid case may in fact be the flu.

Not only are masks impeding breathing, thereby depriving the brain of oxygen and triggering acute anxiety, but what about the inability to view others' facial cues and what this is doing to their sense of connection and feeling of being seen and loved over the long term? The mask situation itself during this time of Covid-19 could be a set-up for massive PTS/trauma, highly damaging physiological and psychological problems in the future. Time will tell.

Here are some further tips and suggestions to develop trust with children as you help to ease their anxiety:

- Ask directly but gently what is bothering them.
  Create a space, even if just in your tone, to let them speak.
  (And make sure you have stuffed animals and toys they can hang onto.)
- Find the cause but don't belabor it – i.e., don't stress them further. Is it fear during Covid-19, bullying, sibling rivalry,

unclear expectations, too much screen time or a poor diet causing fatigue, or seeing or hearing parents worry or argue?

- Encourage them to draw or paint or dance or sing what's bothering them.
- Make sure not to judge or ridicule their feelings.
- Teach them breathing exercises. Make it fun through images and sounds, (the five senses) and counting.
- Teach them how to visualize. Add humming.
- Write down affirmations.
- Make sure their diet is filled with organic vegetables, fruit and protein.
- Connect with nature… help them to feel supported.
- Praise them, highlight their curiosity or other attributes to draw them out if they are shy.
- Encourage them to have fun and to exercise. (Not easy to be stuck behind a screen and not enjoy their friends.)
- Try essential oils like lavender or ylang ylang.
- Let them sip on chamomile tea. Or if they have ragweed allergies try tulsi/holy basil (can also spritz when cold). Add stevia or monk fruit for sweetness if needed. Rose or ginger and turmeric tea can also be calming. Always sip.
- Learn about food allergies, molds and mycotoxins, and probiotics and how the gut influences anxiety. Remember fermented foods affect the brain through the gut–brain connection. (See Chapter 4 and my book *Surviving a Viral Pandemic*.)
- Homeopathy – Consult a professional for their particular needs.
- Botanical – See Chapter 6 or consult a naturopathic or integrated doctor or herbalist. Children's doses are usually half of an adult dose. Under 2 years old will be a quarter. This is something your health professional will determine as there are often other factors to consider unique to the individual.

- Start with essential oils. Lavender, rose, ylang ylang. Diffuse in the bedroom nightly. Grow a garden with them. Walk in a forest. (Boosts immunity.)
- Hydrotherapy – Go to the beach or a lake, even a stream. Try lukewarm, not cold. Or simply immerse in nature.

Two comorbidities: Addiction and schizophrenia

I offer two comorbidities with trauma at their core as common examples of treating PTS – addiction because it's such a massive problem in North America and schizophrenia because it is the most extreme psychosis and, if balancing the biochemistry and telling or revising the story is successful for a person with schizophrenia, we can be assured this will help those with less extreme comorbidities.

Addiction

For my basic treatment guide, see Appendix 6: Visit Guidelines.

Today, more than at any previous time on earth, we can find mood-altering substances and activities that take us to a dangerous level of living that snaps onto our neurotransmitters like Lego blocks and won't let go. Addiction, one of the common comorbidities of PTS/trauma, happens through 'a craving for the object of addiction, loss of control over its use, and continuing involvement with it despite adverse consequences'.[3] Another definition comes from psychologist Dr. John Bradshaw: 'Addiction is a pathological relationship to any mood-altering experience that has life damaging consequences.'[4]

We generally think of addiction in terms of stimulants and prescription drugs but it can be to:

- Food
- Tobacco
- Need for a relationship (positive or negative)
- Love
- Anger or any excessive emotion
- Sex
- Gambling
- The Internet
- Computer games
- Television
- Work.

The brain controls our emotions and behaviors, as we have seen, by sending chemical messages along a complex electrical circuitry. These signals are carried by neurotransmitters that connect with designated receptors to restore or maintain homeostasis to make us feel better.[5]

Addiction changes the brain first by upsetting the way it registers pleasure and then by distorting other normal drives such as learning and motivation. As an anonymous loved one who knows from experience wrote me:

> *The constant ingesting of addictive substances short circuits the way the brain normally works to attain pleasure and satisfaction. The focus is no longer on participating in society as you may have done once, but on getting more drugs etc, or addictive activity, so you can stay in balance enough to do the remaining things of which you are capable while high. The problem is that once the chemistry of addiction is in place, the body adjusts to this new state of being which in turn informs the brain that it needs ever-increasing amounts and strengths to experience the same release of stress and unpleasantness as when the substance*

was initially introduced into the system. Ergo the oft-used expression, 'the higher you are, the harder you fall'!

Three neurotransmitters are largely responsible for addiction; they create a 'wanting' to regain homeostasis… the greater the imbalance the greater the 'wanting'. These neurotransmitters are:

- Dopamine – rules pleasure and reward; doing self-care, completing a task, feeling good about activities...
- Norepinephrine (or noradrenaline) – mobilizes the brain for action and increases focus and energy.
- Serotonin – stabilizes mood and increases with exercise, meditation, forest bathing or being in nature.

My father woke up every night to have a cigarette; he and my mother indulged in a cocktail before dinner, wine during dinner and an aperitif afterwards. Maybe their addictive behavior was what originally interested me in trauma recovery.

I was very lucky/blessed to have Carolyn Beaupré, Delegate for BC/Yukon for AA (Alcoholics Anonymous) as my Kitsilano clinic's colon therapist. I learned so much and she attracted a lot of people with addictions as well as prostitutes to the clinic. (Yes, you can learn a lot from prostitutes, especially when you have had a sheltered childhood.) I went to AA with patients several times and did my own non-alcoholic 12 Step program.

I have loved working with survivors with addictions because I know they are in fact full of life, and helping to re-route their craving for drink or drugs or sex through creativity never gets old. Yes, addicts may seem self-absorbed or lie and cheat, but tread lightly with your judgment. Far from being 'bad' people, addicts are quite simply passionate people who feel deeply, who need something to expunge their psychological pain, expressed in the form of physical obsessions or yearnings.

This doesn't excuse negative behavior but remember the importance of brain chemistry and help balance it through first decreasing inflammation and oxidative stress while decreasing triggers, the many faces of stress. Get them to tell their story. Understand what makes them tick. What trauma has not been resolved? How deeply were they wounded? If you are going to commit to working with addicts, remember their specialness. Just be prepared; it can be a wild ride.

Balancing biochemistry helps them with abstinence, therefore make sure to check out Chapter 5. Blood sugar issues are high on the list as are allergies, so regular eating of low glycemic foods helps. Overtaxed livers can be supported with dandelion (*Taraxacum officianalis*) and milk thistle (*Silybum marianum*) – these are two botanicals that are essential to add.

My sense of people with addictions is that it is more important to balance the biochemistry first... and the story will come. Fluctuating blood sugar levels and toxic lymph must be addressed to curb lethal possibilities.

One researcher hypothesized alcoholism was due in part to the fact cell membranes consist in part of polyunsaturated fatty acids (PUFAs), and that ethanol-induced derangement of fatty acid metabolism can be averted by the fatty acid, gamma-linolenic acid (GLA).[6] If this hypothesis bears out, then bypassing the blocked delta-6-desaturase enzyme with supplemental help by GLA from evening primrose oil, borage seed oil, or blackcurrant oil could be beneficial.

Make sure to check:
- Blood sugar. Be aware of reactive hypoglycemia (page 92). Suggest sugar substitutes: stevia, monk fruit, sweet potato syrup.
- Gut flora.

(See Appendix 6 for my full Visit guidelines including lab tests – page 325.)

At the minimum:

- Add B complex vitamins, minerals including chromium 200 mcg daily.
- A detox superfood like spirulina or phytoplankton dail.
- Encourage them to go to a group like AA or NA.
- Offer a pathway for them to tell their story. This can be in your office, in a workshop, or on retreat with someone you trust to refer them to.

Schizophrenia

Schizophrenia is the severest expression of disordered thoughts and feelings – including hallucinations and delusions. There is no doubt that a traumatic experience (PTS) or a lifetime of trauma (ACE) can induce schizophrenia. Depleted nutritional stores and a sensitivity to foods must be addressed, balancing the brain and body chemistry. (Sadly, recreational drugs like cannabis can cause an increased risk of psychosis, as rare as this may be.)

And listen for the story. I think what many of us miss in treating people with any kind of diagnosis is that we let the diagnosis confuse or scare us. Even a person on the street seeming to talk nonsense is trying to figure something out and is not to be feared.[7]

Early on in practice I was influenced by two Canadian psychiatrists who had been using LSD to treat alcoholics with delirium tremens (DTs). As I had experience personally with LSD, my ear was to the door of their discoveries.

Drs. Abram Hoffer and Humphrey Osmond, with the 60s backlash against LSD and the government making it illegal, turned their attention to people diagnosed with schizophrenia, believing trauma can induce this psychotic state by depleting nutritional stores.[8, 9] Their book, *The Hallucinogens*, describes their discovery of adrenochrome from the oxidation of adrenaline, the compound they believed produced a similar effect to schizophrenia on the metabolism. Their study included 5000 schizophrenic patients over a 50-year period, with a high recovery rate. According to their data, the natural recovery rate was 50% if three basic elements were met: shelter, good food, and attention to personal dignity and respect.

Consider the following: (Again see standard treatment guidelines Appendix 6.)

- The adrenals are often the bell ringers of disease; stress topples our weakest link. First on the list are high doses of B vitamins particularly B3 (niacin or niacinamide) and vitamin C and CoQ 10 for the mitochondria to boost energy stores.

- Hoffer and Osmond discovered when nutritional therapy was added, 90% of those with acute schizophrenia (less than two years of symptoms or had several remissions and relapses) recovered within two years and 65–75% of chronic schizophrenics were much improved or well within 10 years.

- In contrast, fewer than 10% of schizophrenic patients treated with drugs alone recover.[10]

- Dietary studies by Kraft and Westman showed that long-term symptoms of schizophrenia can resolve through a ketogenic (high fat, low carb) diet.[11]

- There are many studies from the 60s and 70s that suggest B6, B12 under 200 mg/d, folic acid, homocysteine, zinc will all help.

- Studies abound in eliminating gluten, known to cause inflammation, with communities that do not eat grains having few if no cases of schizophrenia.[12, 13]

- Researcher Dohan observed hospital admissions for schizophrenia decreased during WW II in countries where bread consumption was minimal.[14] He also noted a decrease in several South Pacific islands where grains are rare. Again, a complete mind–body workup with a diet journal is essential before creating a treatment plan.

- Probe the root of the symptoms – could it be anxiety that is leading to paranoia… to past experiences particularly of trauma? Let them talk about the experience.
- If hearing voices: help to track the triggers and to develop an empowering relationship with the voices.

One aspect often not taken into consideration with psychosis is parasites,[15] although any infectious agent can increase psychotic symptoms that have altered neurotransmitter balance and affected behavior. That's why a full lab work-up by a naturopathic or integrated physician is essential; they will have a program to eradicate them, using plant medicine such as wormwood, clove oil, berberine, oregano oil, the Ayurvedic herbs triphala and neem, among many others. Besides testing for parasites, I suggest the minimum (labs are costly) of a hair analysis for mineral ratios, urine for thyroid levels and whatever else is clearly indicated. Of particular importance:

- **Lab tests:** Food allergies, inflammation and gut function.
- **Nutrition:** (see Chapter 5: Optimizing your matabolism)
  Gluten free and minimize grains as much as possible.
  Balance blood sugar to reduce hypo- or hyper-glycemia.
  High doses of vitamin C and Bs particularly B3.
  Restore minerals including chromium and zinc.
  Address gut function. Daily detox.
- **Botanicals:** Ashwagandha. (This can be safely added even if on medication.)
- **Homeopathy:** A professional homeopath is needed if you aren't one.
- **Expressive arts:** Encourage a daily still-point therapy such as mindfulness or meditation, to build a strong center before encouraging them to tell or revise their story by channeling their imagination into the expressive arts.
- **Lifestyle:** Reduce stress (to decrease cortisol) especially with adolescents.

- **Family dynamics:** Must be addressed or at least understood as adolescent stress is a major trigger for schizophrenia. They need all the resources possible. [16, 17] (See Chapter 7: Trauma-informed care.)

A NOTE TO THE CLINICIAN

We are in a precarious time. Just from living in a society rife with chaos and hate is creating trauma. We are all feeling it as Covid-19 continues to express itself, not by the virus per se but by what it has opened up, lifting the veil on both greed for money and greed for control. The divisions between vaccinated and unvaccinated are filled with animosity. There are many things to question, to have an opinion about. We need open minds, an ability to discuss difficult and confusing topics in our offices, clinics, and around the dining room table. We need to learn to listen to each other, to educate, to support our bodies and minds in medical freedom and care for the Earth. Between fighting for our rights and learning about various experiences we have not had to delve deeper into the human experience. For instance, what you personally believe about gender dysphoria (GD) or vaccine mandates will inform your recovery and/or work. Do as much research as you need to truly understand the wider issues so you can be best informed when talking with the person sitting across from you.

As part of knowing yourself and being honest with yourself, be prepared to recognize when you've mis-stepped, as in being dismissive, or angry, or just not there. You can't and won't always be right; you will make mistakes, hopefully easily corrected. So don't let your ego get in the way. Cherish the growth of trust. This is what will

---

let you in to truly help. You might want to recite this prayer to whatever you call your Source. It is a Hawaiian prayer:

I'm sorry
Please forgive me
Thank you
I love you

There are so many ways to do this work. Yet it demands honesty and trust to build compassion and emotional strength. This has been my way and I hope it will encourage you to widen your approach. Because whatever the case, how you have hoped to help, or been thrown into it for your own healing, know that the effect of one person rising, letting go of helplessness and grabbing onto their inner power, helps all of us, no matter what part we play in trauma recovery.

Our children, our teens, need this, our sanity and centeredness more than ever.

ASSIGNMENT #15

1. Design a basic health protocol for an adult family member with anxiety. What is the reasoning at the forefront of your plan?

2. How do imagination, mindfulness and the expressive arts tie in to healing PTS/trauma?

3. What are the major factors in optimizing the brain in trauma recovery? What is and what role does glutathione play?

4. What is one thing during COVID-19 you have learned or experienced that has helped you feel more balanced?

Epilogue

Presidential historian Jon Meacham, in his book, *The Soul of America*, underlines the value of examining the past to protect yourself against what the future may bring.[1] If we apply this to mental health care, we can further understand how medical history plays a vital role in the present reality. By understanding this we can better determine what heals in trauma recovery, opening the door to those of us hoping to change conformist treatment of PTS, C-PTS and ACE with any form of comorbidity due to a traumatic experience.

When we look back and trace history forward, we can see what went wrong. We can see the imbalances that generated a mental health care system that is fraught with quick fixes and barbaric practices leaving Nature's cures not only in the dust and dismissed in these 'modern' times but viewed as quackery, too simple to earn the respect of the psychiatric and medical establishment.

Fortunately, epigenetics has come to the rescue in the last decade to confirm that natural medicine is filled with truths, that nature is science and holds many answers to mental and emotional issues in a world obsessed with drugs to cure them. Probing the cause that spun out into an unmanageable sequence of thoughts and feelings can be reeled in. We simply need to give natural modalities a chance, to learn about them, to trust them, to employ them, and to offer the body and brain what they need for optimal function to maximize mood and behavior.

Drawing on the ancient knowledge of plants and mantras and music to state-of-the-art research of the arts, homeopathy, foods, and brain supplements that augment systemic and neural pathways, natural medicine offers the safest and most thorough way to recover from trauma, to recapture and empower our life force.

An old friend once said to me, 'You feel fear, but you do it anyway'. And it's true, I have been determined to get past childhood and adolescent trauma that left me angry and confused. I turned to Eastern religion, nature, and creativity for answers. These things nourished me and reminded me of the *joie de vivre*, the feeling of freedom when I was unburdened by life's nasty events, experiences that pulled me into timidity, speechlessness, even dissociated states.

And that's what must happen in trauma recovery. We embrace 'what is', the entire presentation of symptoms, until the pain of trauma is shredded on the ground, recycled into our joyous intentions for our lives, unfettered and no longer encumbered. You, whether a clinician or a survivor, must feel the fear and keep moving forward. Because truly, what choice do we have if our goal is for another and/or ourselves not only to survive but to thrive? To build an empowered and happy core, particularly when our outer world, society, teems with chaos and disconnection?

This cure or respite lies in a health-based model of medicine, not the disease-based one we have been floundering within for years that dehumanizes people by forcing foreign substances down our throats. Now is the time to bring out all that we know about manipulating the physiological and psychological pain response system as well as allow 'the hungry ghosts' to speak their truth in the form of an expressive art piece.

The current socio-economic climate, particularly in small towns that have lost manufacturing and other jobs over the last decades, the reality of child abuse and human trafficking, the stress of political concerns including vaccine mandates and climate extremes, are all contributing factors that have us on edge. And then when it happens to us, our family... a mother is raped, a child commits suicide, we aren't allowed to say a final goodbye to a dying loved one... or we are homeless... so much from every direction that can wound us piles on top of us, and we give over to despair, perhaps becoming addicted or the thoughts and feelings become so strong we are labeled psychotic. At the minimum, we experience depression as we grapple with the alternating dance of high anxiety.

The inclusion of natural medicine and the expressive arts in government and private rehabs and clinics must be given a high priority if we want to seriously address addiction, because there is no question that addiction is distorting the whole western world. Killing it. Losing generations. And understanding the deeper distortion of our reality that comes with helplessness and ignorance of what we can do for ourselves or each other or as a community.

Right now, the majority of North Americans are not taught how to control creeping emotions, not educated to detect triggers, not reinforced to keep blood sugar and other biochemistry on an even keel… and then when something happens and someone hands out a pill to suppress pain or the deadly emotion… well, it's just too easy, and oftentimes fatal.

Whatever the source or manifestation of our unease, physiological or physical, it comes down to the fact we need to fill the shadows of our hunger before it destroys us further. More than ever, we need to understand what healing means, where to look. We must stop looking for something outside of ourselves to feel good about ourselves, to distract us from the pain of being alive on this fraught planet.

We need a revival, particularly in the realm of healthcare. It is long overdue. Can we move forward to another social transformation where the #MeToo, assault weapon awareness, clean water and food, and medical freedom movements usher in a revolution so that basic rights and dignities underscore our mental and physical lives?

As we consider the intricacies and specifics of individual symptoms of mental health, and its link to the physical, can we reinvest in our communities to make deep and long-lasting changes, changes that will make every part of our lives that much easier?

When I was a teenager I loved reading books by Kahlil Gibran, who said: 'Out of suffering have emerged the strongest souls; the most massive characters are seared with scars.'[2] If this is true then those of us who have experienced trauma, who have had our days and nights shaped by tragedy, can offer a path forward that will not only help individuals but also society to awaken to truth, to a journey that we can be proud of and excited by, whatever the challenge and suffering.

Why Indigenous North Americans, in another era prior to being compromised by the spread of European viruses, rarely became ill remains a curiosity to me. For one thing, they had their tribe, a community which is essential in being and staying whole and their connection to the land, the seasons, its bounty.

What would Samuel Thomson, a farmer turned doctor, in the 19th century US, have to say about mental health care in the 20th and 21st centuries? Founder of the first self-help movement, Thomson believed that every person should be their own physician. Thomsonian Medicine appealed to the settlers who had brought cures from the home country and continued to care for their own as a way of life, integrating wholeness and a human's inherent ability to heal. And they learned from the people already here.

Dating back to the 17th century, an assortment of doctors and healers, and various medical associations with wide-ranging philosophies and treatment modes, engaged in a healthy competition for clients. The sick had lots of alternatives, places to go, and doctors to choose until… zap… at the turn of the next century, the Flexner Report of 1910 put an abrupt halt to medical availability.

While the public was initially resistant to the 'scientific' takeover, pressured by a rising tide of consumerism propagated by the 'robber barons' coupled with the availability of 'miracle drugs', by the middle of the 20th century, most of the American population had acquiesced.

From across the ocean, Ivan Illich, an Austrian philosopher (1926 to 2002) critiqued his fellow humans love affair with the 'quick fix', observing that 'modern medicine had little if nothing to offer chronic pain management, oncology and palliative care, or therapy of complex psychiatric disorders'.[3]

It is my hope that this book will be helpful in forging a way forward that allows people to live empowered and happy lives after tragedy strikes. The first thing we must do is adhere to the laws of nature.

We've had decades of a re-emergence of medical systems that consider the whole person yet still we are met by the tyranny of one medical system bullying all others, or worse, confining people to locked wards, offering dangerous pharmaceuticals without understanding the human mind or brain. I had hoped by this time for far more awareness from the powers that be. Now baby boomers, the '70s activists, are growing old, wondering 'what have we done?'

Truly, where do we stand in 2022? For one thing, we aren't standing at all. America is on its knees, its hands tied by Big Brother, Big Pharma and Big Agro.

At this point we must be willing to combine the latest advances in trauma research, such as neuroplasticity and epigenetics, with the 'tried and true' methods of natural medicine, by treating the source and not the symptom, balance the biochemistry, and gently guide the story of the initial event to the surface, and out into the open where it can disintegrate amidst sunshine and truth.

As I finish this, Robert F. Kennedy Jr's book, *The Real Anthony Fauci* has been released, vaccine mandates – thanks to so many brave workers and organizations – may be coming to an end, and the people who have understood health are or will soon be vindicated and the hate will stop for those of us who have realized how corrupt our government is and how easy it has been to manipulate those who don't know their bodies and their minds. Let alone the Constitution.

The damage from the spike protein, experimental gene therapy with its onslaught of side effects of heart inflammations, seizures, uncontrollable movements and so on, compete now with the need to address the mental and emotional trauma that governments have created through keeping people away from loved ones as they lay dying; mandates – vaccines and masks, particularly with children; all the lockdowns and isolation; the suicides and overdoses, as well as the knowingly unvaxxed hated and scorned, barred from restaurants, libraries, grocery stores, concerts and games.

Where do we go from here?

It is my heartfelt belief this book will help to strengthen bodies and minds as well as share ideas of how to express yourself or help a family member, patient or client, feelings that have been stirred by this global disaster, truly a crime against humanity.

We must look to each other now, reach out and heal the hate, reach in and empower our voice if it continues to be silent, no matter what side you have found yourself on. With compassion and insight, we will heal ourselves and our planet. It may take time but every day if we find a way to grow love, peace and understanding for ourselves and our precious and so beautiful planet, it will be so worth it.

Gilda Radner said, 'There's always something'. Let's make that something a stepping stone each day, each moment to realize the divine preciousness that is each of us and work toward its manifestation without delay, to heal our deepest wounds individually and as community, as country, basking in the divine light of Mother Earth.

For those who have not survived to share their stories, we grow strong in their honor, shining love on those beings who

Epilogue

crossed to the other side for no fault of their own. We work to pick the world up, dust off the wrongs, bring it closer to justice.

Our voices, our hearts, must not stop reaching out until all hands and hearts are joined, truly socially engaged to bring us all into love and acceptance and wholeness.

Truth expressed shall set us free.

Appendices

Appendix 1

Epigenetics

While a detailed discussion of epigenetics is beyond the scope of this book, it does support the need for natural medicine as a primary platform in the treatment of PTS. Hence this brief section.

Epigenetics, literally 'on top of genes', is an emerging and dynamic branch of biology which looks at how our behaviors and environment can cause changes in the ways our genes are expressed; it dovetails beautifully with the principles of naturopathic medicine and the expressive arts, even if all is not known. In 2000, psychiatrist and researcher Eric Kandel won the Nobel Prize for demonstrating that learning involves changes in the strength of communication between neurons (nerve cells), and that these synapses, or points of contact, are captured by the **hippocampus**, thought to be the center of emotion and memory. Kandel's work was with snails, but it does relate to humans. Understanding how the brain works begins the work of trauma recovery, with neuroplasticity and its expression offering the reality that we can change our brains, ergo we can heal from a traumatic experience.

Kandel and others demonstrated that when 'a single neuron develops a long-term memory for sensitization, it might go from having 1300 to 2700 synaptic connections, a staggering amount of neuroplastic change'.[1, 2] By and large, Kandel's work shows that, when we learn, our minds also affect which genes in our neurons are transcribed; therefore, we can shape our genes, which in turn shapes our brain's microscopic anatomy.

Remember, our genes have both a template and a transcriptive function. The template is genetics, our genes replicate, making copies of themselves that are passed from generation to generation. This is beyond our control. Transcription, on the other hand, is epigenetics, meaning our genes are influenced by what we do and think. From this, we may conclude that the science of neuroplasticity is essentially epigenetics in action.

Knowing that the brain is both malleable (neuroplasticity) and that our genetic code (nucleotides that form the basic structural unit of DNA) can be altered (epigenetics) due to its ability to 'change its own structure and function in response to activity and mental experience'[3] gives us a tremendous boost and rationale to lay out modalities practiced by drugless practitioners like naturopathic physicians who are trained with the requisite skills for modulating biochemistry and reducing symptoms of PTS naturally.

While it's a young science, the bottom line is that knowledge of epigenetics can help in treatment because we are learning what to add or limit to have the best effect on the brain as well as various health conditions or diseases. For example, the MTHFR gene can be a concern because it has a common gene mutation with a potentially wide, negative effect through impaired detoxification. (We then can offer natural substances to enhance this pathway.) Other substances, called epigenetic factors, such as the brain-derived neurotrophic factor or BDNF, can play a crucial role in optimizing brain health.

Epigenetics confirms this ancient philosophy by linking our unique DNA to diet, nutraceuticals, lifestyle, and environmental factors as well as our psychological makeup which includes the joy of discovery of the expressive arts. Adding lab data analysis as it pertains to new 'markers' of metabolic function, including recently discovered unique risk factors from inherited DNA to the treatment plan, is not much of a leap.

Appendix 2

Homeopathic medicines

Homeopathy is a system that must be learned before trying it out in the case of PTS/trauma. Leave it to the experts. Have an experienced homeopath on speed dial to refer out to. That said, having a vial of 10M Aconite for an emergency for direct aftermaths of violence is a good idea. Check my website for more. See Resources.

Remember, *any* homeopathic medicine is possible.

ACONITE: The 'acute' remedy in a violent or nonviolent shock:

- an earthquake, explosion or terrorist attack
- immediately after trauma or years later
- deep, phobic situations after fright or shock
- a state of ANGUISH in mind and body
- physical and mental restlessness
- head bursting, oppressed breathing on least motion
- symptoms are worse at night and after midnight.

ARGENTUM NITRICUM: great anxiety about health:

- nervous, anticipatory fear
- impulsive
- needs an editor, verbose
- craves sugar.

ARSENICUM ALBUM: difficult to distinguish from aconite:

- same great anxiety, fears and restlessness
- felt in the pit of the stomach
- needs constant company (better in the next room), thinks personal death is imminent
- moans and groans and weeps with fear
- burning pains anywhere and high fever but still chilly
- symptoms are worse after midnight to 3 pm

ARSENICUM IODATUM: hyperactive (especially children) with tremendous restlessness:

- anxious and hyper, especially meth heads
- vertigo
- emaciation
- scaly skin.

BELLADONNA: acuteness of all senses, delirius, can be hallucinating:

- excited mental state
- vertigo
- heat, redness, flushed, throbbing, burning — anywhere
- glaring eyes
- throbbing carotids
- dryness of mouth and throat
- There is an interesting article[1] about treating a veteran with many different homeopathic medicines in which Belladonna acted the best.

CAMPHORA OFFICINARUM: one of the main remedies used for shock:

- state of collapse with icy coldness of the whole body but patient still wants to throw covers off
- coldness in a particular spot
- fear at night when alone
- urinary tract infections (UTIs).

CAUSTICUM: compulsive anxiety with lots of fears:

- concerned about injustice
- very sympathetic
- hoarse.

DYSENTERY CO (bowel nosode): This is another medicine I have not used but received this information from a European homeopath through Dana Churchill NMD; said to be a medicine to give when other anti-anxiety remedies fail:

- anticipation anxiety (like *Argentum nitricum*)

- total restlessness
- chronic state of anxiety with palpitations and discomfort in cardiac area (she suggests not lower than 200C, preferably 1M; if 200 C...sip for three days then wait a few months)
- after being given a lot of homeopathic medicines ...has a picture of a lot of medicines.

HELLEBORUS: stupefaction:

- staring
- low vitality but mania
- forgets what just said
- general muscular weakness
- sighing.

IGNATIA AMARA: deep grief or hysteria:

- easily offended, can be very defensive
- ailments after grief like headaches (common in those suffering PTS)
- sighing
- suspicious
- symptoms worse after eating sweets
- dislikes fruit
- complaints improve when traveling.

KALI ARSENICUM: tremendous anxiety (similar to Arsenicum album):

- restlessness
- fear of heart disease – has palpitations with periodicity, every other day
- considered of late to be top for PTS in veterans or anyone who has witnessed devastation
- PTS with night terrors and restlessness
- reserved, conservative people who have kept the trauma inside for a long time then get very anxious
- often have asthma or skin diseases like psoriasis.

LYCOPODIUM: love of power but low self-confidence:
- anxiety about conflicts, health
- gut issues
- bullying to those close and with less authority, subservient to those in charge.

MERCURIUS: anxiety—broken down:
- stammering, tremors (especially of hands)
- impulse to strike out, even kill someone considered to be offensive
- toxic: offensive breath, excessive salivation.

NATRUM MURIATICUM: Grief, suppressed emotions:
- suppressed symptoms come out in headaches, herpes
- reserved but easily hurt feelings
- sad but cannot weep
- depression
- aversion to company
- fears someone will break into the house, storms, darkness, claustrophobia
- symptoms often worse in morning about 10 am
- hates or loves salt.

OPIUM: Complaints from fright—insomnia, tremors, also from joy:
- feel renewed fear if triggered to remember the traumatic event
- warm blooded and aggravated by heat
- painlessness of normally painful complaints
- narcolepsy
- constipation with no urge.

PHOSPHORUS: Very anxious:
- wants sympathy and is sympathetic
- lots of fears: being alone, death, dark, thunderstorms
- worried something bad will happen like an earthquake or terror attack
- thirsty for cold drinks

- easily dehydrated.

PHOSPHORICUM ACIDUM: Nervous exhaustion:

- adrenals are flagged after a long physical illness or endurance or emotional lability.

RHUS TOXICODENDRON: helpless, crying:

- extreme restlessness, constantly trying to change position
- progressive stiffness from overuse or the restlessness
- can't sit still
- red tip on tongue; the rest is coated and dry.

STAPHYSAGRIA: suppressed anger:

- very sweet, elicits your sympathy
- 'overly' sensitive
- history of abusive parent or older sibling.

STRAMONIUM: violence – convulsive:

- can be very frightening; tendency to rage
- fears a lot including death, dark, water (even a shower or head under water)
- night terrors with no memory of the event
- child can be very placid in office.

SULPHUR: anxiety about their health or their family, can be irrational:

- hypochondria
- egotism/always thinks they know what's best for them
- may not disclose emotional problems
- procrastinates
- headaches on the weekends
- thirsty for ice cold drinks
- doesn't want to wash.

VERATRUM, ALBUM and VIRIDE: similar

- disconnected to those around them
- haughtiness
- mania – acute or chronic psychosis
- viride – has red streak down tongue.

VERBENA: I do not have experience using verbena homeopathically, only botanically; I include it because it is used a lot in the UK and India in acute depression to help raise spirits; I have read in *Boerke* and elsewhere that it is:

- good for weaning off meds
- brightens up mental powers and prepares one for the appropriate polycrest or constitutional medicine
- give verbena first 6C sip in water for a day or two or MT 10 gtts in cup of water twice a day for a few weeks (four to five, or until they feel better) during acute depression to help decrease allopathic meds then give constitutional Aurum metallicum or Ignatia
- great for depression, called 'homeopathic Prozac'.

VIOLA ODORATA: hysteria:

- confusion
- wants to cry but doesn't know why
- trembling in legs
- wrists, mainly right.

Remember, there are many other remedies that may be appropriate.

Appendix 3

Plants to support the brain

Bacopa monnieri (water hyssop) – supports cognitive function

Black cumin (oil) – anti-inflammatory.

Ginkgo biloba – for mental clarity; contains glycosylated flavonoids that decrease inflammation, increases brain circulation, improves mood

Ginseng – for mental energy and stamina; contains ginsenosides; stimulates neurotransmitters so they can synthesize protein for brain fuel

Hericium erinaceus (Lion's mane mushroom) – anti-inflammatory, neuroprotective and nootropic effects; improves cognitive function, memory and learning

Rhodiola rosea – for mental energy, strength, endurance

Schisandra – increases resistance to stress; increases cognitive and emotional balance.

Foodlike plants that support the brain include:

Curcumin (turmeric) – reduces inflammation; also promotes blood flow; increases oxygen; strong antioxidant activity while supporting vascular and cell integrity.

Grape seed (oil) – antioxidants: high in proanthocyanins; has gallic acid; inhibits neurodegeneration

Rosemary, saffron and any other culinary herbs – full of antioxidants so anti-inflammatory.

Appendix 4

Dr. Heather's womb exercise

I devised this exercise for my workshop 'Moving to Healing'. It was a type of psychodrama perfect for sexual abuse survivors; extremely powerful!

Preparation:

- The woman in the center of the circle is the woman working or WW. She is lying down on her back.
- The other women are seated around her body.
- The facilitator F (me) is at the top of her head, outside the circle depending on the number of participants and availability of space.
- The participants become parts of her body: the head/brain, arms (two), legs (two) chest, abdomen, stomach.
- The number depends on how many people there are who can take over an area.
- The woman working (WW) becomes her womb.

Action:

- Using the imagery of the five senses as described earlier (page 167), the facilitator leads the visualization, attempting to allow WW's womb to speak.
- Sometimes there will be silence; we keep still and focus until we sense what the body is saying, for instance, it may be that it is too painful to be in her womb, and we need to move up to her abdomen; this gives a distance to the womb and will allow the abdomen instead to reflect the fear without being invasive.
- We must always respect what the body is trying to tell us and go slowly.

- In this example, the woman who is playing the abdomen can put her hand on WW's abdomen to generate its voice through speech or the five senses.
- The abdomen participant can voice her intuitive thought, but the facilitator must be careful to discern what is said, asking the abdomen participant to pause, to get clarification from WW.
- At this point WW is able to confirm or deny, a process that usually allows her to continue her own story.
- For example: WW: 'I can't get closer to my womb. It's crying. It's no wonder I have so many gut issues.'
- Therefore, we pause on the gut, allowing its voice to come forward.
- If there is silence still from the room, we can open one by one as we go around the circle and let every part of her body have a say, always pausing to see if WW senses its truth or if not.
- At any time, WW can elaborate, often with some prodding from the facilitator to help the story unfold.
- If the womb continues to shade its truth, the next step is throwing off energy through physical activity which frees limiting emotion (fear or sadness and so on). For example: WW kicking her legs or throwing out her arms.
- This usually elicits a stronger emotion which, as facilitator, I bring her back to, to see if she can now move into her womb.
- Again, we use five senses (color, sound, texture, images, smell) to draw out her story.

To finish:
- Affirmations can be done by WW.
- For example: 'I love myself', 'I love my womb and all it's been through', and so on.

- The women begin a song or a chant, circling WW... often 'You are so beautiful...'

Session length:
- These sessions can last upwards of three hours.

Appendix 5
Writing: A sample poem

The Missing Scene: He speaks again to the ghost of his father
By Jim Natal

Do not turn your back on me and point to all the junctions
I have missed through sheer spirit lethargy, ebb of vision,
and lack of your favorites, drive *and* determination.

Do not remind me on this platform, cold and sick at heart,
of my fallings, too quick to quit, to cut my meager losses,
my denial of your faith, my failure to construct a temple,
as your father did before you, or to become, like you,
a pillar that even Samson could not pull down.

I am shackled to pillars of my own. But you should know that,
you, with your rear-view vision through the ether.

Clear, clear.

Eleven years not a sign from you, not a simple manifestation
no matter how low I scraped, how much I needed righteous
counsel. And now that my mother has passed over,
you return again just this once, you say. But I know different.
You ride me like a mule, burdened with your example.

Oh, how I wish I could follow you at first scent of morning,
first weaseling of the light. But that would be giving in again.

Not yet, not yet.

Were you this tired, this disgusted, as purpled bags began
to accumulate beneath the eyes, as biceps and thighs shrink back
from athletic grace, hair white and thinning, falling everywhere?

Did you consciously choose not to examine too closely, keep
your eye on the living and not on the life—children, house, job,
marriage a mantra loud enough to drown every mermaid,
art a distraction condoned, though forbidden by the prayer book;
separate dishes for milk and meat, business and poetry.

Compared to you—always compared to you—I am directionless.
There is no magnetic north anymore, my soul a lode of ferrous ore
that sets the needle spinning. Is there is no rest from it?
I was slow that morning, preoccupied and late to your bedside.

Forgive, forgive.[294]

Appendix 6

Visit guidelines for clinicians

The first visit

1. Normally 1½ to 2 hours, homeopathic and nutritional.
2. If, by the end of case-taking, there has been no mention of trauma/unresolved psychological stress, including in childhood, ask. This takes a level of trust. I have found people will know their experience of trauma but usually haven't linked it to their condition. At some point you can suggest the two are linked – that is, the mind (the lingering experience – if it is) and the body (symptoms, condition or disease).
3. The same is true about their creative interests, their love of music, art, writing and so on. You need to find what moves them, their passion.
4. Use pre-made up pages laid out for a Diet Journal: include space for emotions and bowel habits. They take it home and bring it back on the next visit. In this way you will see what is getting in their way of biochemical balance or, as Hahnemann said, 'Remove obstacles to cure'.
5. Lab testing: Consider lab testing by assessing basic parameters. What do you want to know? (This can be left for the second visit.) Possibilities include:
blood sugar imbalance
digestion – enzymes, dysbiosis, food allergies, overeating
nutrients, hydration
toxic overload – heavy metals, pesticides, mycotoxins etc.

brain chemistry – neurotransmitters
hormones – adrenals, thyroid, sex hormones
musculoskeletal alignment

6. Biomarkers of inflammation, the root of the physiological imbalance in PTS/trauma, include CRP, a protein.
   - In regulatory pathways we can check methylation, levels of glutathione, phases of liver function, yeast and alcoholic metabolism, specific allergies, neurotransmitters, toxic minerals, thyroid function, cardiac and lipids, immunoglobulins and mitochondrial function.
   - Blood, urine, saliva will be appropriate for different tests.
   - When affordability or insurance is an issue, hair analysis from a reputable lab can tell you enough to begin with.

7. Suggest daily homework, which could be breathwork, meditation, imagery/creative processes; make it interesting and fun, such as breathing into the sound of birds or music.

8. Remember, this is a person with some level of PTS/trauma; make sure to give them at least some calming substance (magnesium, a botanical like ashwagandha, an essential oil like lavender), especially if you are studying the case and won't have the homeopathic medicine for a few days or a week.

The second visit

1. This will generally not be the homeopathic follow up.
2. It will either consist of a straight naturopathic visit to assess any lifestyle changes and lab results (time the visit so these are back) or a counseling or psychotherapy session.

- A priority with survivors is to restore sleep, bolster the adrenals and mitochondria and calm the nervous system.
- It can also be that what we are working towards is a stronger resilience, to balance biochemistry optimally.
3. Discuss diet based on their journal and suggest changes gently.
4. Review lab work:
    - Determine what is appropriate individually: food allergies, hormones, toxicity and so on.
5. Once the biochemistry is known and they are on a plan, consider deeper psychological counseling; talk to them if this is something they want.
6. Discuss goals and what you have for them, whether it's homeopathic medicine, botanicals, hydrotherapy, nutritional therapy, art therapy and so on.
    - The goal is to reduce the activity of the amygdala and restore the PFC, not in a couple weeks but as quickly as possible without of course re-igniting anxiety.
    - This is the time to begin assessing their triggers, probably the best way to get a sense if you are helping.

The third visit

1. Reinforcement of goals.
2. If this is the follow up to homeopathy, afterwards you can include a 5-minute visualization, chakra toning or a longer Tracking (see page 193) session… even then if 10 to 15 minutes…
3. Give them homework. For example, you can ask them to make a meal with anti-inflammatory foods. Get them to bring the recipes and ask them why these are good

ones for calming, to balance their gut and brain. Help to
educate.

4. Or you can go deeper and ask them to track their inner
voice daily:
   - Is it helping by encouraging?
   - Hurting by shaming?
   - Is the judge a bully?
   - Can you get it to be funny or somewhat humorous or
     absurd?
   - The inner voice has a huge effect on thoughts
     and feelings and can sabotage any progress to
     re-empowerment.
   - Dreams are a great way in. Have them write them
     down as per Swami Radha's interpretation that is
     based on the person's own perception... no books
     needed.

5. As you help them move from helplessness to
empowerment, remind them that the goal is to slow
down:
   - Meditate.
   - Go into nature.
   - Practice mindfulness.
   - Try to laugh with yourself and to become more self-
     aware. This includes the practitioner!

6. Suggest:
   - Breathwork – 4 in 8 out, throughout the day for
     1-2 minutes at a time.
   - Regularly scheduled meditation, even 1 minute a day.

Appendix 7

Sleep

Sleep may be the single most important factor in determining and maintaining good health, up there with good food and feeling part of a community. It affects every part of the mind and body and is especially important as a thorough brain detox. Resilience, essential to recovering from a traumatic event, relies on a rejuvenated brain.

See Chapter 5. Once food allergies, blood sugar, gut support and nutrient-dense foods are accessed and implemented, sleep usually comes much more easily.

That said, sometimes our brain is just too active with thoughts and feelings, which is why writing in a journal can start a survivor on unravelling the true nature of their insomnia.

Here are some other considerations:

1. Circadian rhythm[1, 2, 3, 4, 5] and our pineal gland: Our 24-hour natural clock responds to light and dark. The pineal gland is part of the endocrine system that regulates so many bodily functions including thought, intuition and even clairvoyance, and is thought to be a door to higher consciousness. Unfortunately, it can calcify, primarily as a result of exposure to fluoride and pesticides.
   - Iodine chelates fluoride (and other heavy metals).
   - Turmeric helps as well
   - Citrus fruits daily is a recommendation along with foods with chlorophyll (dark leafy greens, spirulina, chlorella) and boron (avocados, beans, walnuts, bananas)

- Vitamin K2 is in dark leafy greens as well as grass-fed meat and dairy – what Weston Price called Activator X.
- Chaga mushrooms are also said to help decalcify and activate the pineal gland.

2. Sunshine:
   - When the sun's rays hit the retina, the brain releases serotonin, the happy neurotransmitter that flips over to melatonin at night.
   - This also increases sulfate synthesis, boosting detoxification.
   - Provides vitamin D that dramatically boosts the immune system.

3. Glymph system: The brain has its own detoxification system that functions at night and controls our hormone levels:
   - After only a night of disturbed sleep, cortisol, TSH and ghrelin (hunger hormone) levels can rise.
   - Or conversely those affecting testosterone, growth hormone and insulin sensitivity can decrease, resulting in:
     - feelings of emotional distress
     - food sensitivities
     - blood sugar dysregulation.

4. Sleep deprivation or excessive sleep and increases inflammation.

5. In chronic insomnia:
   - The adrenal glands are the first to become exhausted, leading to a possible decline in daytime cognition, possible depression, and increased anxiety.
   - Thyroid disruption (or is an indication).
   - May need the amino acid tyrosine – this is high in spirulina and phytoplankton.

6. Frequent nightmares can promote:
   - A vicious cycle that triggers difficult memories.

- Autoimmune disease because of its association with adrenal gland function and deeper negative feelings.
7. Increase intestinal permeability that can lead to:
   - insulin resistance
   - weight gain or loss
   - immune dysfunction including:
     ○ allergies
     ○ increased potential for infections
     ○ metabolic syndrome (diabetes, hypertension)
     ○ parasites.[6]
8. Nutrients that can help include:
   - Foods high in BDNFs, brain-derived neurotrophic factors and flavonoids.
   - Check allergies and intolerances.
   - Protein before bed for better quality sleep.
9. Vitamins and minerals:
   - Get tested. Depending on deficiencies you might just take spirulina or phytoplankton. The added bonus is they both contain iodine.
   - Magnesium: calms and is said to mimic the action of the sleep hormone, melatonin.
   - Vitamin A: deficiency may alter brain waves in non-REM sleep causing less restorative sleep.
   - Vitamin B1 (thiamine) and B2 (riboflavin): essential to produce the sleep hormone, melatonin.
   - Vitamin B3 (niacin): increases REM sleep, improves quality and length of sleep by converting tryptophan to serotonin.
   - Vitamins B6 and folate: cofactors for several neurotransmitters including serotonin and dopamine that regulate sleep.
   - Folate: methylation pathways for optimal detox.
   - Vitamin B12: normalizes circadian rhythms, both oral and IV.

10. Botanicals:
    - Magnolia can decrease cortisol levels, and so calms before bed.
    - Valerian, popular but is fickle, can also do nothing.
    - Scutellaria (when insomnia is accompanied by agitation).
11. Homeopathy: you can try low potencies but check with your homeopath:
    - Coffea cruda
    - Nux vomica.
12. Hydrotherapy:
    - a cold dunk can bring the PNS in line promoting sleep, or just a cold splash of water on the face can help.
13. Detox:
    - Check toxic metals through hair analysis or urine test.
14. Breath work:
    - Count for 4 on inhales, hold for 7, exhale for 8.
15. Sound frequency: Also called brainwave entrainment, this method stimulates the brain by using a pulsing sound, light, or electromagnetic field to enter a specific state such as inducing sleep. The pulses encourage the brainwaves to align to the frequency of a given beat.

Appendix 8

Acute PTS

This book is about lingering psychological trauma, engaging professionals and laypeople in the many treatment options and activities available to maximize trauma recovery. But what if this hasn't lingered – say a traumatic event happened 5 minutes or 2 hours ago? The following can help in an acute attack whether a shooting, an assault, a terrifying earthquake or other such event.

General suggestions for survivors or helpers

- Find help and safety as soon as it is safe and you are able.
- If a sexual assault as much as you want to shower, first get a rape kit. Demand it.
- Homeopathic Aconitum (see page 313) given immediately, all high potency. One dose of 10 M every hour, although lower potencies more frequently if that's what you have available. Arsenicum (second choice to Aconitum for the fear, third Scutellaria). Arnica if hurt physically can also be indicated.
- Get something to squeeze, to pour the fear and shock out of the muscles.
- Rock back and forth or in a circle on sitting bones.
- Hum if it's safe.
- Try to feel your/their pulse. Count into it. Breathe into it: inhale for 4, breathe out for 4. Breathe in for 4, out for 5. Continue breathing in as slowly as possible for 4 and add 1 beat out on the exhale. So 4 in, 5 out, 4 in, 6 out until you get to 8. You can pause between in and out but only to the count of 4 initially.

- Feel the light, sun or not, surrounding you.
- Try the following from the Incredible String Band:

  'May the long time sun shine upon you/me/us [in this case suggest using *me*]
  'All love surrounds me and the pure light within me guides my way on.'

Think it, hum it, chant it; whatever works for you. (This song, turned mantra, was written by Scottish musician and band member, Mike Heron.[1] New to meditation as a teenager in the 60s I was lucky to attend an Incredible String Band concert. It was incredible!) Or simply hum 'mmm'. This will help the thyroid gland that is working with your adrenals and vagus nerve to calm you. You can also put your hands in prayer pose to increase GABA. (Don't worry if you don't think you are religious or spiritual.)

- Sip water or teas like chamomile, diluted green tea with its high levels of l-theanine.
- Take *Ashwagandha* or *Scutellaria* and/or *Glyccyrhiza*/licorice botanically. (See Chapter 6 for other choices.)
- Cold cloth to the face – this increases vagus nerve activity. (Look up vagal activity in Index for more.)
- See drheatherherington.com for an acute trauma kit.

Appendix 9

The International Trauma Questionnaire (ITQ)[1]

Note: Reproduced with the kind permission of Marylène Cloitre.

Overview

The attached instrument is a brief, simply-worded measure, focusing only on the core features of PTSD and CPTSD, and employs straightforward diagnostic rules. The ITQ was developed to be consistent with the organizing principles of the ICD-11, as set forth by the World Health Organization (WHO), which are to maximize clinical utility and ensure international applicability through a focus on the core symptoms of a given disorder. The ITQ is freely available in the public domain to all interested parties. Evaluation of the measure continues particularly as it relates to the definition of functional impairment for both PTSD and CPTSD and possibly the content of the items as they might relate to being predictive of differential treatment outcome.

Diagnostic algorithms

These are as follows:

> **PTSD:** A diagnosis of PTSD requires the endorsement of one of two symptoms from the symptom clusters of (1) re-experiencing in the here and now, (2) avoidance, and (3) sense of current threat, plus endorsement of at least one indicator of functional impairment associated with these symptoms. Endorsement of a symptom or functional impairment item is defined as a score of >2.

CPTSD: A diagnosis of CPTSD requires the endorsement of one of two symptoms from each of the three PTSD symptoms clusters (re-experiencing in the here and now, avoidance, and sense of current threat) and one of two symptoms from each of the three Disturbances in Self-Organization (DSO) clusters: (1) affective dysregulation, (2) negative self-concept, and (3) disturbances in relationships. Functional impairment must be identified where at least one indicator of functional impairment is endorsed related to the PTSD symptoms and one indicator of functional impairment is endorsed related to the DSO symptoms. Endorsement of a symptom or functional impairment item is defined as a score of >2.

An individual can receive a diagnosis of either PTSD or CPTSD, not both. If a person meets the criteria for CPTSD, that person does not also receive a PTSD diagnosis.

Scoring instructions are available at the end of this guide (page 339).

The questionnaire

Instructions: Please identify the experience that troubles you most and answer the questions in relation to this experience, starting with a brief description of the experience and when it occurred.

Brief description of the experience:

Appendix 9

When did the experience occur? (circle one)
  a. less than 6 months ago
  b. 6 to 12 months ago
  c. 1 to 5 years ago
  d. 5 to 10 years ago
  e. 10 to 20 years ago
  f. more than 20 years ago

Below are a number of problems that people sometimes report in response to traumatic or stressful life events. Please read each item carefully, then circle one of the numbers to the right to indicate how much you have been bothered by that problem in the past month.

	Not at all	A little bit	Moderately	Quite a bit	Extremely
P1. Having upsetting dreams that replay part of the experience or are clearly related to the experience?	0	1	2	3	4
P2. Having powerful images or memories that sometimes come into your mind in which you feel the experience is happening again in the here and now?	0		2	3	4
P3. Avoiding internal reminders of the experience (for example, thoughts, feelings, or physical sensations)?	0	1	2	3	4
P4. Avoiding external reminders of the experience (for example, people, places, conversations, objects, activities, or situations)?	0	1	2	3	4
P5. Being "super-alert", watchful, or on guard?	0	1	2	3	4
P6. Feeling jumpy or easily startled?	0	1	2	3	4

In the past month have the above problems:

	Not at all	A little bit	Moderately	Quite a bit	Extremely
P7. Affected your relationships or social life?					
P8. Affected your work or ability to work?					
P9. Affected any other important part of your life such as parenting, or school or college work, or other important activities?					

Below are problems that people who have had stressful or traumatic events sometimes experience. The questions refer to ways you typically feel, ways you typically think about yourself and ways you typically relate to others. Answer the following thinking about how true are the following for you?

	Not at all	A little bit	Moderately	Quite a bit	Extremely
C1. When I am upset, it takes me a long time to calm down.					
C2. I feel numb or emotionally shut down.					
C3. I feel like a failure.					
C4. I feel worthless.					
C5. I feel distant or cut off from people.					
C6. I find it hard to stay emotionally close to people.					

In the past month, have the above problems in emotions, in beliefs about yourself and in relationships:

	Not at all	A little bit	Moderately	Quite a bit	Extremely
C7. Created concern or distress about your relationships or social life?					
C8. Affected your work or ability to work?					
C9. Affected any other important parts of your life such as parenting, or school or college work, or other important activities?					

1. Diagnostic scoring for PTSD and CPTSD

PTSD

If P1 or P2 > 2 criteria for Re-experiencing in the here and now (Re_dx) met

If P3 or P4 > 2 criteria for Avoidance (Av_dx) met

If P5 or P6 > 2 criteria for Sense of current threat (Th_dx) met AND

At least one of P7, P8, or P9 > 2 meets criteria for PTSD functional impairment (PTSDFI)

If criteria for 'Re_dx' AND 'Av_dx' AND 'Th_dx' AND 'PTSDFI' are met, the criteria for PTSD are met.

CPTSD

> If C1 or C2 > 2 criteria for Affective dysregulation (AD_dx) met
>
> If C3 or C4 > 2 criteria for Negative self-concept (NSC_dx) met
>
> If C5 or C6 > 2 criteria for Disturbances in relationships (DR_dx) met
>
> AND
>
> At least one of C7, C8, or C9 > 2 meets criteria for DSO functional impairment (DSOFI)

> If criteria for 'AD_dx' AND 'NSC_dx' AND 'DR_dx', and 'DSOFI' are met, the criteria for DSO are met.

PTSD is diagnosed if the criteria for PTSD are met but NOT for DSO.

CPTSD is diagnosed if the criteria for PTSD are met AND criteria for DSO are met.

Not meeting the criteria for PTSD or meeting only the criteria for DSO results in no diagnosis.

2. Dimensional scoring for PTSD and CPTSD

Scores can be calculated for each PTSD and DSO symptom cluster and summed to produce PTSD and DSO scores.

PTSD

> Sum of Likert scores for P1 and P2 = Re-experiencing in the here and now score (Re)
>
> Sum of Likert scores for P3 and P4 = Avoidance score (Av)
>
> Sum of Likert scores for P3 and P4 = Sense of current threat (Th)
>
> PTSD score = Sum of Re, Av, and Th

DSO

Sum of Likert scores for C1 and C2 = Affective dysregulation (AD)

Sum of Likert scores for C3 and C4 = Negative self-concept (NSC)

Sum of Likert scores for C5 and C6 = Disturbances in relationships (DR)

DSO score = Sum of AD, NSC, and DR

Bibliography

Ballentine R. *Radical Healing.* New York: Three Rivers Press. 1999.

Barrus C. *Nursing the Insane.* New York: MacMillan Co; 1908. Reprinted October 1915. Reprinted by Bibliolife.

Bastyr students. *Naturopathic Treatment Notebook.* NCNM (NUNM) Library reprint. 1984.

Boyle W, Saine A. *Lectures in Naturopathic Hydrotherapy.* Sandy: Eclectic Medical Publications, 1988: 17-18

Breggin PR. *Toxic Psychiatry.* New York: St Martin's Press; 1991.

Breggin PR. *Covid-19 and the Global Predator: We are the Prey.* Ithaca, New York: Lake Edge Press; 2021.

Brown ER. *Rockefeller Medicine Men.* L.A.: University of California Press;1981.

Cayleff SE. *Wash and Be Healed.* Philadelphia: Temple University Press. 1991.

Cayleff SE. *Nature's path: A History of Naturopathic Healing in America.* Baltimore: Johns Hopkins University Press; 2016.

Cass H. *8 Weeks to Vibrant Health.* New York: McGraw-Hill; 2004.

Colbert D. *Deadly Emotions.* Nashville, TN: Thomas Nelson Inc; 2003.

Cowan T. *Vaccines, Autoimmunity etc.* VT: Chelsea Green Publishing; 2018.

Czeranko S. *Mental Culture in Nat. Med.* Portland OR: NUNM Press; 2017.

De Schepper L. *Hahnemann Revisited: A Textbook of Classical Homeopathy for the Professional.* Full of Life Publishing; 1999.

Doidge N. *The Brain That Changes Itself.* New York: Penguin; 2007.

Doidge N. *The Brain's Way of Healing.* New York: Penguin; 2016.

Dowling M. *Sergeant Rex.* New York: Atria Publishing; 2012.

Duke J. *The Green Pharmacy.* Erasmus, Pennsylvania: Rodale; 1997.

Edelman GM. *Second Nature.* New Haven, CT: Yale Univ Press; 2006.

Freeman D, Freeman JR. *Anxiety: A Very Short Intro.* Oxford Univ Press; 2012.

George N. *The Little Paris Bookshop.* New York: Crown Publishers; 2015

Gottfried S. *The Hormone Cure.* New York: Scribner; 2013.

Gotzsche PC. *Deadly Medicines and Organized Crime.* London: Radcliffe; 2013.

Handley JB. *How to End the Autism Epidemic.* White River J, VT: Chelsea Green Publishing; 2018.

Hari J. *Los Connections.* New York: Bloomsbury; 2018.

Herington HL. *Flawed.* Vancouver; 2006.

Herington HL. *Surviving a Viral Pandemic through the lens of a naturopathic medical doctor.* Los Angeles; 2020.

Hirsch M. *The Generation of Postmemory: Wriitng and Visual Culture After the Holocaust.* New York: Columbia University Press. 2012.

Humphries S, Bystrianyk R. *Dissolving Illusions: Disease, Vaccines and the Forgotten History.* Createspace; 2013.

Hutchens AR. *Indian Herbology of North America.* Windsor, Canada: Merco; 1973.

Jaynes J. *The Origin of Consciousness in the Breakdown of the Bicameral Mind.* 2nd Ed. Boston: Houghton Mifflin; 1990.

Bibliography

Kennedy RF. *The Real Anthony Fauci*. New York: Skyhorse Publishing; 2021.

Kipper D. (Steven Whitney). *The Addiction Solution*. Emmaus, PA: Rodale; 2010.

Kuhne L. *The New Science of Healing*. Unknown; 1891.

Lawlis F. *The PTSD Breakthrough*. Naperville, Illinois: Sourcebooks; 2010.

Leeds J. *Power of Sound*. Rochester, VT.: Healing Arts Press; 2001.

LeBaron M, Acland AF, MacLeod C. *The Choreography of Resolution*. American Bar Association; 2014.

Levy FJ. *Dance and Other Expressive Art Therapies: when words are not enough*. New York: Routledge; 1995.

Lovello WR. *Stress and Health* 3rd Ed. Los Angeles: Sage: 2016.

Lyon MR. *Healing the Hyperactive Brain*. Calgary, AB: Focused Publ.; 2000.

Maltz W. *The Sexual Healing Journal: A Guide for Survivors of Sexual Abuse*. 3rd Ed. New York: William Morrow; 2012.

Manookian L. (documentary film) *The Greater Good*

Marks-Tatlow T. *Clinical Intuition in Psychotherapy*. New York: Norton; 2012.

Matsakis A. *Loving Someone with PTSD*. Oakland, CA: New Harbinger; 2013.

McGilchrist I. *The Master and his Emissary*. New Haven, CT: Yale Univ. Press; 2009.

Mead JH, Lommen ET. *Slim, Sane & Sexy*. Or. City, OR: Calaroga Pub.; 2008

Moynihan R, Cassels A. *Selling Sickness*. New York: Nation Books; 2005.

Myhill S. *Diagnosis and Treatment of Chronic Fatigue Syndrome and Myalgic Encephalitis*. London, UK: Hammersmith Health Books; 2017.

Northrup C. *Women's Bodies, Women's Wisdom*. New York: Bantam; 1998.

Ogden G. *Extraordinary Sex Therapy.* U.K: Taylor and Francis; 2017. (And many more books, videos and articles.)

Pizzorno J, Murray M. *Encyclopedia of Natural Medicine (1990)* and numerous other books since.

Porges SW. *The Polyvagal Theory: Neurophysiological Foundations of Emotion, Attachment, Communication and Self Regulation.* New York: W.W. Norton and Co; 2011.

Rama S et al. *Science of Breath.* Honesdale, PA: Himalayan Inst; 1979.

Raja S. *Overcoming Trauma and PTSD.* Oakland, CA: New Harbinger. 2012.

Rosen R. *The World Split Open.* New York: Penguin; 2000.

Seneff S. *Toxic Legacy: how the weedkiller glyphosate is destroying our health and the environment.* White River J, VT: Chelsea Green; 2021.

Shawn T. *Dance We Must.* London, GB: Dennis Dobson, publisher; 1940.

Shawn T. *Every little movement: a book about F. Delsarte.* Pittsfield, MA: Eagle Press;1954.

Sherman A. *Reservation Blues.* Grove Press. 2005.

Silver-Isenstadt JL. *Shameless: The Visionary Life of Mary Gove Nichols.* Baltimore: Johns Hopkins Press; 2016.

Steelsmith L. *Natural Choices for Women's Health.* NY: Three Rivers Pr. 2005.

Stillwagon K. *The Silent Killers.* Todd and Honeywell; 1984.

Sumner J. *American Household Botany.* Portland, OR: Timber Press. 2004.

Teachout Z. *Corruption in America.* Cambridge: Harvard University Press; 2014.

Thompson SB ed. *Born Into Slavery: Voices from the Past. Federal Writers Project;* 2015.

Treuer D. *Rez Life.* Washington, DC: Atlantic Monthly; 2012.

Thomas A. *Healing Family Patterns: Ancestral Lineage Clearing.* Ancestral Wisdom Press. 2018.

Tommey P et al. (documentary film) VAXED ll : The People's Truth

Vaughn B. *Hawthorn: The Tree That Has Nourished, Healed, and Inspired through the Ages*. New Haven CT: Yale University Press. 2015.

Volakova H ed. *I never saw another butterfly*. New York: Schocken Books; 1993.

Wakefield A, Bigtree D. (documentary film) VAXED 1: From Cover up to Catastrophe

Weed S. *Menopausal Years*. Woodstock, New York: Ash Tree Publishing; 1992.

Weiss RF. *Herbal Medicine*. Beaconsfield, England: Beaconsfield Publ.1988.

Willis M. *Plandemic, Fear is the Virus, Truth is the Cure*. New York City: Skyhorse; 2021.

Wolf N. *Outrages*. New York: Chelsea Green; 2020.

Zorn JW, ed. *The Essential Delsarte*. Lanham, MD: Scarecrow; 1968.

Resources

FARMER MARKETS: Please support our community farmers!

BARLOW HERBAL SPECIALTIES: powerful plant medicines and awesome newsletter

DA VINCI LABS: best liposomal vitamin C

DOCTORS' DATA: Hormones, neurotransmitters, stool analysis

FULLSCRIPT.COM: online dispensary

GAIA HERBS: potent herbal products

GREAT PLAINS LABS (GPL): Organic acid test (OAT), mycotoxins and so much more

HAHNEMANN: homeopathic medicines

HEALTH FREEDOM DEFENSE ORGANIZATION and UK MEDICAL FREEDOM ALLIANCE

HEMPLILY: 'Hemplily helps women with symptoms of menopause find harmony and balance again with the amazing hemp plant.' You can find them at hemplily.com

HOMEOPATHY: Homeopathic.com (Dana Ullman)

INTEGRATED THERAPEUTICS: wide range of natural medicine products

MADELEINE HARVEY, FLORENCE RIGGS, and TIFFANY VAN BOXTEL: singing teachers

MOUNTAIN ROSE HERBS: when you want to make your own

PODCAST: Dr. Heather Uncensored, a supplement to this book

RESEARCHED NUTRITIONALS: mitochondrial products

TEECINO TEAS: awesome dandelion blend with ramon seed for energy

VANCOUVER CENTER for Homeopathy – individual treatment

WESTON A. PRICE FOUNDATION: annual conference, information on traditional diets (paleo-keto)

WHOLE HEALTH NOW: homeopathic books and courses

WISE WOMAN HERBALS: herbal products

Acknowledgments

Without the love of my partner, editor, and podcast director, Avi, my grandchildren and my artist bestie, Marianna Mashek, I might not have survived the journey of fleshing out my personal and professional experience of PTS/trauma over the last 35 years.

I would still be sitting in front of my computer if it hadn't been for Georgina Bentliff. She and her publicists – Sophie, Katie, Deirdre and Mary – are rare birds indeed and I am so very grateful.

I deeply thank David Schleich PhD, past president of National University of Natural Medicine, for the Foreword.

To all the people who allowed me to quote them. This list includes Peter Breggin MD, Hyla Cass MD, Peter C Gøtzsche MD, Joseph Pizzorno ND, Mary Minor ND, Sussanna Czeranko ND, Stephanie Seneff PhD, Dana Ullman MPH CCH, M Gerald Fromm PhD, Karl Tomm MD, Brain Klaas, M Bani Younes, dancer and childhood friend Margie Gillis, Tim Cunningham of Clowns Without Borders, Frank Lawless PhD, Marianna Mashek, Florence Riggs, Avi Gross, and solo show people Jessica Johnson, Lynne Jassem and Steve Brock, and Jim Natal for the poem in Appendix 5. I must also thank Marylene Cloistre for permitting the inclusion of the International Trauma Questionnaire (Appendix 8).

I also thank all those who have contributed their expertise to my podcast, Dr Heather Uncensored, an offshoot of the book (see Buzzsprout.com for a full list of amazing interviewees). I can't forget podcast mix engineer Maurice Gainen, webmaster Max Mitchell, artist Julie Mai and Rachel Deltoro ND.

To those who remain close after or because of Covid: my 100-year-old aunt Isabelle, cousins Barb and Florrie, Harv, Veena, Florence, Roberta, Mikki, Kim, Robin (Star and Silas), Michelle, Marcie, Kid, Leanne, Penny, Idelina, Jeff, Janice, Johanna, Anne, Debbie, Dom, Cha Cha, the Huthsteiner sisters, the Sears family, Joseph, Cindy, Taji, Leslie (and Hugo). To Sam and Cynthia and everyone at the Sherman Oaks Farmer's Market and to the workers and my neighbors at Horace Heidt Estate. And as always, to Rebecca Skye.

To the best homeopath ever, Laurie Dack.

To all my patients over the past 35 years – I have learned something from each of you…. I will never ever forget those early years in Kitsilano, especially participants on my retreat 'Moving to Healing' on Galiano Island where *I* learned sooo much…. This book could not have been written without those times.

For my mother who showed me what PTS can be and my father too, but a bit more regulated.

Denis came to me in the end, and it was magical. He and his partner Chris as well as another extraordinary man, Eky, all deceased without need, will forever be alive in my heart. That goes for Carol-Anne Bickerstaff, Georgie Sears, and Nicole Roland too.

And as always to the muses among the palm trees where I live and the faeries sliding over water and around plants at my sanctuary, a nearby lake.

References

Introduction

1. Breggin PR. *Toxic Psychiatry*. New York: St Martin's Press; 1991.
2. Breggin PR. *Psychiatric Drug Withdrawal: A Guide for Prescribers, Therapists, Patients*. New York: Springer Publ; 2012.
3. Lenzer J. Loren Mosher. Quaker Moral Therapy dovetailed with Samuel Hahnemann in Germany/Austria and Phillippe Pinel in France. *Br Med J* 2004; 329(7463): 463.
4. Whitaker R. *Anatomy of an Epidemic*. New York: Broadway Books; 2015.
5. Gøtzsche PC, Smith R, Drummond R. *Deadly medicines and organised crime how big pharma has corrupted healthcare*. London: Radcliffe; 2013.
6. Haque, U. Why We're Underestimating American Collapse: The Strange New Pathologies of the World's First Rich Failed State. Eudaimonia and Co. Jan 25, 2018. https://eand.co/why-were-underestimating-american-collapse-be04d9e55235. (Accessed 30 May 2022)
7. Meerloo JAM. *The Rape of the Mind: the psychology of thought control, menticide and brainwashing*. 1956 Reissued by Martino Publishing, 2015.
8. Keefe RJ. Psychotropic Medication Usage Among Foster and Non-Foster Youth on Medicaid. Presented during the virtual American Academy of Pediatrics 2021. National Conference and Exhibition. file:/// Users/user/Downloads/2021-10-children-foster-psychotropic-medications.pdf
9. Garfield LD, et al. Psychotropic drug use among preschool children in the Medicaid program from 36 states. *Am J Public Health* 2015;105(3):524-529. doi:10.2105/AJPH.2014.302258
10. Citizens Commission on Human Rights International. Total number of people taking psychiatric drugs in the United States. www.cchrint.org/psychiatric-drugs/people-taking-psychiatric-drugs/ from IQVia Total Pt Tracker Database for 2020, extracted January 2021.

11. Cass H. Is it Drugs Not Guns that Cause Violence? A common thread amongst the most horrific school shootings of the past 25 years is that the majority of the shooters were taking psychiatric medication. *Huffington Post* February 2013. www.huffingtonpost.com/hyla-cass-md/is-it-drugs-not-guns-that_b_2393385.html (Accessed 30 May 2022)

12. Flannery MA. The early botanical medical movement as a reflection of life, liberty, and literacy in Jacksonian America. *J Med Libr Assoc* 2002; 90(4): 442-454.

13. Brown ER. *Rockefeller Medicine Men* Los Angeles: University of Calif. Press; 1981.

14. Flexner A. *Medical Education in The United States and Canada*. The Carnegie Foundation, 1910.

15. Stevenson AE. University Speech. Presented at the 1952 Democratic Convention. www.quotationspage.com/quote/3224.html.

16. Klaas B. *Despot's Accomplice* Oxford: Oxford University Press; 2017.

17. Dewa CS, et al. The association of treatment of depressive episodes and work productivity. *Can J Psychiatry* 2011; 56(12): 743-750. doi:10.1177/070674371105601206

18. America's opioid epidemic and its effect on the nation's commercially-insured population. Blue Cross Blue Shield: The Health of America. June 29, 2017. www.bcbs.com/the-health-of-america/reports/americas-opioid-epidemic-and-its-effect-on-the-nations-commercially-insured. (Accessed 30 May 2022)

19. Gurevich MI, Robinson CL. Medication-free Alternatives for Long-term Maintenance of Bipolar Disorder: A Case Series. *Glob Adv Heal Med* 2015; 4(2): 53-60. doi:10.7453/gahmj.2014.064

20. Trowbridge JP. *The Townsend Letter*, Chicken Little and the End of "Conventional" Medicine. December 2016.

21. Nischal A, et al. Suicide and antidepressants: what current evidence indicates. *Mens Sana Monogr* 2012; 10(1): 33-44. doi:10.4103/0973-1229.87287

22. Spatz R, Kugler J. Abnormal EEG activities induced by psychotropic drugs. *Electroenceph Clin Neurophysiol Suppl* 1982; 36: 549-58.

23. Napoleon H. , *Yuuyaraq: The Way of the Human Being* University of Alaska, Fairbanks, College of Rural Alaska, Center for Cross-Cultural Studies; 1991

Chapter 1: The history of the experience

1. Bryan CP (translator): *The Book of Hearts: The Papyrus Ebers*. London, Geoffrey Bles; 1930.

2. Tyrpak S, Crouch B, Berge J. Vestal Virgin: Suspense in Ancient Rome. CreateSpace Independent Publishing Platform; 2011.

3. *The Yellow Emperor's Classic of Medicine*, circa 2600 BC

4. Abdul-Hamid WK, Hughes JH. Nothing New under the Sun: Post-Traumatic Stress Disorders in the Ancient World. *Early Sci Med* 2014; 19(6) :549-557. doi:10.1163/15733823-00196p02

5. Trueman CN. World War One Executions. Historylearningsite.co.uk. The History Learning Site, 31Mr 2015, 1 Oct 2021.

6. Cergan-Reid V. *The Epic of Gilgamesh*The tragic tale of George Smith and Gilgamesh. *The Telegraph* 2013. www.telegraph.co.uk/history/10321147/The-tragic-tale-of-George-Smith-and-Gilgamesh.html.

7. *Iliad*, circa 672 BC

8. Shakespeare W. *Henry IV* Act 2 Scene 3

9 American Psychiatric Association. *DSM-IV Task Force. Diagnostic and Statistical Manual of Mental Disorders : DSM-IV. American Psychiatric Association,* 1994.

10. Blumber J. A Brief History of the Salem Witch Trials: One town's strange journey from paranoia to pardon. Smithsonian. October 23, 2007. www.smithsonianmag.com/history/a-brief-history-of-the-salem-witch-trials-175162489/ (Accessed 30 May 2022)

11. G. W. Wars and Witches: What Caused the Disaster of 1692. http://people.ucls.uchicago.edu/~snekros/The Salem Colonial Current 2015/Indian_Wars_Affecting_Trials.html.

12. Jacobs HA. *Incidents in the Life of a Slave Girl* Boston, MA: Thayer and Eldridge;1861.

13. Dickens M. *Charles Dickens, by His Eldest Daughter (The World's Workers): 4th ed.* Cassell, WI:1891.

14. Slipperjack R. *These are My Words: The Residential Diary of Violet Pesheens* Scholastic Canada. 2016

15. Gajić V. Forgotten great men of medicine: Baron Dominique Jean Larrey (1766-1842). *Med Pregl* 2011; 64(1-2): 97-100.

16. Reilly RF. Medical and surgical care during the American Civil War, 1861-1865. *Proc (Bayl Univ Med Cent)* 2016; 29(2): 138-142. doi:10.1080/08998280.2016.11929390

17. maine.va.gov/about/history.asp

18. Wooley CF. Jacob Mendez DaCosta: medical teacher, clinician, and clinical investigator. *Am J Cardiol* 1982; 50(5): 1145-1148. www.ncbi. nlm.nih.gov/pubmed/6753556. Accessed March 21, 2018.

19. Da Costa JM. *On Irritable Heart: A Clinical Study of a Form of Functional Cardiac Disorder and Its Consequences.* 1871

20. Kardiner A. *The Traumatic Neuroses of War* 1941.

21. Meerloo JAM. *The Rape of the Mind: the psychology of thought control, menticide and brainwashing.* 1956 Reissued by Martino Publishing, 2015.

22. Yehuda R et al. Epigenetic Biomarkers as Predictors and Correlates of Symptom Improvement Following Psychotherapy in Combat Veterans with PTSD. *Front Psychiatry* 2013; 4: 118. doi:10.3389/fpsyt.2013.00118

23. Rodriguez T. Descendants of Holocaust Survivors Have Altered Stress Hormones. *Sci Am Mind* 2015; 26(2): 10-10. doi:10.1038/scientificamericanmind0315-10a

24. Yehuda R, Bierer LM. The relevance of epigenetics to PTSD: implications for the DSM-V. *J Trauma Stress* 2009; 22(5): 427-434. doi:10.1002/jts.20448

25. Pember MA. Intergenerational Trauma: Understanding Natives' Inherited Pain. Indian Country Media Network. www.academia. edu/31720368/Intergenerational_Trauma_Understanding_Natives_Inherited_Pain (Accessed 30 May 2022)

26. Solomon Z. Transgenerational Effects of the Holocaust. In: *International Handbook of Multigenerational Legacies of Trauma.* Boston, MA: Springer; 1998: 69-83. doi:10.1007/978-1-4757-5567-1_4

27. Napoleon H. *Yuuyaraaq: The Way of the Human Being.* University of Alaska, Fairbanks, College of Rural Alaska, Center for Cross-Cultural Studies; 1991.

28. Fromm MG. *Lost in Transmission: Studies of Trauma Across Generations* London, UK: Karnac Books; 2011.

29. Thomas A. *Healing Family Patterns: Ancestral Lineage Clearing for Personal Growth.* Ancestral Wisdom Press; 2011.

Chapter 2: Present considerations

1. Nasses CF. *Journal for the Healing and Diagnosis of Pathological Mental Disorders.* 1818.

2. Kumazaki T. The theoretical root of Karl Jaspers' General Psychopathology. Part 1: Reconsidering the influence of

References

phenomenology and hermeneutics. *History of Psychiatry* 2013; 24(2): 212-226. doi:10.1177/0957154X13476201

3. American Medical Association's *Standard Classified Nomenclature of Disease (MASCND)*.

4. *War Department Technical Bulletin: Medical 203*.

5. American Psychiatric Association. *DSM-II: Diagnostic and Statistical Manual of Mental Disorders, Second Edition*. APA, 1968.

6. American Psychiatric Association. *DSM-III: Diagnostic and Statistical Manual of Mental Disorders, Third Edition*. APA, 1980.

7. American Psychiatric Association. *DSM-III-R: Diagnostic and Statistical Manual of Mental Disorders, Third Edition*. APA, 1987.

8. American Psychiatric Association. *DSM-IV: Diagnostic and Statistical Manual of Mental Disorders, Fourth Edition*. APA, 1994.

9. Shorter E. The history of nosology and the rise of the Diagnostic and Statistical Manual of Mental Disorders. *Dialogues Clin Neurosci* 2015; 17(1): 59-67. doi:10.31887/DCNS.2015.17.1/eshorter

10. Tuke DH. A Dictionary of Psychological Medicine. Vol 1. London, UK: Churchill;1892.

11. Tomm K. *A Critique of the DSM*(1990). Dulwich Centre Newsletter 1990; 1(3): 5-8. (An earlier version was published in 1990, The Calgary Participator: A Family Therapy Newsletter, 2-3).

12. Caplan P. *They Say You're Crazy: How the World's Most Powerful Psychiatrists Decide Who's Normal* Lebanon, IN. Da Capo Lifelong Books. 1996.

13. Williams MT. Can Racism Cause PTSD? Implications for DSM-5. *Psychol Today* May 20, 2013. www.psychologytoday.com/ie/blog/culturally-speaking/201305/can-racism-cause-ptsd-implications-dsm-5 (Accessed 30 May 2022)

14. Gotzche P. *Deadly Medicines and Organised Crime: How Big Pharma has Corrupted Healthcare* CRC Press: Boca Raton Fl. 2013.

15. Simon R. The debate over DSM-5: A step backward. *Psychotherapy Networker* March/April 2014. psychotherapynetworker.org/magazine/article/119/the-debate-over-dsm-5-a-step-backward (Accessed 30 May 2022)

16. Godlee F. Who should define disease? *Br Med J* 2011; 342: d2974. doi: 10.1136/bmj.d2974

17. Hutchinson T. Trauma and PTSD Fort Myers. Tracy Hutchinson, Psychotherapy and Consulting. www.drtracyhutchinson.com/trauma-and-ptsd-fort-myers/ (Accessed 30 May 2022)

18. Bremner JD, et al. Neural correlates of memories of childhood sexual abuse in women with and without posttraumatic stress disorder. *Am J Psychiatry* 1999;156(11): 1787-1795. doi:10.1176/ajp.156.11.1787

19. Miller IW, et al. Depressed patients with dysfunctional families: description and course of illness. *J Abnorm Psychol* 1992; 101(4): 637-646. doi:10.1037//0021-843x.101.4.637

20. Trafficking in children is on the increase, according to the latest UNODC Report. United Nations Office on Drugs and Crime. www.unodc.org/unodc/en/front

21. Van Ameringen M, Mancini C, Patterson B, Boyle MH. Post-traumatic stress disorder in Canada. *CNS Neurosci Ther* 2008;14(3):171-181. doi:10.1111/j.1755-5949.2008.00049.x

22. UN Women, *Progress of the World's Women 2011–2012: In Pursuit of Justice.* 2011. www.unwomen.org/en/digital-library/publications/2011/7/progress-of-the-world-s-women-in-pursuit-of-justice (Accessed 30 May 2022)

23. Statista. Femicide rate in Mexico from 2017 to 2021. www.statista.com/statistics/979065/mexico-number-femicides/ (Accessed 30 May 2022)

24. National Institute of Mental Health. Post-traumatic stress disorder (PTSD). www.nimh.nih.gov/health/statistics/post-traumatic-stress-disorder-ptsd (Accessed 30 May 2022)

25. Vernor D. PTSD is more likely in women than men. National Alliance on Mental Illness. October 8, 2019. www.nami.org/Blogs/NAMI-Blog/October-2019/PTSD-is-More-Likely-in-Women-Than-Men (Accessed 30 May 2022)

26. Glover EM, Jovanovic T, Norrholm SD. Estrogen and extinction of fear memories: implications for posttraumatic stress disorder treatment. *Biol Psychiatry* 2015; 78(3): 178-185. doi:10.1016/j.biopsych.2015.02.007

27. Biometrica. Females still account for around 70% of all trafficked persons. March 8, 2021. www.biometrica.com/females-account-for-70-percent-of-all-trafficking (Accessed 30 May 2022)

28. UN Women. Facts and figures: Ending violence against women. February 2022. www.unwomen.org/en/what-we-do/ending-violence-against-women/facts-and-figures (Accessed 30 May 2022)

29. European Commission. What is gender-based violence. https://ec.europa.eu/info/policies/justice-and-fundamental-rights/gender-equality/gender-based-violence/what-gender-based-violence_en (Accessed 30 May 2022)

References

30. RAINN. Victims of Sexual Violence: Statistics. rainn.org/statistics/victims-sexual-violence (Accessed 30 May 2022)

31. Bradley A. Child abuse in England and Wales: January 2020. Census 2021 January 14, 2020. www.ons.gov.uk/peoplepopulationandcommunity/crimeandjustice/bulletins/childabuseinenglandandwales/january2020 (Accessed 30 May 2022)

32. World Population Review. Rape Statistics by Country 2022. worldpopulationreview.com/country-rankings/rape-statistics-by-country (Accessed 30 May 2022)

33. National Sexual Violence Resource Center. Statistics. www.nsvrc.org/statistics (Accessed 30 May 2022)

34. World Health Organization. Devastatingly pervasive: 1 in 3 women globally experience violence. March 9, 2021. who.int/news/item/09-03-2021-devastatingly-pervasive-1-in-3-women-globally-experience-violence (Accessed 30 May 2022)

35. World Health Organization, Female Genital Mutilation: Fact Sheet No. 241, UN Women, The Violence against Women Prevalence Data: Survey per Country, 2011. www.who.int/news-room/fact-sheets/detail/female-genital-mutilation (Accessed 30 May 2022)

36. Global Estimates of Modern Slavery: forced labour and forced marriage. Geneva, Internationl Labour Organization and Walk Free Foundation, 2017. ilo.org/wcmsp5/groups/public/@dgreports/@dcomm/documents/publication/wcms_575479.pdf (Accessed 30 May 2022)

37. Urban Indian Health Institute. Missing and Murdered Indigenous Women and Girls. A snapshot of data from 71 urban cities in The United States. uihi.org/wp-content/uploads/2018/11/Missing-and-Murdered-Indigenous-Women-and-Girls-Report.pdf

38. NICOA. American Indian Suicide Rate Increases. National Indian Council on Aging. September 9, 2019. www.nicoa.org/national-american-indian-and-alaska-native-hope-for-life-day/ (Accessed 30 May 2022)

39. Peterson C, Sussell A, Li J, *et al*. Suicide rates by Industry and Occupation – National Violent Death Reporting System, 32 States, 2016. *Morbidity and Mortality Weekly Report (MMWR) (CDC)* 2020; 69(3): 57–62. www.cdc.gov/mmwr/volumes/69/wr/mm6903ab.htm

40. World Health Organization. Global and regional estimates of violence against women: Prevalence and health effects of intimate partner violence and non-partner sexual violence. 2013. https://apps.who.int/iris/handle/10665/85239 (Accessed 30 May 2022)

39. Centers for Disease Control and Prevention. Facts about suicide. www. cdc.gov/suicide/facts/index.html (Accessed 30 May 2022)
40. US Department of Veterans Affairs. PTSD: National Center for PTSD. ptsd.va.gov/understand/common/common_veterans.asp (Accessed 30 May 2022)
41. UCLA School of Law Williams Institute. Transgender people over four times more likely than cisgender people to be victims of violent crime. March 23, 2021. williamsinstitute.law.ucla.edu/press/ncvs-trans-press-release/ (Accessed 30 May 2022)
42. Swopes RM, et al. Adverse childhood experiences, posttraumatic stress disorder symptoms, and emotional intelligence in partner aggression. *Violence and Victims 2013;* 28(3): 513–530. doi. org/10.1891/0886-6708.VV-D-12-00026
43. Cook A, et al. Complex Trauma in Children & Adolescents. *Psychol Ann* 2005; 35(5): 398.
44. Herzog JI, Schmahl C. Adverse Childhood Experiences and the Consequences on Neurobiological, Psychosocial, and Somatic Conditions Across the Lifespan. *Front Psychiatry* 2018; 9: 420. doi:10.3389/fpsyt.2018.00420
45. Felitti VJ, Anda RF, Nordenberg D, Williamson DF, Spitz AM, Edwards V, Koss MP, Marks JS. The relationship of selected health risk behaviors, health status and disease in adulthood to childhood abuse and household dysfunction: the adverse childhood experiences (ACE) study. *Am J Prev Med* 1998; 14(4): 245–258.
46. National Conference of State Legislatures. Adverse Childhood Experiences. NCSL December 8, 2021. ncsl.org/research/health/adverse-childhood-experiences-aces.aspx (Accessed 30 May 2022)
47. Prokopez CR, Vallejos M, Farinola R, et al. The history of multiple adverse childhood experiences in patients with schizophrenia is associated with more severe symptomatology and suicidal behavior with gender-specific characteristics. *Psychiatry Res* 2020; 293: 113411. doi:10.1016/j.psychres.2020.113411
48. Talge NM, Neal C, Glover V; Early Stress, Translational Research and Prevention Science Network: Fetal and Neonatal Experience on Child and Adolescent Mental Health. Antenatal maternal stress and long-term effects on child neurodevelopment: how and why? *J Child Psychol Psychiatry* 2007; 48(3-4): 245-261. doi:10.1111/j.1469-7610.2006.01714.x
49. Mlambo-Ngcuka P. Violence against women and grils: the shadow pandemic. UN Women April 6, 2020. www.unwomen.org/en/

References

news/stories/2020/4/statement-ed-phumzile-violence-against-women-during-pandemic (Accessed 30 May 2022)

50. Currie A, Buston C, Freeman E. What is complex PTSD? *The Psychologist* November 12, 2019. thepsychologist.bps.org.uk/what-complex-ptsd (Accessed 30 May 2022)

51. Wall J, Lazarus J. Caleb Parry, Hyperthyroidism and Stress. *Brain Immune: Trends in Neuroendocrine Immunology* October 29 June, 2009. www.brainimmune.com/caleb-parry (Accessed 30 May 2022)

52. Parry CH. *Collections from the unpublished medical writings of C. H Parry.* London, Underwoods: 1825; 2: 11-128.

53. Harmer RG. The Dawn of a New Medicine. learninggnm.com/ (Accessed 30 May 2022)

54. O'Donovan et al. Elevated risk for autoimmune disorders in Iraq and Afghanistan veterans with posttraumatic stress disorder. *Biol Psychiatry* 2015; 77(4): 365-374. doi:10.1016/j.biopsych.2014.06.015

55. Wooley CF. Jacob Mendez DaCosta: medical teacher, clinician, and clinical investigator. *Am J Cardiol* 1982; 50(5): 1145-1148.. pubmed/6753556. (Accessed March 21, 2018.)

56. Da Costa JM. On Irritable Heart: A clinical study of a form of functional cardiac disorder and its consequences. *Am J Med* 1951; 11(5): 559-567. doi:10.1016/0002-

57. Merchant EE, et al. Takotsubo cardiomyopathy: a case series and review of the literature. *West J Emerg Med* 2008; 9(2):104-111.

58. Vaccarino V, et al. Post-traumatic stress disorder and incidence of coronary heart disease: a twin study. *J Am Coll Cardiol* 2013; 62(11): 970-978.

59. Coughlin S. Post-traumatic Stress Disorder and Cardiovascular Disease. *Open Cardiovasc Med J* 2001; 5: 164-170. doi:10.2174/1874192401105010164

60. Yehuda R, Lehrner A, Rosenbaum TY. PTSD and sexual dysfunction in men and women. *J Sex Med* 2015; 12: 1107–1119.

61. Lehrner A, et al. Sexual dysfunction and neuroendocrine correlates of posttraumatic stress disorder in combat veterans: Preliminary findings. *Psychoneuroendocrinology* 2016; 63: 271-275. doi:10.1016/j.psyneuen.2015.10.015

62. Podcast: Dr. Heather Uncensored: Episode 5: Talking with Dr. Brian Hooker about vaccine injury.

63. Podcast: Dr. Heather Uncensored: Episode 39.Talking with Ted Kuntz about vaccine injury.

64. Dhejne C, et al. Mental health and gender dysphoria: A review of the literature, *International Review of Psychiatry 2016;* 28(1): 44-57, doi: 10.3109/09540261.2015.1115753

65. Cook M. Policy shift in Finland for gender dysphoria treatment. *BioEdge* July 25, 2021. www.bioedge.org/bioethics/policy-shift-in-finland-for-gender-dysphoria-treatment/13843 (Accessed 30 May 2022)

66. Littman L. Parent reports of adolescents and young adults perceived to show signs of a rapid onset of gender dysphoria. *PLoS One* 2018; 13(8): e0202330. doi:10.1371/journal.pone.0202330

Chapter 3: A divided perspective

1. Kleisiaris CF et al. Health care practices in ancient Greece: The Hippocratic ideal. *J Med Ethics Hist Med* 2014; 7: 6.

2. Tsiompanou E, Marketos SG. Hippocrates: timeless still. *J R Soc Med* 2013; 106(7): 288-292. doi:10.1177/0141076813492945

3. Emotions and Disease. National Library of Medicine. nlm.nih.gov/exhibition/emotions/balance.html (Accessed 30 May 2022)

4. Biomedicine and Health: Galen and Humoral Theory. www.encyclopedia.com/science/science-magazines/biomedicine-and-health-galen-and-humoral-theory (Accessed 30 May 2022)

5. Galen's four temperaments in 1893 at Chicao's Post-graduate School of Anaesthesia. *Anesthesiology* 2016; 125: 10. doi.org/10.1097/01.anes.0000484134.41701.db pubs.asahq.org/anesthesiology/article/125/1/10/14479/Galen-s-Four-Temperaments-in-1893-at-Chicago-s (Accessed 30 May 2022)

6. Javier H. The four humours theory. *ESSAI* 2014; 12: 21. core.ac.uk/download/pdf/33196432.pdf (Accessed 30 May 2022)

7. North RL. Benjamin Rush, MD: assassin or beloved healer?. *Proc (Bayl Univ Med Cent)* 2000; 13(1): 45-49. doi:10.1080/08998280.2000.11927641

8. Morrell P. Hahnemann and Homeopathy. New Delhi: B Jain; 2003.

9. Editors of Encyclopedia Britannica. Philippe Pinel: French physician. In: *Encyclopedia Britannica.* www.britannica.com/biography/Philippe-Pinel (Accessed 30 May 2022)

10. Shorter E. *A History of Psychiatry : From the Era of the Asylum to the Age of Prozac.* Hoboken, NJ: John Wiley & Sons; 1997.

11. Weiner DB. Philippe Pinel's "Memoir on Madness" of December 11, 1794: a fundamental text of modern psychiatry. *Am J Psychiatry* 1992; 149(6): 725-732. doi:10.1176/ajp.149.6.725

12. Kibria AA, Metcalfe NH. A biography of William Tuke (1732-1822): Founder of the modern mental asylum. *J Med Biogr* 2016; 24(3): 384-388. doi:10.1177/0967772014533059

13. Parry MS. Dorothea Dix (1802–1887). *Am J Public Health* 2006; 96(4): 624-625. doi:10.2105/AJPH.2005.079152

14. Bly N. *Ten Days in a Mad House*. New York: Ian L Muro; 1887. http://digital.library.upenn.edu/women/bly/madhouse/madhouse.html. (Accessed March 25, 2018.)

15. Barrus C. *Nursing the Insane*. New York: The Macmillan Company: 1915.

16. Czeranko S. Helen Wilmans and Mental Culture. *Naturopathic Doctor News and Review November 10, 2017.* http://ndnr.com/nature-cure/helen-wilmans-mental-culture/ (Accessed 30 May 2022)

17. Panciroli P. The Asylum as Utopia in The Homeopathic Landscape: Innovations And Contradictions. *Society and Politics 2019;* 12(1).

18. prezi.com/p/cmmtxfljceov/benedict-and-louisa-lust/

19.Cayleff SE. Nature's Path: A history of naturopathic healing in America. Baltimore, US; Johns Hopkins University Press; 2016. www.academia.edu/33212847/Review_SusanCayleff_NaturesPath.docx (Accessed 30 May 2022)

20. Cody GW. The Origins of Integrative Medicine-The First True Integrators: The Philosophy of Early Practitioners. *Integr Med (Encinitas)* 2018; 17(2): 16-18.

21. Czeranko S. Past pearls: The trials of Benedict Lust. *Naturopathic Doctor News & Review* November 8, 2010. ndnr.com/education-web-articles/past-pearls-the-trials-of-benedict-lust/ (Accessed 30 May 2022)

22. The Naturopath and Herald of Health published by Benedict Lust 1915

23. Flexner A. *Medical Education in The United States and Canada*. The Carnegie Foundation, 1910.

24. Casamajor LC. Charles Burlingame, M.D. 1885-1950. *AMA Arch Neurol Psychiatry* 1950; 64(6): 882-883. doi:10.1001/archneurpsyc.1950.02310300129016 AND A Psychiatrist Speaks: The Writings and Lectures of C. Charles Burlingame, 1885-1950.

25. Deutch A. *The Shame of the States*, in a 1948 *Life* magazine reprinted in Deutsch A. *The Shame of the States*. New York: Arno Press; 1973.

Chapter 4: The brain on fire

1. Lachance L, Ramsey D. Food, mood, and brain health: implications for the modern clinician. *Mo Med* 2015; 112(2): 111-115.

2. Kanoski SE, Davidson TL. Western diet consumption and cognitive impairment: links to hippocampal dysfunction and obesity. *Physiol Behav* 2011; 103(1): 59-68. doi:10.1016/j.physbeh.2010.12.003

3. Hoerster KD, et al. PTSD is associated with poor health behavior and greater Body Mass Index through depression, increasing cardiovascular disease and diabetes risk among U.S. veterans. *Preventive Medicine Reports 2019*; 15.

4. Miller MW, Lin AP, Wolf EJ, Miller DR. Oxidative Stress, Inflammation, and Neuroprogression in Chronic PTSD. *Harv Rev Psychiatry* 2018; 26(2): 57-69. doi:10.1097/HRP.0000000000000167

5. Renoir T, et al. Mind and body: how the health of the body impacts on neuropsychiatry. *Front Pharmacol* 2013; 4: 158. doi:10.3389/fphar.2013.00158

6. Kim TD, Lee S, Yoon S. Inflammation in Post-Traumatic Stress Disorder (PTSD): A Review of Potential Correlates of PTSD with a Neurological Perspective. *Antioxidants*. 2020; 9(2): 107. doi:10.3390/antiox9020107

7. Mariotti A. The effects of chronic stress on health: new insights into the molecular mechanisms of brain-body communication. *Future Sci OA* 2015; 1(3): FSO23. doi:10.4155/fso.15.21

8. Insana SP, Banihashemi L, Herringa RJ, Kolko DJ, Germain A. Childhood maltreatment is associated with altered frontolimbic neurobiological activity during wakefulness in adulthood. *Dev Psychopathol* 2016; 28(2): 551-564. doi:10.1017/S0954579415000589

9. Herzberg MP, McKenzie KJ, Hodel AS, et al. Accelerated maturation in functional connectivity following early life stress: Circuit specific or broadly distributed? *Dev Cogn Neurosci* 2021; 48: 100922. doi:10.1016/j.dcn.2021.100922

10. Anda RF, et al. The enduring effects of abuse and related adverse experiences in childhood. A convergence of evidence from neurobiology and epidemiology. *Eur Arch Psych & Clinical Neuroscience 2006;*. 256(3): 174-186. doi:10.1007/s00406-005-0624-4

11. Ney LJ, Gogos A, Hsu C-MK, Felmingham, KL, An alternative theory for hormone effects on sex differences in PTSD: The role of heightened sex hormones during trauma, *Psychoneuroendocrinology* 2019; 109: 1-12.

12. Herringa RJ. Trauma, PTSD, and the Developing Brain. *Curr Psychiatry Rep* 2017; 19(10): 69. doi:10.1007/s11920-017-0825-3

13. Morey JN, et al. Current Directions in Stress and Human Immune Function. *Curr Opin Psychol* 2015; 5: 13-17. doi:10.1016/j.copsyc.2015.03.007

References

14. Girgenti MJ, Hare BD, Ghosal S, Duman RS. Molecular and Cellular Effects of Traumatic Stress: Implications for PTSD. *Curr Psychiatry Rep* 2017; 19(11): 85. doi:10.1007/s11920-017-0841-3

15. Speer K, Upton D, Semple S, McKune A. Systemic low-grade inflammation in post-traumatic stress disorder: a systematic review. *J Inflamm Res* 2018; 11: 111-121. doi:10.2147/JIR.S155903

16. Michopoulos V, Powers A, Gillespie CF, Ressler KJ, Jovanovic T. Inflammation in Fear- and Anxiety-Based Disorders: PTSD, GAD, and Beyond. *Neuropsychopharmacology* 2017; 42(1): 254-270. doi:10.1038/npp.2016.146

17. Brand SR. The Effect of Maternal PTSD Following in Utero Trauma Exposure on Behavior and Temperament in the 9-Month-Old Infant. *Annals of the New York Academy of Sciences* 2006; 1071(1): 454-458. doi:10.1196/annals.1364.041.

18. Crum KI, Flanagan JC, Vaughan B, et al. Oxytocin, PTSD, and sexual abuse are associated with attention network intrinsic functional connectivity. *Psychiatry Res Neuroimaging* 2021; 316: 111345. doi:10.1016/j.pscychresns.2021.111345

19. Miller MW, Lin AP, Wolf EJ, Miller DR. Oxidative Stress, Inflammation, and Neuroprogression in Chronic PTSD. *Harv Rev Psychiatry* 2018; 26(2): 57-69. doi:10.1097/HRP.0000000000000167

20. Zimmerman A, Halligan S, Skeen S, et al. PTSD symptoms and cortisol stress reactivity in adolescence: Findings from a high adversity cohort in South Africa. *Psychoneuroendocrinology* 2020; 121: 104846. doi:10.1016/j.psyneuen.2020.104846

21. Adam EK, Quinn ME, Tavernier R, McQuillan MT, Dahlke KA, Gilbert KE. Diurnal cortisol slopes and mental and physical health outcomes: A systematic review and meta-analysis. *Psychoneuroendocrinology* 2017; 83: 25-41. doi:10.1016/j.psyneuen.2017.05.018

22. Jain S. Researcher discusses epigenetic transmission of stress and PTSD. *Pscychology and Psychiatry* June 9, 2016. medicalxpress.com/news/2016-06-discusses-epigenetic-transmission-stress-ptsd.html (Accessed 30 May 2022)

23. Yehuda R, Bierer LM. Transgenerational transmission of cortisol and PTSD risk. *Prog Brain Res* 2008; 167: 121-135. doi:10.1016/S0079-6123(07)67009-5

24. Herman JP, Nawreen N, Smail MA, Cotella EM. Brain mechanisms of HPA axis regulation: neurocircuitry and feedback in context Richard Kvetnansky lecture. *Stress* 2020; 23(6): 617-632. doi:10.1080/10253890.2020.1859475

25. Scassellati C, Marizzoni M, Cattane N, et al. The Complex Molecular Picture of Gut and Oral Microbiota-Brain-Depression System: What We Know and What We Need to Know. *Front Psychiatry* 2021; 12: 722335. doi:10.3389/fpsyt.2021.722335

26. Reddy OC, van der Werf YD. The Sleeping Brain: Harnessing the Power of the Glymphatic System through Lifestyle Choices. *Brain Sci* 2020; 10(11): 868. doi:10.3390/brainsci10110868

27. Harris JJ, Attwell D. Is myelin a mitochondrion? *J Cereb Blood Flow Metab* 2013; 33(1): 33-36. doi:10.1038/jcbfm.2012.148

28. Jeanneteau F, Arango-Lievano M. Linking Mitochondria to Synapses: New Insights for Stress-Related Neuropsychiatric Disorders. *Neural Plast* 2016; 2016: 3985063. doi:10.1155/2016/3985063

29. University of Queensland Australia. What is synaptic plasticity? qbi. uq.edu.au/brain-basics/brain/brain-physiology/what-synaptic-plasticity (Accessed 30 May 2022)

30. Naviaux RK. Perspective: Cell danger response Biology-The new science that connects environmental health with mitochondria and the rising tide of chronic illness. *Mitochondrion* 2020; 51: 40-45. doi:10.1016/j.mito.2019.12.005

31. Porges SW. The polyvagal theory: new insights into adaptive reactions of the autonomic nervous system. *Cleve Clin J Med* 2009; 76(Suppl 2):S86-S90. doi:10.3949/ccjm.76.s2.17

Chapter 5: Optimizing our metabolism

1. Winston A, Hardwick E, Jaberi N. Neuropsychiatric effects of caffeine. *Advances in Psychiatric Treatment* 2005; 11(6): 432-439. doi:10.1192/apt.11.6.432

2. Jackson JR, et al. Neurologic and psychiatric manifestations of celiac disease and gluten sensitivity. *Psychiatr Q* 2012; 83(1): 91-102. doi:10.1007/s11126-011-9186-y

3. Pitman RK, Rasmusson AM, Koenen KC, et al. Biological studies of post-traumatic stress disorder. *Nat Rev Neurosci* 2012; 13(11): 769-787. doi:10.1038/nrn3339

4. Russo SJ, Murrough JW, Han MH, Charney DS, Nestler EJ. Neurobiology of resilience. *Nat. Neurosci 2012*; 15: 1475–1484.

5. Wentz LM, Eldred JD, Henry MD, Berry-Cabán CS. Clinical relevance of optimizing vitamin D status in soldiers to enhance physical and cognitive performance. *J Spec Oper Med* 2014; 14(1): 58-66.

References

6. Mocking RJT, Assies J, Ruhé HG, Schene AH. Focus on fatty acids in the neurometabolic pathophysiology of psychiatric disorders. *J Inherit Metab Dis* 2018; 41(4): 597-611. doi:10.1007/s10545-018-0158-3

7. Kuhne L. *The New Science of Healing* 1917.

8. Jacka FN, Cherbuin N, Anstey KJ, Sachdev P, Butterworth P. Western diet is associated with a smaller hippocampus: a longitudinal investigation. *BMC Med* 2015; 13: 215. doi:10.1186/s12916-015-0461-x

9. Seneff S. *Toxic Legacy.* Vermont, USA: Chelsea Green; 2021.

10. Fuglewicz AJ, Piotrowski P, Stodolak A. Relationship between toxoplasmosis and schizophrenia: A review. *Adv Clin Exp Med* 2017; 26(6): 1031-1036. doi:10.17219/acem/61435

11. Winston A, Hardwick E, Jaberi, N. Neuropsychiatric effects of caffeine. *Advances in Psychiatric Treatment* 2005; 11(6): 432-439. doi:10.1192/apt.11.6.432

12. Levinta A, Mukovozov I, Tsoutsoulas C. Use of a Gluten-Free Diet in Schizophrenia: A Systematic Review. *Adv Nutr* 2018; 9(6): 824-832. doi:10.1093/advances/nmy056

13. Jackson JR, Eaton WW, Cascella NG, Fasano A, Kelly DL. Neurologic and psychiatric manifestations of celiac disease and gluten sensitivity. *Psychiatr Q* 2012; 83(1): 91-102. doi:10.1007/s11126-011-9186-y

14. Loguercio C, Festi D. Silybin and the liver: from basic research to clinical practice. *World J Gastroenterol* 2011; 17(18): 2288-2301. doi:10.3748/wjg.v17.i18.2288

15. Allen J, Montalto M, Lovejoy J, Weber W. Detoxification in naturopathic medicine: a survey. *J Altern Complement Med* 2011; 17(12): 1175-1180. doi:10.1089/acm.2010.0572

16. Partrick KA, et al. Ingestion of probiotic (*Lactobacillus helveticus* and *Bifidobacterium longum*) alters intestinal microbial structure and behavioral expression following social defeat stress. *Sci Rep* 2021; 11: 3763. doi.org/10.1038/s41598-021-83284-z

17. Messaoudi M. Beneficial psychological effects of a probiotic formulation (Lactobacillus helveticus R0052 and Bifidobacterium longum R0175) in healthy human volunteers. *Gut Microbes* 2011; 2(4): 256-261.

18. Akiyama T, et al. FMN phosphatase and FAD pyrophosphatase in rat intestinal brush borders: role in intestinal absorption of dietary riboflavin. *J Nutr* 1982; 112(2): 263-268. doi:10.1093/jn/112.2.263

19. Hustad S, et al. Riboflavin, flavin mononucleotide, and flavin adenine dinucleotide in human plasma and erythrocytes at baseline and

after low-dose riboflavin supplementation. *Clin Chem* 2002; 48(9): 1571-1577.

20. Felger JC. Imaging the Role of Inflammation in Mood and Anxiety-related Disorders. *Curr Neuropharmacol* 2018; 16(5): 533-558. doi:10.21 74/1570159X15666171123201142

21. van den Berk-Clark C, Secrest S, Walls J, et al. Association between posttraumatic stress disorder and lack of exercise, poor diet, obesity, and co-occurring smoking: A systematic review and meta-analysis. *Health Psychol* 2018; 37(5): 407-416. doi:10.1037/hea0000593

22. Howland GJ. Ways to conquer PTSD-why diet really matters. Food and Mood Center; 2018. foodandmoodcentre.com.au/2018/09/ ways-to-conquer-ptsd-why-diet-really-matters.

Chapter 6: The healing power of nature

1. Akobeng AK. Principles of evidence based. *Arch Dis Child* adc.bmj.com/ content/90/8/837 (Accessed 31 May 2022)

2. Cayleff SE. *Wash and Be Healed: The Water Cure Movement and Women's Health* 1880 republished by Temple University Press 1991.

3. Staden L. *Naturarzt* page 110

4. Czeranko S. Nature Cure Clinical Pearls: Ludwig Staden, Naturarzt. *NDNR Journal* January 11, 2016. https://ndnr.com/nature-cure/ nature-cure-clinical-pearls-ludwig-staden-naturarzt/ (Accessed 30 May 2022)

5. Bayda S, Adeel M, Tuccinardi T, Cordani M, Rizzolio F. The History of Nanoscience and Nanotechnology: From Chemical-Physical Applications to Nanomedicine. *Molecules* 2019; 25(1): 112. doi:10.3390/molecules25010112

6. Morrell P. Hahnemann and Homeopathy. New Delhi: B Jain; 2003.

7. Holcombe. W. *Yellow fever and its homoeopathic treatment.* New York: W Radde; 1856.

8. Holcombe W. *Photothéque Homéopathique présentée par Homéopathe International.* http://homeoint.org/photo/h2/holcombe.html (Accessed 30 May 2022)

9. Sue Young Histories. Ethelbert Petrie Hoyle 1861-1955. March 28, 2009. www.sueyounghistories.com/2009-03-28-ethelbert-petrie-hoyle-1861-1955/ (Accessed 30 May 2022)

10. Anastopoulos C. *Particle or Wave : The Evolution of the Concept of Matter in Modern Physics.* Princeton. Princeton University Press; 2008.

References

11. Manzalini A, Galeazzi B. Explaining Homeopathy with Quantum Electrodynamics. *Homeopathy* 2019; 108(3): 169-176. doi:10.1055/s-0039-1681037

12. Ullmann D. Critique of Proposed Regulations of Homeopathic Medicines and Alternative Proposals. Mercola News. 2018.

13. Pratte MA, Nanavati KB, Young V, Morley CP. An Alternative Treatment for Anxiety: A Systematic Review of Human Trial Results Reported for the Ayurvedic Herb Ashwagandha (Withania somnifera). *J Altern Complement Med* 2014; 20(12): 901-908. doi:10.1089/acm.2014.0177

14. SATVEDA. Ashwagandha Herb Information. Satveda Herbs Forever. Ashwagandha: Uses, Side Effects, Interactions, Dosage, and Warning. WebMD. www.webmd.com/vitamins/ai/ingredientmono-953/ashwagandha. Published 2018.

15. Al-Qarawi AA et al. Liquorice (Glycyrrhiza glabra) and the adrenal-kidney-pituitary axis in rats. *Food Chem Toxicol* 2002; 40(10): 1525-1527. doi:10.1016/s0278-6915(02)00080-7

16. Duke JA. The Green Pharmacy : The Ultimate Compendium of Natural Remedies from the World's Foremost Authority on Healing Herbs. St Martin's Press; 1998.

17. Yadav AV, Kawale LA, Nade VS. Effect of Morus alba L. (mulberry) leaves on anxiety in mice. *Indian J Pharmacol* 2008; 40(1): 32-36. doi:10.4103/0253-7613.40487

18. Armstrong CG. Skookum root: Hellebore (Veratrum viride). *Ethnobiology Letters* 2018; 9(2): 197–205. doi: 10.14237/ebl.9.2.2018.1298

19. Sarris J, et al. Ayahuasca use and reported effects on depression and anxiety symptoms: An international cross-sectional study of 11,912 consumers. *J Aff Disorders Reports* 2021; 4. doi.org/10.1016/j.jadr.2021.100098.

20. Frecska E et al. The Therapeutic Potentials of Ayahuasca: Possible Effects against Various Diseases of Civilization. *Front Pharmacol* 2016; 7: 35. doi:10.3389/fphar.2016.00035

21. Inserra A. Hypothesis: The Psychedelic Ayahuasca Heals Traumatic Memories via a Sigma 1 Receptor-Mediated Epigenetic-Mnemonic Process. *Front Pharmacol* 2018; 9: 330. doi:10.3389/fphar.2018.00330

22. Labate BC, Cavnar C. *Therapeutic Use of Ayahuasca*. Berlin: Springer-Verlag; 2014.

23. Labate B. Great scientific news of Ayahuasca's therapeutic potentials. *Science Archives* February 26, 2017. www.ayahuasca.com/category/science/ (Accessed 30 May 2022)

24. Fraser GA. The Use of a Synthetic Cannabinoid in the Management of Treatment-Resistant Nightmares in Posttraumatic Stress Disorder (PTSD). *CNS Neurosci Ther* 2009; 15(1): 84-88. doi:10.1111/j.1755-5949.2008.00071.x

25. Rahn B. Cannabinoids 101: What Makes Cannabis Medicine? *Leafly* January 22, 2014. www.leafly.com/news/Cannabis-101/cannabinoids-101-what-makes-Cannabis-medicine (Accessed 30 May 2022)

26. Ganon-Elazar E, Akirav I. Cannabinoids and traumatic stress modulation of contextual fear extinction and GR expression in the amygdala-hippocampal-prefrontal circuit. *Psychoneuroendocrinology* 2013; 38(9): 1675-1687. doi:10.1016/j.psyneuen.2013.01.014

27. Hill MN, et al. Reductions in circulating endocannabinoid levels in individuals with post-traumatic stress disorder following exposure to the world trade center attacks. *Psychoneuroendocrinology* 2013; 38(12): 2952-2961. doi:10.1016/j.psyneuen.2013.08.004

28. De Gregorio D, McLaughlin RJ, Posa L, et al. Cannabidiol modulates serotonergic transmission and reverses both allodynia and anxiety-like behavior in a model of neuropathic pain. *Pain* 2019; 160(1): 136-150. doi:10.1097/j.pain.0000000000001386

29. Lee M. *Smoke Signals* New York: Scribner; 2012

30. Elliott S. Indica vs Sativa: The Difference Between These Two Cannabis Types. *Herb* September 21, 2021. herb.co/marijuana/news/indica-vs-sativa-whats-the-difference (Accessed 30 May 2021)

31. Bassir Nia A, Bender R, Harpaz-Rotem I. Endocannabinoid System Alterations in Posttraumatic Stress Disorder: A Review of Developmental and Accumulative Effects of Trauma. *Chronic Stress* 2019; 3: 2470547019864096. doi:10.1177/2470547019864096

32. Tupper KW, Wood E, Yensen R, Johnson MW. Psychedelic medicine: a re-emerging therapeutic paradigm. *CMAJ* 2015; 187(14): 1054-1059. doi:10.1503/cmaj.141124

33. Toda M et al. Effects of woodland walking on salivary stress markers cortisol and chromogranin A. *Complement Ther Med* 2013; 21(1): 29-34. doi:10.1016/j.ctim.2012.11.004

34. Just A. Return to Nature. Boston: E.P. Dutton :1912 (see www.amazon.com/Return-nature-Adolf-Just/dp/B00089L566 and Czeranko S. Adolf Just (1859-1936). *Integr Med (Encinitas)* 2019; 18(3): 46.)

35. Oschman JL, et al. The effects of grounding (earthing) on inflammation, the immune response, wound healing, and prevention and treatment of chronic inflammatory and autoimmune diseases. *J Inflamm Res* 2015; 8: 83-96.

References

36. Starr P. (see Biblio for book) in: Cayleff S. *Wash and Be Healed.* Philadelphia. Temple University Press. 1987: page19.

37. Wesley J. *Primitive Physic, or an Easy and Natural Method of Curing Most Diseases.* 1702.

38. Nichols MG. *Experience in Water Cure.* New York: Fowler and Wells; 1853.

39. The Water-Cure Journal. New York: Fowlers and Wells; 1851. www.abebooks.com/Water-Cure-Journal-Herald-Reforms-Devoted-Physiology/30357302153/bd

40. Benfield RD, et al. The effects of hydrotherapy on anxiety, pain, neuroendocrine responses, and contraction dynamics during labor. *Biol Res Nurs* 2010;12(1):28-36. doi:10.1177/1099800410361535

41. Shevchuk NA. Adapted cold shower as a potential treatment for depression. *Med Hypotheses* 2008; 70(5): 995-1001. doi:10.1016/j.mehy.2007.04.052

42. Mooventhan A, Nivethitha L. Scientific evidence-based effects of hydrotherapy on various systems of the body. *N Am J Med Sci* 2014; 6(5): 199-209. doi:10.4103/1947-2714.132935

43. Song S, et al. Loss of Brain Norepinephrine Elicits Neuroinflammation-Mediated Oxidative Injury and Selective Caudo-Rostral Neurodegeneration. *Molecular Neurobiology* 2019; 56(4): 2653-2669. doi:10.1007/s12035-018-1235-1

44. Jackson TC, Manole MD, Kotermanski SE, Jackson EK, Clark RS, Kochanek PM. Cold stress protein RBM3 responds to temperature change in an ultra-sensitive manner in young neurons. *Neuroscience* 2015; 305: 268-278. doi:10.1016/j.neuroscience.2015.08.012

45. Bongiorno P. A Cold Splash – Hydrotherapy for Depression and Anxiety. *Psychol Today* July 6, 2014. www.psychologytoday.com/ca/comment/872544 (Accessed 30 May 2022)

46. Shevchuk NA. Adapted cold shower as a potential treatment for depression. *Med Hypotheses* 2008; 70(5): 995-1001. doi:10.1016/j.mehy.2007.04.052

47. Vega JL. Edmund Goodwyn and the first description of diving bradycardia. *J Appl Physiol* 2017; 123(2): 275-277. doi:10.1152/japplphysiol.00221.2017

48. Godek D, Freeman AM. Physiology, Diving Reflex. In: *StatPearls.* Treasure Island (FL): StatPearls Publishing; September 29, 2020.

49. Lubkowska A et al. The Effects of Swimming Training in Cold Water on Antioxidant Enzyme Activity and Lipid Peroxidation in Erythrocytes

of Male and Female Aged Rats. *Int J Environ Res Public Health* 2019; 16(4): 647. doi:10.3390/ijerph16040647

50. Jedema, Hank P et al. Chronic cold exposure increases RGS7 expression and decreases alpha(2)-autoreceptor-mediated inhibition of noradrenergic locus coeruleus neurons. *Eur J Neurosci* 2008; 27(9): 2433-2443. doi:10.1111/j.1460-9568.2008.06208.x

51. Johnson DG, Hayward JS, Jacobs TP, Collis ML, Eckerson JD, Williams RH. Plasma norepinephrine responses of man in cold water. *J Appl Physiol Respir Environ Exerc Physiol* 1977; 43(2): 216-220. doi:10.1152/jappl.1977.43.2.216

52. Yang HJ, Shi X, Ju F, et al. Cold Shock Induced Protein RBM3 but Not Mild Hypothermia Protects Human SH-SY5Y Neuroblastoma Cells From MPP+-Induced Neurotoxicity. *Front Neurosci* 2018; 12: 298. doi:10.3389/fnins.2018.00298

53. Jackson TC, Manole MD, Kotermanski SE, Jackson EK, Clark RS, Kochanek PM. Cold stress protein RBM3 responds to temperature change in an ultra-sensitive manner in young neurons. *Neuroscience* 2015; 305: 268-278. doi:10.1016/j.neuroscience.2015.08.012

Chapter 7: Trauma-informed care

1. Younes MB. *History, Identity, Trauma and Narratives*. In: Toni *Morrison*. Sodertorn University: 2016.

2. Ehlers A, Clark DM. Post-traumatic stress disorder: the development of effective psychological treatments. *Nord J Psychiatry* 2008; 62(Suppl 47): 11-18. doi:10.1080/08039480802315608

3. Rosenberg M. *Nonviolent Communication: A Language of Compassion* Encinatas, CA: Puddle Dancer Press; Second Printing edition (January 1, 2000)

4. Quote from a friend.

5. Varoufakis Y. *Adults in the Room* New York: Farrar, Straus and Giroux; Illustrated edition 2017.

Chapter 8: A way in

1. Porges SW. The polyvagal theory: new insights into adaptive reactions of the autonomic nervous system. *Cleve Clin J Med* 2009; 76(Suppl 2): S86-S90. doi:10.3949/ccjm.76.s2.17

2. Shiffman M. Mindfulness for Anxiety Dissociation. Insight Center, Los Angeles. https://insightcenter.org/schedule/mindfulness-2018-2/

3. Pert C. *Molecules of Emotion*. New York: Simon and Schuster; 1999.

4. Rama S, Ballentine R, Hymes A. *Science of Breath*. Honesdale, PA: Himalayan Institute Press; 1998.

5. Yogapedia. Mantra. Definition – What does Mantra mean? July 16, 2020. yogapedia.com/definition/4950/mantra (Accessed 30 May 2022)

6. The Art of Living Bhramari Pranayama – Humming bee breathing. artofliving.org/in-en/yoga/breathing-techniques/bhramari-pranayama (Accessed 30 May 2022)

Chapter 9: The mind–body connection

1. Pert C. *Molecules of Emotion*. New York. Simon and Schuster. 1999

2. Thibaut F. The mind-body Cartesian dualism and psychiatry. *Dialogues Clin Neurosci*. 2018;20(1):3. doi:10.31887/DCNS.2018.20.1/fthibaut

3. Locke J. *An Essay Concerning Human Understanding* 1689.

4. Reich W. *Character Analysis* 1933

5. Moreno JD. *Impromptu Man : J.L. Moreno and the Origins of Psychodrama, Encounter Culture, and the Social Network*. Bellevue Literary Press; 2014.

6. Ader A, Cohen N. Psychoneuroimmunology: Conditioning and Stress. *Annu. Rev. Psychol.* 1993. 44:53~5

7. Massey J. Mind-Body Medicine Its History and Evolution NDNR. June 1, 2015. ndnr.com/mindbody/mind-body-medicine-its-history-evolution

8. McGilchrist I. *The Master and his Emissary* McGilchrist I. *The Master and His Emissary : The Divided Brain and the Making of the Western World*. Yale University Press; 2009.

9. Werner G. Fractals in the nervous system: conceptual implications for theoretical neuroscience. *Front Physiol*. 2010;1:15. Published 2010 Jul 6. doi:10.3389/fphys.2010.00015

10. Burnett-Zeigler I, Schuette S, Victorson D, Wisner KL. Mind-Body Approaches to Treating Mental Health Symptoms Among Disadvantaged Populations: A Comprehensive Review. *J Altern Complement Med*. 2016;22(2):115-124. doi:10.1089/acm.2015.0038

11. Gawain S. *Creative Visualization*. New York: Bantam Books; 1978

12. Atkinson A, P Adolphs R. Visual Emotion Perception: Mechanisms and Processes. In Barrett LF, Niedenthal PM, Winkielman P. (Eds.) *Emotion and consciousness* (pp. 150–182). The Guilford Press; 2005.

13. Tyng CM et al. The Influences of Emotion on Learning and Memory. Front. Psychol.,24 August 2017 doi.org/10.3389/fpsyg.2017.01454

14. Woolf V. *Holodynamics 2nd Edition* The International Academy of Holodynamics; June 29, 1990.

15. Goldman J. *Healing Sounds: The Power of Harmonics*. Rochestert: Healing Arts Press; 2002.

16. Wagner KD. Do healing frequencies work? *Spirituality & Healing* www. spiritualityhealth.com/articles/2013/12/16/science-behind-healing-sound (Accessed 31 May 2022)

17. Leeds J. Power of Sound. *Alternative Therapies in Health and Medicine* 2008

18. Fox J, Salas J. *Personal Stories in Public Spaces*. New Paltz. NY: Tusitala Publishing; 2019

19. Lawless F. *PTSD Breakthrough*. Napierville, IL: Sourcebooks; 2010.

Chapter 10: The arts as refuge

1. Plato. Music. In: *The Republic* Book III (398-403). Extract available from Theory of Music and take from *The Dialogues of Plato, translated by Benjamin Jowett, Volume Four, The Republic*, edited by M Hare & DA Russell, Sphere Books Ltd., 1970. https://theoryofmusic.wordpress. com/2008/08/04/music-in-platos-republic/. (Accessed 31 May 2022)

2. West ML. *Ancient Greek Music*. Oxford: Clarendon Press; 1994.

3. Delsarte F, Zorn JW. *The Essential Delsarte*. Lanham, MD: Scarecrow; 1968.

4. Levitin DJ. *This Is Your Brain on Music* New York: Plume/Penguin; 2007

5. Robbins A. *The Psycho Aesthetic Experience – An Approach to Depth-Oriented Treatment* New York: Human Sciences Press; 1989.

6. Homer. *The Iliad*. London: New York: Dent; Dutton; 1955,

7. Homer. *The Odyssey* London: New York: W Heinemann; GP Putnam's Sons; 1919.

8. Chase A. Review of "Achilles in Vietnam" by Jonathan Shay. *The White Rhino Report* March 15, 2007. http://whiterhinoreport.blogspot. com/2007/03/review-of-achilles-in-vietnam-by.html. (Accessed 31 May 2022)

9. baltimoresun.com/la-me-veterans-art-20180528-story.html (Not available outside US)

10. Baldwin J. *The Price of the Ticket*. New York: St Martin's Press; 1985.

11. MacKinnon DW. What makes a person creative? *Theory Into Practice* 1966; 5(4): 151-156, doi: 10.1080/00405846609542017

Chapter 11: Writing and visual art

1. Pennebaker J. Writing about Emotional Experiences as a Therapeutic Process. *Psychological Sciences* 1997; 8(3): 162-166. doi/10.1111/j.1467-9280.1997.tb00403.x

2. Rose LK. The Role of Meaning Making in Expressive Writing and Adults with Post Traumatic Stress Disorder: A Literature Review.. *Expressive Therapies Capstone Theses* 2019; 122. https://digitalcommons.lesley.edu/expressive_theses/122 (Accessed 31 May 2022)

3. Meston CM, et al. Effects of Expressive Writing on Sexual Dysfunction, Depression, and PTSD in Women with a History of Childhood Sexual Abuse: Results from a Randomized Clinical Trial. *J Sex Med* 2013; 10(9): 2177-2189. doi:10.1111/jsm.12247

4. Thompson SB ed. *Born Into Slavery: Voices from the Past. Federal Writers Project; 2015. (from the 1930s; many books from this project) Also Born in Slavery: Slave Narratives from the Federal Writers' Project from 1938-1939.*

5. Beston H. *The Outermost House : A Year of Life on the Great Beach of Cape Cod.* Garden City, NY: Doubleday, Doran and Company; 1928.

6. Beston H. *The Firelight Fairy Book.* Alexandria: Library of Alexandria; 1919.

7. Cameron J. *The Artist's Way : A Spiritual Path to Higher Creativity.* New York: Putnam; 1991.

8. Goldberg N. *Writing Down the Bones.* Boulder: Shambala; 1986.

9. Hirsch M. An Interview with Marianne Hirsch. Columbia University Press. https://cup.columbia.edu/author-interviews/hirsch-generation-postmemory (Accessed 31 May 2022)

10. Gross A. In private conversation.

11. Natal J. *Memory and Rain: Poems.* Pasadena: Red Hen Press; 2009.

12. Volavkova H (Ed), Havel V (Afterword). *I Never Saw Another Butterfly: Children's Drawings and Poems from the Terezin Concentration Camp, 1942-1944, 2nd edition.* NYC: Schocken: 1994.

13. Keane C. Featured Member: Charles Anderson, Art Therapy Pioneer. *American Art Therapy Association* February 15, 2018. https://arttherapy.org/charles-anderson-art-therapy-pioneer/. (Accessed 31 May 2022)

14. Why We Rise. https://whywerise.la/ (Accessed 30 May 2022)

Chapter 12: Music and vocalization

1. Pert C. *Molecules of Emotion*. New York: Simon and Schuster; 1999.
2. Plato. Music. In: *The Republic* Book III (398-403). Extract available from *Theory of Music* and take from *The Dialogues of Plato, translated by Benjamin Jowett, Volume Four, The Republic*, edited by M Hare & DA Russell, Sphere Books Ltd., 1970. https://theoryofmusic.wordpress.com/2008/08/04/music-in-platos-republic/. (Accessed 31 May 2022)
3. Leiff J. *Music Stimulates Emotions Through Specific Brain Circuits*. Searching for the Mind. *Human Brain* March 2, 2014 http://jonlieffmd.com/blog/music-stimulates-emotions-through-specific-brain-circuits. (Accessed 31 May 2022)
4. Trimble M, Hesdorffer D. Music and the brain: the neuroscience of music and musical appreciation. *BJPsych Int* 2017; 14(2): 28-31. doi:10.1192/s2056474000001720
5. Langer S. *Feeling and Form: A Theory of Art Developed from Philosophy in a New Key*. New York: Charles Scribner's Sons; 1953.
6. Florence Mercurio Riggs. In private conversation.
7. Hegde S. Music therapy for mental disorder and mental health: the untapped potential of Indian classical music. *BJPsych Int* 2017; 14(2): 31-33. doi:10.1192/s2056474000001732
8. Rogers M. The healing power of your voice: why you should sing! *DIY Musician* August 10, 2015 https://diymusician.cdbaby.com/musician-tips/the-healing-power-of-your-voice-7-reasons-why-everyone-should-sing/. (Accessed 31 May 2022)
9. Thoma MV et al. The effect of music on the human stress response. *PLoS One* 2013; 8(8): e70156. doi:10.1371/journal.pone.0070156
10. Thaut MH, Wheeler BL. Music therapy. In: Juslin PN, Sloboda JA (Eds). *Handbook of Music and Emotion: Theory, research, applications*. Oxford: Oxford University Press; 2010: pages 819-848.
11. Zhang S. The Positive Influence of Music on the Human Brain. *Journal of Behavioral and Brain Science 2020;* 10: 95-104. doi: 10.4236/jbbs.2020.101005.
12. Uvnäs-Moberg K, et al. Self-soothing behaviors with particular reference to oxytocin release induced by non-noxious sensory stimulation. *Front Psychol* 2015; 5: 1529. doi:10.3389/fpsyg.2014.01529
13. Levitin D. *This is Your Brain on Music*. New York: Plume/Penguin; 2007.
14. Lawlis GF. *The PTSD Breakthrough : The Revolutionary, Science-Based Compass Reset Program*. Naperville IL: Sourcebooks; 2010.
15. Composer Avi Gross. In private conversation.

16. Schaefer HE. Music-Evoked Emotions-Current Studies. *Front Neurosci* 2017; 11: 600. doi:10.3389/fnins.2017.00600

17. Landis-Shack N, Heinz AJ, Bonn-Miller MO. Music Therapy for Posttraumatic Stress in Adults: A Theoretical Review. *Psychomusicology* 2017; 27(4): 334-342. doi:10.1037/pmu0000192

18. Zatorre RJ, Chen JL, Penhune VB. When the brain plays music: auditory-motor interactions in music perception and production. *Nat Rev Neurosci* 2007; 8(7): 547-558. doi:10.1038/nrn2152

19. Zwerling I. The creative arts therapies as "real therapies". *Am J Danc Ther* 1989; 11(1): 19-26. doi:10.1007/BF00844263

20. Osborne N. Neuroscience and "real world" practice: music as a therapeutic resource for children in zones of conflict. *Ann N Y Acad Sci* 2012; 1252(1): 69-76. doi:10.1111/j.1749-6632.2012.06473.x

21. Barrett D. How Singing Can Help Heal Thyroid Disease. *I Heart Intelligence* January 22, 2016. http://iheartintelligence.com/2016/01/22/singing-thyroid-disease/. (Accessed 31 May 2022)

22. Bensimon B, Amir D, Wolf Y. Drumming through trauma: Music therapy with post-traumatic soldiers. *The Arts in Psychotherapy 2008;* 35: 34–48.

23. Beck BD, Messel C, Meyer SL, et al. Feasibility of trauma-focused Guided Imagery and Music with adult refugees diagnosed with PTSD: A pilot study. *Nord J Music Ther* 2018; 27(1): 67-86. doi:10.1080/08098131.2017.1286368

24. Vickhoff B, Malmgren H, Åström R, et al. Music structure determines heart rate variability of singers. *Front Psychol* 2013; 4. doi:10.3389/fpsyg.2013.00334

25. Murrock CJ, Higgins PA. The theory of music, mood and movement to improve health outcomes. *J Adv Nurs* 2009; 65(10): 2249-2257. doi:10.1111/j.1365-2648.2009.05108.x

Chapter 13: Movement and dance

1. Delsarte F, Zorn JW, ed. *The Essential Delsarte.* Lanham, MD: Scarecrow; 1968.

2. Lanzendorfer J. The sorrow of Isadora Duncan. *KQED* May 28, 2017. www.kqed.org/arts/13310956/isadora-duncan-sorrow-amelia-gray-book (Accessed 31 May 2022)

3. Duncan I. *My Life.* New York: Liveright (Reissued Ed); 1996

4. Halprin D (interview). Through Trauma and Tragedy: From one stage to the next. *Performers and Creators*

Lab January 23, 2019 performersandcreatorslab.com/
dariahalprinthroughtraumaandtragedy. Interview with Daria
Halprin. (Accessed 31 May 2022)

5. Levy FJ, et al. *Dance and Other Expressive Art Therapies: When Words Are
Not Enough*. Oxfordshire: Routledge;1995.

6. Koch SC, et al. Effects of Dance Movement Therapy and Dance on
Health-Related Psychological Outcomes. A Meta-Analysis Update.
Front Psychol 2019; 10: 1806. doi:10.3389/fpsyg.2019.01806

7. Pericleous IA. Healing Through Movement: Dance/Movement Therapy
for Major Depression (Thesis). *Columbia Univ Acad Commons* 2011.
doi.org/10.7916/D8ZC88V2

8. Merleau-Ponty M. *Phenomenology of Perception*. Oxfordshire: Routledge;
1945.

9. Jassem L. In private conversation.

10. American Dance Therapy Association. What is dance/movement
therapy? adta.memberclicks.net/what-is-dance movement-therapy
(Accessed 30 May 2022)

11. European Association Dance Movement Therapy (EADMT). What
is dance movement therapy (DMT)? eadmt.com/what-is-dance-
movement-therapy-dmt (Accessed 31 May 2022)

12. Siegel E V. *Dance-Movement Therapy : The Mirror of Ourselves : A
Psychoanalytic Approach*. Human Sciences Press; 1984.

13. Kleinlooh ST, Samaritter RA, van Rijn RM, Kuipers G, Stubbe JH.
Dance Movement Therapy for Clients With a Personality Disorder:
A Systematic Review and Thematic Synthesis. *Front Psychol* 2021; 12:
581578. doi:10.3389/fpsyg.2021.581578

14 .Roth G. 5rhythms.com.

15. Gillis M. In private conversation.

16. LeBaron M, MacLeod C, Aclan AF *The Choreography of Resolution*.
American Bar Association; 2014.

17. Mashek M. Personal Essay.

Chapter 14: Acting

1. T. Campbell. Valedictorian Stanzas. Written June 1817. In: *The Poetical
Works of Thomas Campbell*. Scotland: W Scott; 1885.

2. Aristotle. *The Poetics*. One interpretation perfect for artists: https://
classicalwisdom.com/philosophy/tragedy-poetics/

3. Cunningham T. Quote: Clowns Without Borders. clownswithoutborders.
org

4. Rabbi Zalman Schachter-Shalomi. partnershipsinaging.unc.edu/
   itineraries-winter-2009/#shalomi. Also see his books, including *From
   Age-ing to Sage-ing*.
5. Brock S. Comments on his solo show, on request.
6. Kane M. *Moonlodge*. Performance. Vancouver East Cultural Centre.
   1990. Group Interview with Margo and director Corey Payette & PJ
   Prudat. youtube.com/watch?v=Cm09TU6hM3E. 2017.

Chapter 15: Putting it all together

1. Anna Liotta. In Conversation. *Unlocking Generational Codes.* New York:
   Aviva; 2012
2. Alexander PE. Masking Children: Tragic, Unscientific and Damaging.
   American Institute for Economic Research March 10, 2021.
3. *Understanding Addiction: How Addiction Hijacks the Brain*. Harvard Help
   Guide. helpguide.org/harvard/how-addiction-hijacks-the-brain.
   htm.
4. Bradshaw J. *Healing the Shame that Binds You*. 1988
5. Nemade R, et al. Biology of Depression – Neurotransmitters. *MentalHelp.
   net* 2007. www.mentalhelp.net/articles/biology-of-depression-
   neurotransmitters/. (Accessed 31 May 2022)
6. Segarnick DJ, Mandio Cordasco D, Agura V, Cooper NS, Rotrosen J.
   Gamma-linolenic acid inhibits the development of the ethanol-
   induced fatty liver. *Prostaglandins Leukot Med* 1985; 17(3): 277-282.
   doi:10.1016/0262-1746(85)90116-7
7. Herington HL. The Meaning of Emotion. *ALIVE Magazine May 2002:*
   76-77.
8. Hoffer A, Osmond H. *The Hallucinogens*. Academic Press; 1967.
9. Tanne JH, Humphry Osmond. *Br Med J* 2004; 328(7441): 713. ncbi.nlm.
   nih.gov/pmc/articles/PMC381240/
10. Lakhan SE, Vieira KF. Nutritional therapies for mental disorders. *Nutr J*
    2008; 7: 2. doi.org/10.1186/1475-2891-7-2
11. Kraft BD, Westman EC. Schizophrenia, gluten, and low-carbohydrate,
    ketogenic diets: a case report and review of the literature. *Nutr Metab*
    2009; 6: 10. doi.org/10.1186/1743-7075-6-10
12. Bressan P, Kramer P. Bread and Other Edible Agents of Mental Disease.
    Front Hum Neurosci 2016; 10: 130. doi:10.3389/fnhum.2016.00130
13. Levinta A, Mukovozov I, Tsoutsoulas C. Use of a Gluten-Free Diet in
    Schizophrenia: A Systematic Review. *Adv Nutr* 2018; 9(6): 824-832.
    doi:10.1093/advances/nmy056

14. Dohan FC. Wheat "consumption" and hospital admissions for schizophrenia during World War II. A preliminary report. *Am J Clin Nutr* 1966; 18(1): 7-10. doi:10.1093/ajcn/18.1.7

15. Torrey EF, Yolken RH. Toxoplasma gondii and schizophrenia. *Emerging Infectious Diseases* 2003; 9(11): 1375–1380. doi.org/10.3201/eid0911.030143

16. Corcoran C, et al. Trajectory to a first episode of psychosis: a qualitative research study with families. *Early Interv Psychiatry* 2007; 1(4): 308-315. doi:10.1111/j.1751-7893.2007.00041.x

17. Gomes FV, Grace AA, Adolescent Stress as a Driving Factor for Schizophrenia Development—A Basic Science Perspective, *Schizophrenia Bulletin 2017*; 43(3): 486–489. doi.org/10.1093/schbul/sbx033

Epilogue

1. Meacham J. *The Soul of America.* New York: Random House; 2018.
2. Gibran K. *Broken Wings.* Lebanese publisher, 1912.
3. Illich I. *Medical Nemesis.* New York: Random House; 1977.

Appendix 1: Epigenetics

1. Faria MA. The neurobiology of learning and memory – as related in the memoirs of Eric R. Kandel. *Surg Neurol Int* 2020; 11: 252. https://surgicalneurologyint.com/surgicalint-articles/the-neurobiology-of-learning-and-memory-as-related-in-the-memoirs-of-eric-r-kandel/

2. Kandel E, Rather D. Neuroplasticity with Nobel Laureate Eric Kandel in conversation with Dan Rather. Wonder Collaborative, 2022. https://wondercollaborative.org/neuroplasticity-with-nobel-laureate-eric-kandel/#:~:text=Kandel%20won%20the%20Nobel%20Prize,into%20a%20life%20of%20science.

3. Doidge N. *The Brain That Changes Itself.* New York: Viking; 2007.

Appendix 2: Homeopathic medicines

1. Malerba L. A veteran with PTSD gets help from homeopathy. *Huffpost* July 19, 2012. www.huffpost.com/entry/homeopathy-ptsd_b_1649398

Appendix 7: Sleep

1. Stenvers DJ, Scheer FAJL, Schrauwen P, la Fleur SE, Kalsbeek A. Circadian clocks and insulin resistance. *Nat Rev Endocrinol* 2019; 15(2): 75-89. doi:10.1038/s41574-018-0122-1

2. McHill AW, et al. Later circadian timing of food intake is associated with increased tolerance in both the morning and evening. *Sleep* 2014; 37(10): 1715-1719.

3. Rubio-Sastre P, Sheer FAJL, Gomez-Abellan P, Madrid JA, Garaulet M. Acute melatonin administration in humans impairs glucose tolerance in both the morning and evening. *Sleep* 2014; 37(10): 1715-1719. doi: 10.5665/sleep.4088

4. McHill AW, Phillips AJK, Czeisler CA, et al. Later circadian timing of food intake associated with increased body fat. *Am J Clin Nutr* 2017; 106(5): 1213-1219. doi: 10.3945/ajcn.117.161588

5. Tan DX, et al. Pineal Calcification, Melatonin Production, Aging, Associated Health Consequences and Rejuvenation of the Pineal Gland. *Molecules* 2018; 23(2): 301. doi:10.3390/molecules23020301

6. Ali T, Choe J, Awab A, Wagener TL, Orr WC. Sleep, immunity and inflammation in gastrointestinal disorders. *World J Gastroenterol* 2013; 19(48): 9231-9239. doi:10.3748/wjg.v19.i48.9231

Appendix 8: Acute PTS

1. Mike Heron. Biography. mikeheron.co.uk/bio.html

Appendix 9: International Trauma Questionnaire

1. Cloitre M, Shevlin M, Brewin CR, Bisson JI, Roberts NP, Maercker A, Karatzias T, Hyland P. The International Trauma Questionnaire: Development of a self-report measure of ICD-11 PTSD and Complex PTSD. *Acta Psychiatrica Scandinavica* 2018; 138(6): 536-546. doi: 10.1111/acps.12956

Background publications for Appendix 9

Brewin CR, Cloitre M, Hyland P, Shevlin M, Maercker A, Bryant RA, et al. A review of current evidence regarding the ICD-11 proposals for diagnosing PTSD and complex PTSD. *Clinical Psychology Review* 2017; 58: 1-15. doi: 10.1016/j.cpr.2017.09.001.

Hyland P, Shevlin M, Brewin CR, Cloitre M, Downes AJ, Jumbe S, et al. Validation of post-traumatic stress disorder (PTSD) and complex PTSD using the International Trauma Questionnaire. *Acta Psychiatrica Scandinavica 2017;* 136: 313-322. doi: 10.1111/acps.12771.

Karatzias T, Shevlin M, Fyvie C, Hyland P, Efthymiadou E, Wilson D, et al. Evidence of distinct profiles of posttraumatic stress disorder (PTSD) and complex posttraumatic stress disorder (CPTSD) based on the new ICD-11 trauma questionnaire (ICD-TQ). *Journal of Affective Disorders 2017;* 207: 181-187. doi.org/10.1016/j.jad.2016.09.032

Shevlin M, Hyland P, Roberts NP, Bisson JI, Brewin CR, Cloitre M. A psychometric assessment of Disturbances in Self-Organization symptom indicators for ICD-11 Complex PTSD using the International Trauma Questionnaire. *European Journal of Psychotraumatology* 2018; 9: 1. doi: 10.1080/20008198.2017.1419749

Index

abdominal (diaphragmatic) breathing, 170–171
abuse
  child, 24–25
  prevalence, 24–25
  sexual, 9, 153, 154, 201, 222, 258, 264
Aconitum/Aconite, 114, 313
  acute PTS, 333
ACTH (adrenocorticotropic hormone), 84, 101, 247
acting, 267–280
action potentials, 69–70
active listening, 149
acute PTS, 333–334
addiction, 36, 292–296
adenosine triphosphate (ATP), 79, 80, 81, 103
Ader, Robert, 185
adolescents, 62
  and schizophrenia, 298, 299
adrenal glands, 68, 69, 297, 317
  see also hypothalamic-pituitary-adrenal (HPA) axis; sympathetic-adrenomedullary axis
adrenaline (epinephrine), 67, 70, 71, 76, 77, 85, 92, 163, 296
adrenochrome, 296
adrenocorticotropic hormone (ACTH), 84, 101, 247
adverse childhood experience (ACE), 31–32
  brain and, 31, 32, 65
  HPA axis and, 84–85
  neurotransmitters and, 70–74
African-Americans, 143
Alaskan Natives, 10, 27
alcoholism, 10, 277, 294, 295
Alexander, Paul F, 290
Alexander the Great, 3
allergens, food, 96–97
allopathic (orthodox/Western) medicine, 112, 177–178

historical perspectives, 42, 46–47, 50, 52–53, 54–55, 108–109
  parental trust, 289
alpha-linolenic acid (ALA), 91, 103, 295
alpha-lipoic acid, 95
America see United States
American Dance Therapy Association, 262
American Medical Association (AMA), 52, 53
American Psychiatric Association (APA), 5, 15, 17, 18, 20, 21, 22
amygdala, 31, 64, 65, 66, 71, 72, 74, 81, 83, 85, 154, 163, 246, 247, 248, 252, 259, 270, 288, 327
  cannabis and, 121
Anderson, Charles, 238
antioxidants, 74, 85, 93, 94, 95
anxiety
  cold water therapy and, 127
  homeopathic medicines, 313, 314, 315, 316–317, 317
  tracking and, 195
  see also fear
Argentum Nitricum, 313
Aristotle, 42, 267
aromatherapy (essential oils), 137, 291, 292
arrhythmias (cardiac), 35
Arsenicum
  in acute PTS, 333
  Arsenicum Album, 313
  Arsenicum Iodatum, 314
arts and crafts, 211–280
  expressive arts, 56, 111, 153, 162, 223, 225–280
    art therapy, 213–214, 238–239
    schizophrenia and, 298
  as refuge, 211–223
  visual art, 237–240
Asclepius, 268
ashwagandha, 84, 116–118, 298, 326, 334
asylums (insane), 43–44, 45

Index

Burlingame, Charles, 54
butyrate, 100–101

California Poppy, 119
Cameron, Julia, 230, 236
Camp Discovery, 207
Campbell, Thomas, 267
Camphora officinarum, 314
Canada
    historical perspectives, 6
    prevalence, 23
cannabis, 120, 121–123
Caplan, Paula, 20
cardiovascular disease, 35
Carnegie and the Carnegie Foundation, 51, 52
Carrol, Otis G, 130
case-taking, homeopathic, 145, 286, 325
catecholamines, 35, 70–71, 79
Caustica, 314
Cayleff, Susan, 108
CBD (cannabidiol), 122–123
CBT, 207–208
celebrity culture, 215–216
cell
    danger/defense response, 66, 79, 80–81, 85
    membranes *see* membranes
    vibrations, 109, 203
central nervous system (CNS), 67
    gut and, 90
    see also brain
chaga mushrooms, 330
chakras, 173
chamomile, 119
chanting, 176, 211, 245, 249
chaos theory, 188
Character analysis, 184
characters in story-writing, 235
chi gong (qi gong), 176
children, 288–292
    abuse, 24–25
    adverse experiences *see* adverse childhood experiences
    art and music in schools, 220–221
    German concentration camps and Holocaust
        children as survivors of, 237
        children of survivors of, 230–231
    as Globals (generational code), 287
    neurological, 37
    trauma transmitted from parents to, 8–11, 62, 143
    see also adolescents; parents

Chinese medicine, traditional, 108, 191
chiropractic, 109
Churchill, Dana, 314
circadian rhythms, 75, 329, 331
citric acid (Krebs) cycle, 80, 104
Civil War (American), 5–6, 7
Cloitre, Marylene, 32–34
clowning, 268, 274
Cochrane, Elizabeth Jane, 45–46
coenzyme Q10, 82
cognitive behavioral therapy, 207–208
cold water therapy, 126–139
    alternating hot and, 135–136
    options, 134–137
colon hydrotherapy, 99
comedy *see* humor
Committee on Statistics of the American Medico-Psychological Association, 5
communication with survivor, 144–145
    non-verbal, 187, 214, 238
    sensitivity of clinician, 150–151, 187
    see also interaction
community
    children and, 287
    descendants of community trauma, 9
    of helpers, healing and the, 150, 156
    humor and, 270
comorbidities, 32–34, 292–296
    addiction, 36, 292–296
    schizophrenia, 36, 292, 296–299
    treatment and, 197–202
compassion, 38, 150, 306
complex PTS/PTSD (C-PTS/PTSD), 32
    diagnosis/measuring instruments, 335, 336, 339–341
concentration camps of WWII and Holocaust, 4, 9, 230–231, 237
consciousness, stream of (writing), 231, 234
consultation *see* visit
contemplation, simple, 169
contrast plunge and contrast shower, 135–136
coronavirus *see* Covid-19
corticotropin-releasing hormone (CRH), 84, 247
cortisol, 75–78, 84
    paradox, 76–77
Covid-19 (and SARS-CoV-2/coronavirus), 27, 32, 47–48, 299
    children, 288, 289, 290, 291
    inoculation, 54, 289
crocodile pose, 175

Index

Index

Index

Index

Index

Endorsements

'This remarkable book is about what has been missing, about what all this time has been hiding in plain sight – natural medicine solutions in a world where conventional medicine has severe limitations.'

David J Schleich, PhD, President, National University of Natural Medicine, USA

'This book has arrived at precisely the right moment in human history! We are at the last fork in the road: change and thrive or perpetuate our blindness and become extinct as a species. More and more of us have come to realize that pharmaceutical methods, which "solve" one problem only to create two more, are not the answer. The way forward is to *realign with nature* – using the natural world (i.e., plants) and natural methods to heal our individual and collective trauma. Dr Herington uses history and science to propose how we can save ourselves and move toward mental wellness. A must read for anyone looking for real and effective answers to hard questions.'

Lisa Samet, ND, author of *Emotional Repatterning: Healing Emotional Pain by Rewiring the Brain*

'This remarkable book is a touchstone for healers, patients and survivors of complex post-trauma syndrome (C-PTS) who want to eschew the American Psychiatric Association's persistent pathologizing of human experience. It is about PTS, ACE and other conditions with psychological trauma at the core. It is a book about what has been missing. It is a book about natural medicine solutions. It is a book as comprehensive as it is precise and functional.

'Dr Herington stares down toxic psychiatry squarely with outstanding, well-researched information, clinical pearls, and proven protocols. She celebrates the extraordinary utility of lifestyle, food, and detoxification options, 'drugless therapies' and a gold mine of naturopathic treatments such as homeopathy, hydrotherapy and botanical medicine. There's more: with equal gusto she delivers exceptional insight into the potential of still-point therapies, the mind-body connection and the all-encompassing expressive arts. Naturopathic physicians welcome this remarkable work. Especially now.'

Sussanna Czeranko, ND BBE, naturopathic doctor, author and presenter

'Dr Herington invokes ancient wisdom in a way that many will perceive to be modern day medical heresy. She recognizes trauma as an unavoidable fact of life. It is not something to pathologize, medicate and suppress; it is something to acknowledge, navigate and overcome with courage, context, compassion and creativity. Herington backs up her thesis with well-researched science in a very readable and accessible book. She circumnavigates the tyranny of Big Pharma by going back to basics: 1) stabilize and deeply restore physical health by following and honouring steadfast natural laws; 2) provide a variety of multisensory lexicons by which to release and transform trauma into psychological, emotional and spiritual healing. If we are to survive as a species, this is a medical model we are in desperate need of embracing.'

Michelle Gibson, PhD, psychologist

'Dr. Herington's book is a must-read for everyone suffering from PTS and ACE (adverse childhood experience), and for healthcare practitioners who seek alternatives to the standard drug treatments provided by Western medicine. Dr. Herington includes well-researched historical and modern sources for the care of trauma subjects and reviews a broad spectrum of sources for a whole-body approach to wellness. The statistics she shares are stark and compelling that PTS and ACE are major issues in the lives of millions of people. Although complex science and medical facts may be a challenge to some readers, the general information on finding and using alternative remedies is readable and accessible. This is a reference book to keep for anyone dealing with PTS and ACE.'

Ariann Thomas, BS JD, international healer, teacher and speaker

'Dr Heather puts her heart and soul into this compassionate, considerate and thoughtful book about transforming trauma. Let the healing begin as you are guided through these insightful pages.'

Christina Bjorndal, ND, naturopathic doctor and author of *Beyond the Label: 10 Steps to Improve your Mental Health with Naturopathic Medicine* and *The Essential Diet; Eating for Mental Health.*

'This is a powerful and insightful guidebook for those with PTS and those caring for them. Herington spells out all the steps one needs to take to make a successful transformation.'

Jonathan Collins, MD, Publisher, *Townsend Letter*